# CAN WE COOK

## by Jackie Olden

THE KNAPP PRESS
LOS ANGELES

Library of Congress Cataloging-in-Publication Data

Olden, Jackie, 1934-
    Can We Cook.

    Includes index.
    1. Cookery.    I. Title.
TX715.0444  1987          641.5          87-3998
ISBN 0-89535-189-7

# TABLE OF CONTENTS

Appetizers and Beverages ...............   3

Soups and Sandwiches ..................  21

Salads and Dressings ...................  43

Sauces and Marinades ..................  65

Eggs, Cheese, Pasta, Pizza, Etc. ...........  79

Vegetables ..............................  99

Meats ................................. 117

Poultry ............................... 145

Seafood .............................. 167

Breads ............................... 183

Sweets and Treats ..................... 199

# Appetizers
# and
# Beverages

# MARINATED MUSHROOMS

25 fresh mushrooms
1 hard-cooked egg yolk, mashed
1/3 cup malt vinegar
1/2 cup vegetable oil
Salt and pepper to taste
2 teaspoons chopped parsley
1 teaspoon prepared mustard
1 tablespoon brown sugar

Mix together all ingredients except mushrooms. Bring to a boil and add mushrooms. Cook 5 to 6 minutes. Refrigerate and marinate overnight. Serve with toothpicks.

Makes 1-1/2 cups.

# LITTLE MUSHROOM TURNOVERS

3 packages (3 ounces each) cream cheese
1/2 cup butter, room temperature
1-1/2 cups flour

Preheat oven to 375°.

Mix the cream cheese and butter thoroughly. Add the flour and work with fingers or pastry blender until smooth. Chill well for at least 30 minutes.

While pastry is chilling, make the mushroom filling. Then roll the dough to 1/8-inch thickness on a lightly floured surface and cut into rounds with a 3-inch cutter. Place 1 teaspoon of Mushroom Filling on each and fold the dough over filling—to look like a very small dumpling. Press the edges together with a fork. Prick top crusts to allow steam to escape.

# MUSHROOM FILLING

3 tablespoons butter
1 large onion, chopped
1/2 pound mushrooms, finely chopped
1/2 teaspoon thyme
1/2 teaspoon salt
Freshly ground black pepper to taste
2 tablespoons flour
1/4 cup sweet or sour cream

In a skillet, heat the butter, add the onion, and brown lightly. Add mushrooms and cook 3 minutes, stirring often.

Add thyme, salt and pepper and sprinkle with flour. Stir in cream and cook gently until thickened. Cook approximately 15 minutes until golden brown.

# CALIFORNIA SUSHI ROLL

1/2 cup vinegar
1/2 cup sugar
1 cup warm cooked rice
2 tablespoons sesame seeds
1/2 cup cooked crabmeat
3 tablespoons fish roe (may be Golden Caviar)
1/2 avocado, chopped
Wasabi paste

To prepare rice for this or any other sushi dish, rice must be pickled. Combine vinegar and sugar in an enamel saucepan and bring to a boil. Cook, stirring, until sugar is completely dissolved. Remove from heat. Stir 2 tablespoons of vinegar-sugar mixture into the cooked, still warm, rice. Warm rice absorbs the mixture more completely. Stir sesame seeds into rice.

Press pickled rice into a square on a small serving platter. Cut rice into squares, and leave rice squares in place. Press each square lightly so that rice clings, and place a small dab of Wasabi paste on each.

Press a bit of crabmeat, fish roe, and avocado on each square.

# POT LUCK DIP

1 loaf round French bread
1 loaf French bread (does not need to be round),
        cut into pieces for dipping
1 package chopped spinach, defrosted and
        moisture squeezed out, but not dry
1 cup mayonnaise
1 cup sour cream
1 package Knorr's leek soup
2 green onions, chopped
1/2 can water chestnuts, chopped

Cut top from round bread. Scoop out bread, leaving 1/2-inch inside. Save inside bread for dipping. Cut other loaf into pieces for dipping.

Combine remaining ingredients. To take to pot luck, carry in bowl until ready to serve. Place in bread and serve with bread around the platter. As it disappears, the crust can be eaten also. Wonderful!

## Handy Hints

KETCHUP: Great on hamburgers, but even better on copper. A little goes a long way on polishing copperware with a steel wool soap pad.

TANG INSTANT BREAKFAST DRINK: Any similar product will also work to keep hard water stains from forming on dishes. Stir a half teaspoonful of Tang into your dishwater when washing the dishes by hand, or add to the dishwater detergent in your dishwasher.

# RESOLUTION MEATBALLS

1-1/2 pounds ground beef
1/4 cup bread crumbs
1 tablespoon catsup
1 egg, beaten
1-1/4 teaspoons salt
Olive oil
1 small onion, chopped
1/2 cup bourbon
1/4 cup sweet vermouth
2 dashes of bitters
1 beef bouillon cube
1/3 teaspoon oregano
1 teaspoon dry mustard

Combine ground beef, bread crumbs, catsup, egg, 1 teaspoon salt and 1/4 cup water. Mix well; shape into small balls.

Brown meatballs well in oil in skillet. Remove and drain.

Saute onion lightly in skillet drippings; add 1 cup water, bourbon, vermouth, bitters, bouillon cube and remaining seasonings. Cook, stirring, until bouillon cube is dissolved and sauce is heated through.

Return meatballs to skillet; simmer for 5 minutes. Refrigerate overnight for better flavor. Reheat in chafing dish to serve.

Makes 40 meatballs.

# ADOBE HACIENDA DIP

1 pound ground beef
4 tomatoes, peeled and diced
3 green onions, chopped
1 (4 ounce) jar pimentos, diced
Salt and pepper to taste
1 (2-3/4 ounce) bag slivered almonds,
    blanched in butter
3 cloves garlic, crushed
1 (6 ounce) can tomato paste
2 Jalapeno peppers, chopped
3/4 cup seedless raisins
1/4 teaspoon oregano

Cover meat with 3/4 cup water, salt and pepper. Simmer 1/2 hour. Add remaining ingredients and heat for 5 minutes. Serve hot with tortilla chips.

## Handy Hints

WALNUTS: To conceal surface scratches on wood furniture, rub the meat of the walnut into the scratches. Some artistic filling in with a permanent magic marker of the same color as the wood will also hide the scratches from sight.

## CHUTNEY TUNA PUPUS

1 (7-ounce) can tuna, drained
3/4 cup mango chutney, chopped
1/4 cup green pepper, chopped
1/4 cup onion, chopped
2/3 cup mayonnaise
Pastry for three 9" pie shells
1 egg, slightly beaten

Flake tuna with a fork and combine with chutney, pepper, onion and mayonnaise. Roll pastry to 1/8" thickness and cut into 2-1/2" squares. Place 1 teaspoon of the tuna mixture in the center of each pastry square. Fold opposite corners together to form a triangle, pinching the edges together and sealing with the beaten egg. Cut small vents in the top of each pastry and brush with the egg. Bake at 500° for 8 to 10 minutes.

These pupus may be made a week ahead and stored in the freezer. You can bake them, unthawed, just before serving.

Makes 5 dozen.

## MEXICAN CHEESE FONDUE

2 pounds processed American cheese, cubed
2 (7-ounce) cans green chile salsa
1 (4-ounce) can green chiles, diced
1 package taco seasoning mix
1 loaf French bread, cubed

Combine all ingredients except bread in crock cooker. Cover and cook for 2 to 3 hours on Low, stirring once after about an hour; or cook at High heat for 30 minutes or more, stirring often until ingredients are smoothly blended. Set crock cooker to Low for serving. Let guests dip bread through the fondue on long forks or skewers.

Serves 10.

## SPICY TUNA DIP

1 (13-ounce) can tuna
1 (6.5-ounce) jar or can jalapeno chiles, chopped
1 onion, minced
1/2 cup mayonnaise
Chopped cilantro

Mix tuna with chopped jalapeno chiles and jalapeno liquid. Add onion to tuna mixture. Stir in mayonnaise until consistency is mushy. Sprinkle cilantro on top and serve with tortilla chips, if desired.

Makes 1-1/2 cups.

# HUNGARIAN SURPRISES

1 pound pork bulk sausage
1 pound ground round steak
1 pound Velveeta cheese
1/2 teaspoon garlic powder
1/2 teaspoon Worcestershire sauce
1 teaspoon oregano
2 loaves party rye bread
Paprika

Brown sausage and steak in separate skillets. Drain in colander to get off all the fat. Put both meats into a skillet and break up cheese in the meat. Slowly melt cheese and then add the seasonings. Spread on bread slices and dust with paprika.

Freeze on cookie sheets and then package in plastic bags. Bake frozen at 350° for 15 to 20 minutes.

Yields approximately 50 appetizers.

# GUACAMOLE STUFFED CELERY

1 bunch celery, chilled
2 ripe avocados, mashed
1/2 cup minced onion
1-1/2 tablespoons lemon juice
1-3/4 teaspoons salt
4 drops Tabasco
1 cup tomatoes, chopped

Cut off leafy portion of celery. Separate into ribs. Rinse in cold water. Wrap in plastic bag and refrigerate. In a medium bowl, combine avocados, onion, lemon juice, salt and Tabasco. Stir in tomatoes. Refrigerate covered if not stuffing celery right away. When ready to use, fill each rib with about 3 to 4 tablespoons of guacamole mixture. This can be served whole or in bite-sized pieces. Will make about 2-1/2 cups guacamole.

# MOCK LIVER PATE

1/2 pound fresh liver sausage
1 (3-ounce) package cream cheese
2 to 4 tablespoons mayonnaise
2 hard-boiled eggs, finely chopped
1 teaspoon minced onion
Sieve egg yolk or minced parsley for garnish

Combine first five ingredients and shape into a ball. Garnish with additional sieved hard-boiled egg yolk or minced parsley. Serve with crackers.

## SPINACH AND CHEESE APPETIZERS

2 (10-ounce) packages frozen chopped spinach, thawed
2 cups herb-flavored bread crumbs
4 eggs
3/4 cup butter, melted
1 white onion, grated or finely minced
1/2 cup shredded Swiss cheese
1/4 cup grated Parmesan cheese
1 clove garlic, minced

Squeeze thawed spinach dry of liquid. Place in a large mixing bowl and add remaining ingredients. Blend well, cover and refrigerate 2 to 3 hours.

Roll into 1-inch balls. Place on lightly greased cooking sheet. Bake at 350° for 15 minutes.

Note: These can be made ahead of time and frozen. Remove from freezer a few minutes before baking.

Yield: 50 hot appetizers.


## MEATBALLS A LA CAFE

1-1/2 pounds ground beef
3/4 cup soft bread crumbs
1/2 cup light cream
1/2 cup onion, chopped
1 egg
1/4 cup parsley, chopped
1-1/2 teaspoons salt
1/4 teaspoon pepper
1/4 teaspoon nutmeg

Combine all ingredients and form bite-sized meatballs. Fry until browned all over and serve with gravy from a chafing dish.

GRAVY:
3/4 cup beef broth
1/4 cup water
2 tablespoons flour
1/2 teaspoon instant coffee

Combine all ingredients in a small saucepan; heat until smooth and thickened.


## ONION BITES (APPETIZER)

2 cups flour
1 cup butter
1 package onion soup mix
1 pound cheddar cheese, grated

Mix all ingredients and make a roll. Refrigerate or freeze. Let stand at room temperature a few minutes. Slice and bake 10 minutes at 375°.

# LOW CALORIE PATE

(Approximately 170 calories per serving)

1 onion, finely chopped
1/2 teaspoon margarine
1 whole chicken breast, boned and thinly sliced
1 tablespoon brandy
1 teaspoon salt
1/4 teaspoon white pepper
1/4 teaspoon nutmeg
1/2 teaspoon thyme
1/2 teaspoon basil
1/2 teaspoon allspice
1/2 teaspoon lemon peel
3/4 pound ground turkey
3/4 pound ground veal
1 egg
2 egg whites
3 tablespoons nonfat dry milk powder
1/4 cup chopped parsley
2 shallots, chopped
2 cloves garlic, minced
2 bay leaves
Peppercorn

Saute onion in margarine until tender (do not brown). Let chicken strips marinate in brandy with the salt, pepper and nutmeg. Combine the ground meats with the onions, spices, egg, one egg white and the powdered milk. Mix well.

Spoon half the meat mixture into a 4 x 7-inch loaf pan. Mix together the parsley, shallots, garlic and remaining egg white; spread over the meat mixture. Top with remaining meat mixture. Arrange marinated chicken in a layer over the top. Decorate with bay leaves and a few peppercorns. Cover the pan with foil and bake at 350° in a pan containing 1 inch hot water for 1-1/4 to 1-1/2 hours. Let cool and then chill. Slice and serve on lettuce leaf with Cornichon pickles & pumpernickle bread.

# HONEY BAKED CHICKEN WINGS

2 pounds chicken wings
1/2 cup melted butter or margarine
1/2 cup honey
1/4 cup prepared mustard
1 teaspoon salt
1 teaspoon curry powder

Place chicken pieces in a shallow pan. Combine all the ingredients and pour over chicken wings. Bake at 350° for 1 hour or until done, basting every 15 minutes until chicken is tender and nicely browned.

Serves 6 to 8.

# APPETIZER CHEESECAKE

Melted butter or margarine
1 (6-ounce) box cheese crackers, finely crushed
1/2 cup finely chopped stuffed green olives
1/2 cup finely chopped celery
1 medium-sized green pepper, finely chopped
1 small onion, chopped
2 tablespoons lemon juice
1 teaspoon salt
1 teaspoon Worcestershire sauce
Dash of Tabasco and paprika
2 cups sour cream

Brush the bottom and sides of a springform pan with butter. Cover bottom of the pan with half the crushed crackers.

Mix all remaining ingredients. Carefully spread mixture over cracker crumb base. Scatter remaining crumbs evenly over the top. Cover with waxed paper and refrigerate for at least 24 hours before serving.

To serve, remove from spring pan. Place cake, still on bottom, on serving platter. Garnish top with sliced olives. Serve with thin wheat crackers.

Great new idea for an appetizer. Serves 10-12.

# CHEESE FONDUE

1 clove garlic
3 cups dry white wine
2 pounds natural Gruyere cheese, grated
4 teaspoons cornstarch
6 tablespoons Kirsch or sherry
Freshly ground black pepper

Rub the bottom and sides of an earthenware casserole or fondue pot with the garlic. Add the wine and heat to a boiling point but do not boil.

Add the cheese, stirring constantly, with a wooden spoon. When the cheese is creamy and barely simmering, add the cornstarch blended with the Kirsch. Stir until the mixture bubbles. Add pepper to taste.

Place the casserole over an alcohol burner with a low flame. Keep the fondue pot hot but not simmering. If it becomes too thick, add a little more wine.

To serve, accompany with cubes of crusty bread for dipping into the casserole of melted cheese.

Serves 16.

This is really a fun appetizer and it is delicious. Just make sure you set the casserole or fondue pot on a tray.

# BEST EVER CHICKEN LIVER PATE

1/2 cup sweet butter
1 pound fresh chicken livers
1 small onion, finely chopped
1 clove garlic, crushed
Salt and pepper
4 teaspoons beef consomme
4 teaspoons cognac
1 package (8 ounces) cream cheese
1 small wedge roquefort cheese
1 package (1/4 ounce) clear gelatin
1/4 cup water
1 can (10-1/2 ounces) beef consomme
Several large black pitted olives, cut into rounds

In a large skillet saute livers, onion and garlic in butter until golden. Season to taste and remove from the heat.

In your blender set at CHOP, blend liver mixture with beef consomme, cognac, cream cheese, roquefort and a little freshly ground black pepper. Stop blender occasionally to stir.

Dissolve clear gelatin in 1/4 cup water. Pour the beef consomme, which is boiling, less the 4 tablespoons already used, over the gelatin mixture.

Line a 1 pound mold with black olive rounds. Pour in a little of the consomme to cover the olives. Let cool until jelled. Add the liver mixture. Pour the rest of the consomme over all. Cool. Put into refrigerator until jelled.

Unmold and slice 1/2 to 3/4-inch thick. Serve cold on a lettuce leaf garnished with a few cornichons. Serve with slices of baguette-shaped French bread and have a pot of Dijon-type mustard on the table.

# BEEF CUBES ORIENTAL

1/2 cup soy sauce
1/4 cup sesame oil
1/4 cup dry sherry
1 tablespoon finely chopped ginger root
1 tablespoon sugar
2 large garlic cloves, minced
1-1/2 to 2 pounds boneless top sirloin, cut into 1/2" cubes

Combine the first six ingredients in a glass bowl; stir to blend. Add meat cubes and marinate overnight. Turn meat several times.

Remove meat from marinade, reserving liquid.

Broil meat 3 to 4 inches from heat for about 10 minutes. Place in chafing dish. Heat marinade just to boiling and pour over meat. Serve with cocktail picks.

Makes about 40 bites . . . for Christmas appetizers. This is a delicious sampling of East meeting West at your holiday bash.

## CORNED BEEF CANAPES

3/4 pound sharp cheddar cheese, grated
1 (12-ounce) can corned beef, chopped
1 tablespoon Dijon mustard
1 tablespoon Worcestershire sauce
1 clove garlic, chopped
1 small onion, chopped
Mayonnaise
Cocktail rye bread rounds

Mix all the ingredients with enough mayonnaise to make it very moist. Spread on rye rounds. Put under the broiler until the cheese melts. Makes a bunch.

Delicious! This is a favorite of all the men in my family.

## FRIED JACK CHEESE

1/2 pound jack cheese
1/2 cup flour
2 lightly beaten eggs
1/4 teaspoon salt
1/2 cup olive oil
1 ounce of your favorite liqueur
Lemons

Cut jack cheese into 2-inch squares, 1-inch thick. Roll in flour and dip into the eggs which have been combined with the salt and olive oil. Fry in hot oil just long enough for the cheese to turn golden in color. Warm your favorite liqueur and pour over the cheese and flambe. Squeeze halved lemons over flaming cheese. Serve immediately.

Serves 4.

## ACAPULCO SHRIMP

12 jumbo shrimp
1 (8-ounce) block jalapeno cheese
6 slices bacon
1-1/2 cups flour
1 cup milk
Salt and cayenne to taste
Oil for frying

Peel, de-vein and butterfly shrimp down the back. Season well with salt and pepper. Cut cheese into 1/4-inch cubes. Insert 1 slice of cheese into back center of each shrimp. Wrap shrimp with bacon and secure with toothpick. Dip shrimp in flour, milk, and then flour again. Deep fry until golden and crisp.

Serves 6 as an appetizer.

# SWISS 'N RYE BOAT FOR SUPER BOWL SUNDAY

1-1/2 pounds grated Swiss cheese
1/4 pound crumbled roquefort cheese
1 teaspoon dry mustard
2 tablespoons soft butter
1 teaspoon Worcestershire sauce
2 teaspoons snipped chives
12 ounces beer
1 (3 to 5 pound) oval or round rye loaf, unsliced
1 extra loaf of party rye for dipping
Paprika
Snipped parsley

Hollow out the round loaf of bread, reserving as much as possible for dipping, cut into cubes.

Put all ingredients except beer into a bowl to soften, for at least 1/2 hour or more. Add beer slowly and beat until smooth and fluffy. Fill bread with cheese mixture. Cover with plastic wrap and refrigerate.

When serving, garnish with paprika and parsley. Serve on a large bread board with extra and reserved rye. Make ahead and be ready for the gang.

Serves 15 to 20 guys.

# NEW YEAR'S EVE CRAB MOLD

2 (8-ounce) packages cream cheese
1/2 pound sharp cheddar cheese, grated
1 (3-ounce) package roquefort cheese
1 teaspoon garlic salt
1/2 teaspoon curry powder
2 tablespoons Worcestershire sauce
1 teaspoon paprika
1 tablespoon mayonnaise
1 tablespoon lemon juice
1 (6-ounce) can crab meat

Have all ingredients at room temperature. Combine cheeses, garlic salt, curry, Worcestershire sauce, paprika, mayonnaise, lemon juice and crab meat in a mixing bowl. Mix thoroughly with an electric mixer. Turn mixture into a greased 1-quart mold. Chill several hours or overnight. Unmold and garnish with parsley.

Serve with crackers of your choice.

A nice way to say "Happy New Year."

## Handy Hints

HAIR SPRAY: To remove ink stains on fabric, just spray on and wash. The cheaper the brand, the better.

# BUFFALO CHICKEN WINGS
# WITH BLEU CHEESE SAUCE

2 tablespoons finely chopped onion
1 small garlic clove, minced
1/4 cup minced fresh parsley
1 cup mayonnaise or salad dressing
1/2 cup sour cream
1/4 cup finely crumbled bleu cheese
1 tablespoon lemon juice
1 tablespoon white wine vinegar
1/4 teaspoon salt
1/4 teaspoon black pepper
Pinch of cayenne pepper
1/2 cup (1 stick) unsalted butter
1/4 cup bottled hot sauce
25 chicken wings (about 4-1/2 pounds)
About 1-1/2 quarts vegetable oil or lard
Celery sticks for garnish

In a medium bowl, combine the onion, garlic, parsley, mayonnaise, sour cream, bleu cheese, lemon juice, vinegar, salt, black pepper and cayenne, whisk until blended. Cover and refrigerate the bleu cheese sauce until 30 minutes before serving.

In a large skillet, melt the butter over moderately low heat and add the hot sauce, mix well and set aside. (This makes a medium hot sauce. For a hotter or a milder sauce, adjust the ingredients accordingly.)

Cut the wings into three pieces at the joints, discard the tips or reserve for stock. Pat the chicken dry.

In a deep fryer or a heavy, deep skillet, heat the oil to 385°. Fry the chicken in batches for about 10 minutes, until brown and crisp. Drain on paper towels.

When all of the chicken has been fried, rewarm the hot sauce mixture in a large skillet. Add the chicken and turn to thoroughly coat each piece. Turn off the heat, cover and let stand for 5 minutes.

Serve the chicken accompanied with the celery and the reserved bleu cheese dressing for dipping.

4 to 6 appetizer servings.

## Handy Hints

COLA: To clean the toilet bowl — First, use a plunger to lower the level of water below the dirt ring. Then empty a can of Pepsi or Coke on the ring and let it soak for a few minutes. A couple of brush strokes will finish the job.

LEMON OIL: To remove not-too-serious hard water build up on bathroom tile surfaces. Be generous with the oil while rubbing the shower stall walls.

## APHRA DE JACQUES*
### (Fried Jack Hors d'Oeuvres)

1-1/2 pounds Monterey Jack cheese (7 x 3-inch block)
30 cloves fresh garlic
4 cups peanut oil (more as needed)
1 tablespoon Italian seasoning
3 eggs, beaten
2 cups all purpose flour
3 cups French bread crumbs**
3 tablespoons chopped fresh parsley
1 small jar marinara sauce

Slice cheese into 30 slices about 1/4-inch thick. Peel garlic and slice each clove lengthwise into about 6 ovals.

Heat oil in deep, heavy saucepan over medium-low heat. Add garlic ovals and simmer 5 to 7 minutes, being careful not to burn or brown cloves. Remove slices as they float to surface and are light brown in color. Drain on paper towel. Reserve oil for cheese.

Mince garlic and mix with Italian seasoning. Spread half the cheese slices evenly with garlic mixture. Press remaining cheese slices on each to make 15 bars. Cut each bar into 2 pieces.

Dip into beaten egg, then the flour. Dip flour-coated pieces into egg again, then into bread crumbs mixed with parsley. Be sure to cover all sides.

Reheat oil to medium-high and fry cheese in oil a few pieces at a time until lightly browned (takes about 2 minutes). Skim particles and oil as they accumulate. Drain cheese on paper towels and keep warm until all are fried. Serve with toothpicks and marinara sauce for dipping.

Makes about 30 pieces.

** Use day old bread and prepare crumbs in food processor. Dry packaged crumbs may be used but are not as attractive when fried.

* Finalist, 1984 Gilroy Garlic Festival Recipe Contest

## HOT BROCCOLI DIP

2 packages (10 ounces each) chopped broccoli
2 jars Kraft American cheese with garlic
    or Old English Sharp
1 can mushroom soup
1 small can chopped mushrooms
1 package Lipton onion soup mix
1 cube butter

Cook broccoli and drain.

In a saucepan, melt cheese and add the remaining ingredients. Stir well and add broccoli.

Keep heated in a chafing dish or fondue pot. Serve with any type of crudites. Easy and delicious.

## SANGRIA

1 bottle dry red wine (fifth)
1 pint club soda
1/4 cup orange juice
1/4 cup lemon juice
1 ounce cognac
4 slices lemon
4 slices orange
1/4 cup simple syrup (see recipe below)
2 cinnamon sticks
8 ice cubes

Mix all ingredients together. Pour into a clear glass pitcher.

## SIMPLE SYRUP

2-1/2 cups sugar                        1-1/4 cups water

Combine ingredients in saucepan. Stir over low heat until sugar is dissolved. Cover pan and simmer 2 minutes. Store in jar and refrigerate.

## EASY WHISKEY SOURS FOR PARTY TIME

1 can frozen lemonade, thawed
2 lemonade cans water
1 lemonade can bourbon
3 tablespoons sugar

Mix well above ingredients and store in refrigerator. Shake well before serving. Garnish with navel orange slice and maraschino cherry on a pick.

## HOW TO MAKE BAILEY'S IRISH CREAM!

1 cup Irish whiskey
1 can sweetened condensed milk (Eagle brand)
2 teaspoons Hershey's chocolate syrup
1 tablespoon creamed coconut (can get at liquor stores)
   (Coco Casa Cream of Coconut by Holland House 16-ounce)
8 ounces of whipping cream

Mix all ingredients but whipping cream in a blender. Add 8 ice cubes and blend again. Then add whipping cream. (Blend, don't whip.)

Makes ersatz Bailey's Irish cream.

## ORANGE MICHAEL (Julius' poor relation)
## (MIKE ROY'S SPECIAL)

2 cups fresh orange juice
2 cups shaved ice (enough sugar to sweeten juice to taste)
1/8 cup powdered egg white
1/8 cup non-fat milk

Whirl in a blender and strain into serving glass.

# LIQUEURS

Blackberry, blueberry, elderberry, huckleberry, juniper berry:

> 4 cups fresh berries
> Sliced and scraped peel of one lemon
> Pinch of tarragon or cloves
> 3 cups vodka or 2 cups vodka
> and 1 cup brandy or sweet white wine
> 1 cup sugar syrup

Lightly crush berries with a fork. Add to vodka with lemon peel and cloves. Steep 3 months. Strain. Crush the berries through the filters to squeeze out all the juices. Add sugar syrup to taste. Mature 4 to 6 weeks.

# FROZEN BERRY LIQUEURS

When fresh berries are unavailable, you can make liqueurs with frozen berries. You may experiment with one 10-ounce package of any berries and make small batches:

> 1 (10-ounce) package strawberries, raspberries or any berry
> 1-1/2 cups vodka or 1 cup vodka and 1/2 cup brandy
> 1/4 cup sugar syrup

Add juice and berries to alcohol. Stir and steep one week. Strain. Crush berries through strainer and filter. Taste. Add sugar syrup as necessary. Many frozen fruits are already pre-sugared. If using unsugared fruits without syrup, treat them as fresh fruits but reduce the amount of water when making the sugar syrup because of the water content in the frozen fruits. Makes about 2 cups.

# BANANA LIQUEUR

> 2 medium-size bananas, peeled
> 1 teaspoon vanilla extract or a 2-inch length of vanilla bean
> 1 cup sugar syrup
> 3 cups vodka

Mash the bananas and add the vanilla and cooled sugar syrup to the vodka. Shake gently. Steep one week. Strain and filter. It may be consumed now, but a 2 to 3 month maturing period will result in a richer flavor. Makes 4 cups.

# WEDDING CHAMPAGNE PUNCH

> 1 quart strawberries
> 1/2 cup lime juice
> 1 bottle sparkling burgundy
> 1 bottle sauterne
> 2 bottles pink champagne

Puree strawberries in blender. Pour strawberries, lime juice and wines over ice block in punch bowl.

Makes 25 4-ounce servings.

# BRIDE'S CHAMPAGNE PUNCH

48 ounces lemonade (you may use 4 6-ounce cans
    frozen lemonade concentrate plus 4 cans water only)
48 ounces pineapple juice (you may use 4 6-ounce cans
    frozen pineapple juice plus 4 cans water only)
2 quarts ginger ale (or use 3 quarts if you want
    to omit the champagne
1 quart sparkling water
2 quarts dry champagne
Block ice
Fresh strawberries for garnish

Mix the first 5 ingredients and pour over block of ice in a punchbowl. Float the strawberries. Serves 50.

This is a lovely champagne punch that has just a whisper of the bubbly for the bride who does not want a strong punch but would like to serve champagne on her wedding day.

# MIKE ROY'S CHAMPAGNE PUNCH

1/2 cup lemon juice
1/2 cup water
1 cup sugar
3 ounces brandy
3 ounces Curacao
3 ounces maraschino juice
1 bottle sparkling water
3 bottles champagne

In a punch bowl, dissolve sugar in water and lemon. Add brandy, Curacao and maraschino. Mix well. Just before serving, pour in chilled sparkling water and champagne. Stir gently. Garnish with fresh strawberries or pineapple.

Makes 35 4-ounce servings.

# GIN SPARKLERS FOR THE FOURTH

1 (6-ounce) can frozen lemonade, slightly defrosted
1 (6-ounce) can frozen pineapple juice, slightly defrosted
2 cups club soda, chilled
1-1/2 to 2 cups gin
4 to 6 ice cubes

Place half the ingredients at a time in a blender. Mix until smooth. Repeat with remaining ingredients. You may freeze the sparklers. Defrost at room temperature for 1 hour before serving. Return to blender and process until smooth.

Makes 12 4-ounce servings.

# HOLIDAY PUNCH

4 cups cranberry juice
4 cups apple juice
1/2 cup lemon juice
1 quart ginger ale
1 can pineapple spears
20 ice cubes

Chill juices, ginger ale and pineapple spears.

Drain and halve pineapple spears (save juice for holiday salads).

Combine cranberry, apple and lemon juices. Place ice cubes in punch bowl and add juices, ginger ale and pineapple spears. Garnish with maraschino cherries.

This is a delightful non-alcoholic punch, but it can be spiked very nicely with vodka, rum or brandy.

Makes 20-25 servings.

# OLD FASHIONED EGG NOG

8 large eggs, separated
8 fully rounded tablespoons sugar
1/2 cup whipping cream
1 cup good whiskey

Beat egg yolks until thick and lemon colored. Add the sugar gradually, and beat until sugar is dissolved. Pour the whiskey, very slowly, over the yolks and beat well. Stir in the whipping cream.

Now fold in stiffly beaten egg whites. When ready to serve, fill glasses and top with a dash of nutmeg. The egg nog should be made and served. It should not stand very long before serving.

Serves 8.

# BRANDY EGG NOG DELUXE

6 egg yolks
3/4 cup sugar
1/2 teaspoon vanilla
1/4 teaspoon nutmeg
1-1/2 cups brandy
1/3 cup bourbon
3 cups whipping cream, chilled
2 cups cold milk
6 egg whites
6 tablespoons sugar

Beat egg yolks until light. Gradually add 3/4 cup sugar, vanilla and nutmeg. Stir in brandy and bourbon, chill. Stir in cream and milk. Beat egg whites until soft peaks form, add remaining sugar, beating to stiff peaks. Fold into yolk mixture. Serve at once.

24 4-ounce servings.

# Soups
# and
# Sandwiches

# SUMMERTIME BEET AND ZUCCHINI SOUP

1 pound beets, peeled and grated
1/4 cup red wine vinegar
4 tablespoons sweet butter
1 tablespoon oil
1 onion, sliced
2 green onions, chopped
2 carrots, peeled and sliced
1 apple, peeled and sliced
1 pound green cabbage, thinly sliced
2 zucchini, sliced
4 cups chicken stock
Salt and pepper to taste
Sour cream and fresh dill for garnish

Soak 1/3 of the beets in the vinegar and sugar.

Heat butter and oil in a soup kettle. Saute the onions about 5 minutes. Add the remaining beets, carrots and apple; cook 15 minutes. Add the cabbage and zucchini to the soup pot and cook 3 minutes.

In another pan, bring the chicken stock to a boil. Pour over the vegetables and cook 10 minutes. Add the beets and vinegar. Season with salt and pepper.

Serve garnished with a dollop of sour cream and a sprig of fresh dill.

Serves 6.

This soup is so easy and delightful and can be served hot or cold. A nice way to begin any dinner party.

# HARVEST BEAN SOUP

1 red pepper pod
1/4 cup of the following: lentils, pearl barley, split green peas,
     blackeyed peas, large and small lima beans, red, pinto,
     small white and great northern beans
1 (2-pound) can tomatoes
1 large onion, chopped
Juice of 1 lemon (optional)
1 teaspoon chili powder (optional)
Salt and pepper to taste

Put pepper pod aside. Wash bean mix in a bowl of cold water and remove any stones or beans that float. Place beans in a larger pot, cover with fresh water and soak overnight.

Next day, drain, rinse and add 2 quarts of water and a ham bone, ham hock, cubed ham or Spam. Bring mixture to a boil, then lower heat. Simmer approximately 2 hours, stirring frequently.

Add remaining ingredients and simmer for 20 minutes.

Serves 12.

## MAIN DISH MINESTRONE SOUP

3 slices bacon, finely chopped
1 cup chopped onion
1/2 cup chopped celery
2 large cloves garlic, minced
1 teaspoon crushed basil
1 can Campbell's beef broth
1 can Campbell's bean with bacon soup
1-1/2 soup cans water
1 (16-ounce) can tomatoes, undrained
Olive oil
1/2 cup macaroni (any kind)
Salt and pepper to taste
1 cup chopped cabbage
1 cup chopped zucchini

Brown bacon, drain fat. Add enough olive oil to cook onion, garlic, celery and basil until tender.

Stir in soups, water and tomatoes. Bring to a boil, cover and reduce heat. Simmer 30 minutes. Add macaroni and cook to almost done. Add cabbage and zucchini and cook to tender crisp.

## CHILI FOR HOT DOGS

1 medium-size onion, chopped
1 pound ground beef
1/4 pound good-quality bulk sausage
1 (6-ounce) can tomato paste
1 (8-ounce) can tomato sauce
1 tablespoon Worcestershire sauce
1 tablespoon chili powder or to taste
Liquid hot pepper to taste

In a skillet, cook onion, beef and sausage together. Drain off excess fat and discard.

Add remaining ingredients and simmer for 10 to 15 minutes. Add water, if necessary, to keep from being dry.

---

A hobby is something you get goofy about to
keep from going nuts about things in general.

---

Electronic gadgets make my home perk.
But I'm still needed to make them all work.

---

If you can't read the handwriting on the wall,
your children are probably still very young.

## AVOCADO BISQUE

3 large fully ripe avocados
1 cup chicken broth
1 cup light cream
1/4 teaspoon onion salt
1 teaspoon salt
1 pinch white pepper
1/4 cup light rum
1 teaspoon lemon juice
Lemon slices
Whipped cream

In a blender, blend together avocado pulp, chicken broth until smooth. Add cream, seasonings and rum, blend again. Cover cannister and place in refrigerator overnight. Just before serving add lemon juice and blend again. Serve with a garnish of lemon slice and a dollop of whipped cream.

Serves 4.

## CREAMED CORN SOUP

2 cups corn kernels
1 medium onion, finely chopped
1/3 teaspoon sugar
1 teaspoon salt
1/8 teaspoon pepper
1-1/2 cups chicken stock
1 quart milk
2 tablespoons butter
2 tablespoons flour
1 egg

Combine vegetables in stock and simmer for 20 minutes. Add seasonings and milk and bring to a boil. Cream together the flour and butter and stir into the soup. Beat egg. Puree the soup, return to pot. Add a little stock to the egg, whisk into soup. Garnish with parsley.

## QUICK CHICKEN BROTH

Canned Campbell's or Swanson's chicken broth
1 onion, quartered
Parsley stems
Celery chunks
Carrot chunks
Steero Chicken Stock Base

Place canned broth and vegetables in pot. Add a tablespoon or so of chicken stock base, depending on how many cans of broth you are using. Bring to a boil and simmer for 1 hour. Strain and use in any recipe calling for chicken broth. Use of this will greatly enhance the flavor of any soup.

## WOODY'S EVERYDAY CHILI

6 pounds coarse ground chuck
2 medium-sized cans tomatoes, chopped
3 green bell peppers, cubed
2 large onions, chopped
3 teaspoons salt
8 tablespoons chili powder
2 teaspoons oregano
2 teaspoons cumin
5 cloves garlic, chopped
3 cans beef broth

Brown the meat. Add the broth, spices and the garlic. Simmer for 45 minutes. Add peppers and simmer 5 minutes; add onions and simmer 5 minutes; add tomatoes and simmer 5 minutes, or until the onions are tender. Add the juice of 2 limes and simmer another 5 minutes.

Yields 2 gallons.

## COLD CUCUMBER SOUP

1 leek, diced
3 cucumbers, peeled and diced
3 tablespoons butter
1 tablespoon lemon juice
6 cups chicken broth
1 teaspoon dill weed
1/4 cup farina
Salt and pepper
1/2 cup sour cream
Thin slices unpeeled cucumber

Saute leek in butter until translucent. Add cucumbers, lemon juice, chicken broth and dill weed. Bring to a simmer and add farina. Simmer 25 minutes. Blend soup in blender. Add salt and pepper and sour cream. Chill several hours and serve garnished with thin slices of cucumber. Serves 6.

## SUBSTITUTE FOR CREAM SOUPS

2 cups instant non-fat dry milk crystals
3/4 cup corn starch
1/4 cup instant chicken bouillon
2 tablespoons dried onion flakes
1/2 teaspoon pepper
1 teaspoon basil (optional)
1 teaspoon thyme (optional)

Combine all ingredients and mix well. Store in an airtight container. Makes 3 cups mix or 9 cans soup.

To reconstitute, combine 1/3 cup mix with 1-1/4 cups water in pan. Stir over low heat until thick. Add 1 tablespoon butter or margarine. (Makes 1 can of soup.)

# CREAM OF ASPARAGUS SOUP

4 cups yellow onions, chopped (about 4 large)
1 stick sweet butter
2 quarts chicken stock, defatted
2 pounds asparagus
1/2 cup heavy cream or buttermilk (if serving soup cold)
Salt and freshly ground pepper to taste

Melt the butter in a large pot and simmer the onions until they are very soft, about 25 minutes, stirring the major part of the time. Add the chicken stock and bring to a boil.

Meanwhile, trim the tips from the asparagus and reserve. Cut about 1 inch from the bottom ends of the asparagus spears and chop into 1/2-inch pieces and drop into the boiling chicken stock. Simmer for 45 minutes.

Puree the soup and return to the pot. Add the reserved tips and simmer 5 minutes. If serving the soup hot, season with salt and pepper and serve. If serving the soup cold, remove from heat, cool, stir in the cream or buttermilk and refrigerate covered. Season to taste and serve very cold.

Serves 6 to 8.

This is a delightful soup to place on any holiday table.


# CHICKEN AND EGG NOODLE SOUP

1-1/2 quarts chicken stock
2 fryer chickens, cut up
1 celery stalk, chopped
1 carrot, chopped
6 green onions, chopped
1 onion, chopped
1 cup dry white wine
1/2 cup romano cheese, grated
1 bay leaf
8 peppercorns
1 tablespoon salt
1 (8-ounce) package egg noodles

Cover chicken parts with stock and bring to a boil. Add celery, carrot, onions, wine, bay leaf, peppercorns and salt. Simmer 1-1/2 hours or until chicken meat falls off bones.

Strain broth, skim off fat and return to heat. Stir in cheese and simmer 30 minutes. Cool chicken and pick off meat. Dice and reserve.

Add noodles and cook until just tender. Return chicken meat and serve garnished with additional cheese, if desired.

Serves 6.

# JACKIE'S CIOPPINO

1/2 cup cooking oil
2 onions, chopped
10 cloves garlic, mashed
1 large green pepper, chopped
6 to 8 shallots, diced
1/2 pound mushrooms, sliced
1 (1-pound 13-ounce) can tomatoes
1 (6-ounce) can tomato paste
1 pint oysters with liquor
2 cups burgundy or any dry red wine
1-1/2 teapoons salt
1 teaspoon freshly ground pepper
Dash of tabasco
1/2 teaspoon basil
1/2 teaspoon oregano
1/2 teaspoon cumin
1 tablespoon chili powder
3 medium potatoes, diced
3 pounds white fish, cut into chunks
1 pound crabmeat
1 pound raw shrimp, shelled and deveined
4 tablespoons chopped parsley

In a stock pot heat oil and saute onions, garlic, green pepper, shallots and mushrooms until onions and pepper are limp, about 3 to 4 minutes. Do not brown. Add tomatoes, tomato paste, oyster liquor and wine. Bring to a simmer; add salt, pepper, tabasco, basil, oregano, cumin, chili powder and the potatoes and simmer 25 minutes. Now add the fish chunks and cook over high heat 5 minutes. Add crabmeat, oysters and shrimp and simmer for another 3 to 5 minutes, or until the shrimp turn pink. To serve, place cioppino in a soup bowl and serve sprinkled with parsley. Be sure to give each guest a soup spoon and a fork. Serve with thick slices of Italian garlic bread. This dish is one of my favorites and will serve 8 hearty eaters.

# CREOLE GUMBO

Shell 2-1/2 pounds raw shrimp, remove the black vein, and set the shrimp aside.

Heat 1 generous tablespoon butter, add 1 generous tablespoon flour, and make a brown roux. Add 1 large white onion, chopped, and 1/2 cup finely cut parsley and green onions mixed. Cook for a few minutes and add 2 quarts hot water and the liquor from 1 pint oysters. Season with 1 bay leaf, celery salt, and a pinch of thyme, salt, cayenne, and black pepper to taste. Boil slowly for 40 minutes, add the shrimp and cook 20 minutes longer.

Reduce the heat, add 1 pint oysters, and 1/4 cup finely cut parsley and green onion. Add also 1 tablespoon gumbo file powder. Serve the gumbo in a soup tureen and put 1 generous spoonful of fluffy dry rice in each soup bowl.

Serve with toasted french bread spread with garlic butter.

# C.V. WOOD'S WORLD-CHAMPIONSHIP CHILI

1 (3-pound) stewing chicken
1-1/2 quarts water or 4 (10-3/4 ounce) cans chicken broth
1/2 pound beef suet or 1/2 cup oil
1/4 cup finely chopped celery
7 cups peeled, chopped tomatoes
2 teaspoons sugar
4 pounds flank steak
6 long green chiles, peeled
1 tablespoon ground oregano
1 tablespoon ground cumin
1/2 tablespoon MSG, optional
1 tablespoon pepper
4 teaspoons salt
5 tablespoons chili powder
1 teaspoon cilantro
1 teaspoon thyme
1 cup beer
2 cloves garlic, finely chopped
5 pounds thin center cut pork chops
3 medium onions, cut in 1/2-inch pieces
1 pound Jack cheese, shredded
1 lime

Cut stewing chicken in pieces. Combine with water in large pot and simmer for 2 hours. Strain off broth and reserve chicken for other use. Canned chicken broth may be substituted. Render suet to make 6 to 8 tablespoons drippings.

In 2-quart saucepan combine celery, tomatoes and sugar. Simmer 1-1/2 hours.

Trim all fat from flank steak. Cut in 3/8-inch cubes. Boil peeled chiles for 15 minutes or until tender. Remove seeds and cut in 1/4-inch squares. Mix oregano, cumin, MSG, pepper, salt, chili powder, cilantro and thyme with beer until all lumps are dissolved. Add tomato mixture, chiles, beer mixture and garlic to chicken broth.

Pour 1/3 of suet dripping into skillet, add 1/2 pork chops and brown. Repeat for remaining pork.

Add pork to broth mixture and cook slowly for 30 minutes. Brown flank steak in remaining drippings about 1/3 at a time. Add to pork mixture and cook slowly for about 1 hour. Add onions and peppers. Simmer 2 to 3 hours longer, stirring with wooden spoon every 15 to 20 minutes.

Cool 1 hour. Refrigerate for 24 hours. Reheat chili before serving. About 5 minutes before serving time add cheese (if you are reheating only a part of the chili, use 1/6 pound cheese to each quart). Just before serving, add juice of lime and stir with wooden spoon. Makes 6 quarts.

# BOUILLABAISSE

1/4 cup olive oil
1 can (1 pound-12 ounces) tomatoes, chopped
1/2 cup onion, chopped
3 cloves garlic. chopped
1/4 teaspoon fennel seeds
1/2 teaspoon crushed thyme
1 bay leaf
2 tablespoons parsley, chopped
1/2 teaspoon rosemary, crushed
1/4 cup celery, minced
2 slices orange
2 slices lemon
1 cup dry white wine
2 cans (10-1/2 ounces each) condensed chicken broth
1/4 teaspoon saffron, crushed
4 pounds assorted raw seafood: lobster, crab meat, cod,
     red snapper, clams, whiting, cut into bite-size pieces
Salt

In a Dutch oven or deep kettle, heat olive oil. Add remaining ingredients except fish and salt. Bring to a boil, lower heat and simmer until vegetables are tender, about 15 minutes. Remove bay leaf, lemon and orange slices.

If you are using lobster, drop into boiling water and cook only until shell turns red. Drain and drench with cold water.

Cut the seafood, including lobster shell, into 1-inch pieces. Add fish pieces to soup. Simmer 10 minutes or until the fish is cooked. Season to taste with salt.

Serve bouillabaisse in soup bowls topped with toasted French bread slices or croutons and chopped parsley.

Serves 6.

# CONSOMME MADRILENE

2 cups chicken broth
2 cups canned bouillon
2 cups canned tomatoes
1 medium onion, sliced
2 whole cloves
1/2 cup carrots, sliced and pared
1 stalk celery, diced
3 whole black peppers
1 teaspoon salt
1 teaspoon sugar

Combine all ingredients. Simmer, covered, for 1 hour. Strain. Serve hot or cold.

Yields 4 cups.

## JELLIED CONSOMME MADRILENE

Sprinkle 1 envelope of unflavored gelatin over 1/2 cup cold broth or water to soften. Stir into hot strained soup until dissolved. Refrigerate until set, then beat with fork. Serve in bouillon cups, topped with lemon slices.

Yields 4 cups.

## CREME VICHYSSOISE

4 leeks or 3 peeled medium onions
2-1/2 cups diced peeled potatoes
2 cups canned chicken broth
1 tablespoon butter
2 cups milk
1 cup heavy cream
2 teaspoons salt
1/4 teaspoon pepper
2 tablespoons minced chives
1/4 teaspoon paprika

Cut the leeks and about 3 inches of their green tops into fine pieces. (If using onions, chop them fine.) Cook with the potatoes in about 3 cups boiling water until very tender. Drain, then press through a fine strainer into a saucepan. Add the broth, butter, milk, cream, salt and pepper, and mix thoroughly. Reheat to blend.

Serve hot or cold, garnished with chopped chives and paprika.

Makes 6 servings.

## SHE CRAB SOUP

2 tablespoons butter
1 tablespoon flour
1 quart milk
2 cups white crab meat with roe
5 drops onion juice
1/4 teaspoon mace
1/4 teaspoon pepper
Grated rind of 1 lemon
1/2 teaspoon salt
1/4 pint heavy cream (whipped)
4 to 6 tablespoons dry sherry

In top of double boiler, melt butter and blend with flour until smooth. While stirring constantly, add the milk slowly. Then add the crabmeat and roe plus all the seasonings except the sherry. Cook over low heat for 20 minutes. Serve in warm cups with one teaspoon of sherry and a topping of whipped cream.

Serves 4 to 6.

# SUMMER LIME SOUP

4 chicken breasts
10 cups chicken broth
1 onion, quartered
3 cloves garlic, chopped
6 peppercorns
Salt to taste
1/2 teaspoon oregano
1/2 onion, chopped
1 large fresh Anaheim chili, peeled and chopped
2 tomatoes, peeled and chopped
5 limes cut into half, plus 1 lime sliced thin
1/2 cup cilantro leaves
2 avocados, peeled and sliced
6 corn tortillas, cut into wedges
Oil

Put chicken breasts, broth, onion, garlic, peppercorns, salt and oregano in a soup pot. Bring to a boil, cover and simmer for 30 minutes. Remove chicken, cool and shred. Saute onion. Add chili and tomatoes. Cook a few minutes. Add to soup pot.

Add the juice of the 5 limes (depending on the strength of the limes, you may add 1 more). Bring to a boil, reduce heat and simmer for 20 minutes. Add chicken and cilantro. Simmer 10 minutes more.

Fry tortilla wedges until crisp. Drain and keep hot. To serve the soup, add the avocado slices, lime slices and, at the last minute, drop in hot tortilla wedges.

Serves 6.

# CUCUMBER SOUP A LA SCANDIA

3 medium cucumbers
2 tablespoons butter
1/2 cup chopped onion
2 bay leaves
1 tablespoon all-purpose flour
3 cups chicken broth
1 teaspoon salt
1 cup light cream
2 tablespoons lemon juice
1/4 teaspoon dried dill weed
Sour cream

Pare cucumbers, slice 2, add chopped onion. Cook in butter with bay leaves until tender, but not brown. Blend in flour, add broth and salt. Simmer covered for 20-30 minutes. Run mixture through a sieve. Chill well. Skim off any fat. Scoop out and discard any seed of remaining cucumber. Grate and add to chilled mixture. Add cream, lemon juice and dill weed. Served in chilled cups with a dollop of sour cream. Sprinkle dill over top for garnish.

Makes 6 servings.

# BORSCHT

3 beets, peeled
1 carrot, peeled
1 medium-sized onion, peeled
1 turnip, peeled
1 cup shredded red cabbage
1 tablespoon butter
1-1/2 quarts beef stock
3 tablespoons red-wine vinegar
1 teaspoon brown sugar
Salt and pepper to taste
2 tablespoons cornstarch blended with cold water
Sour cream or yogurt
Lemon slices or chopped chives

Finely shred the beets, carrot, onion, turnip and cabbage.

Using a large soup kettle, saute vegetables in butter until glazed. Pour in beef stock and add vinegar, sugar, salt and pepper. Cover and simmer 45 minutes. Blend in a paste of cornstarch and water and cook until thickened.

Ladle into bowls and garnish with a spoonful of sour cream or yogurt and lemon slices or chives.

Makes 8 servings at 50 calories per serving.


# HEARTY LENTIL SOUP

1-1/4 cups dry lentils
5 cups water
4 slices bacon, cut into small pieces
1 onion, chopped fine
1 clove garlic, crushed
1 carrot, sliced thin
1 green pepper, chopped
1 tomato, chopped
3 tablespoons butter
3 tablespoons flour
1 (10-1/2-ounce) can consomme or stock
2 teaspoons salt
2 teaspoons vinegar

Soak lentils overnight. Cook for 1 hour in water in which they soaked.

Cook bacon pieces in large skillet until almost crisp. Saute vegetables with bacon and fat until they are almost limp (5 minutes). Drain off the bacon drippings. Add vegetables and bacon to cooked lentils.

In same skillet, melt butter and stir in flour to make a smooth paste. Add consomme, season with salt and vinegar, and cook until smooth and slightly thickened. Add this sauce to lentil mixture; stir, cook over low heat for 30 minutes or longer. May be mixed in blender for smoother consistency.

Serve with crisp French bread and green salad. For variety, slice Vienna sausage into soup before serving.

Makes 8 servings.

## NEW YORK CREAM OF CABBAGE SOUP

       1 green cabbage, shredded
       3 onions, minced
       1 green pepper, chopped
       2 slices pimiento, chopped
       1 bouquet garni
       1 teaspoon salt
       Pepper to taste
       4 cups scalded milk
       1 cup sour cream
       Pinch of nutmeg
       2 tablespoons butter
       4 strips bacon, cooked and crumbled

Place shredded cabbage, onions and green pepper in a kettle; pour in boiling water just to cover vegetables. Add pimiento, 1 bouquet garni, salt and pepper. Cover and simmer until cabbage is tender, onions soft, and the water reduced by half.

Blend milk with sour cream and nutmeg; stir into cabbage. Add butter; cook soup over very low heat until it thickens, stirring occasionally.

Sprinkle crumbled bacon over top of each serving.

Makes 6 servings.


## CHICKEN AND COCONUT MILK SOUP
### (Gaeng Dom Yam Gai)

       5 cups "thin" coconut milk
       1 small chicken, sectioned and cut into bite-sized pieces
       3 stalks lemon grass, bruised and cut into 1-inch lengths
       2 teaspoons Laos powder (Ka)
       3 green onions, finely chopped
       2 tablespoons coriander leaves, chopped
       4-6 fresh Serrano chilies, seeded and chopped
       Juice of 2 limes
       3 tablespoons fish sauce (Nam Pla)

In a saucepan, bring the "thin" coconut milk to a boil. Add the chicken pieces, lemon grass and Laos powder. Reduce heat and simmer until the chicken is tender, about 15 minutes. Do not cover, as this will tend to curdle coconut milk.

When the chicken is tender, add the green onions, coriander leaves and chilies. Bring the heat up just below boiling. Remove the pan from heat, stir in lime juice, fish sauce and serve.

Serves 6 to 8.

NOTE: Beef, cut into thin strips, or firm white fish pieces may be substituted for chicken.

# HOT AND SOUR SHRIMP SOUP (THAI)

1 tablespoon vegetable oil
Shells from shrimp (see below)
8 cups chicken stock
1-1/2 teaspoons salt
3 stalks lemon grass, cut into 1-inch lengths
4 citrus leaves
1 teaspoon lime zest, slivered
2 green Serrano chilies, slivered
2 pounds fresh (green) shrimp (approximately
    20 count per pound), shelled and deveined
1 tablespoon fish sauce (Nam Pla)
Juice of 2 limes
1 red Serrano chili, slivered
2 tablespoons coriander leaves, coarsely chopped
3 green onions (including some green) coarsely chopped

Heat the oil in a saucepan and fry the shells until they turn pink. Add the chicken stock, salt, lemon grass, citrus leaves, lime rind and green chilies. Bring to a boil, cover, reduce heat and simmer 20 minutes. Strain the mixture through a sieve, return the liquid to a saucepan and bring to a boil. Add shrimp to this boiling "stock" and cook them for 2 to 3 minutes. Reduce heat to simmer and add the fish sauce and lime juice. Stir and immediately remove from heat to prevent overcooking. Pour the soup into a tureen, sprinkle with red chilies, coriander leaves and green onions. Serve piping hot.

# EASY CHEESE CHOWDER

1/2 cup carrots, chopped
1/2 cup celery, chopped
2 cups water or chicken stock
4 ounces butter
1 medium onion, chopped
4 ounces flour
1 quart boiling milk
1 quart chicken broth
1 (14-ounce) jar Kraft Cheese Whiz
Salt, pepper and cayenne to taste
1 tablespoon prepared mustard
1/2 cup green onions, chopped

Boil vegetables in water for 5 minutes. Saute onions in butter for 1 minute. Add flour and blend well. Add boiling milk and chicken broth, stirring with a whisk. Add cheese, seasonings, mustard and vegetables, including water in which they were boiled, and chopped green onions. Bring to a boil and serve. This freezes well and will reheat beautifully.

Serves 12.

## EASY ITALIAN VEGETABLE SOUP

8 strips bacon fried crisp (reserve drippings)
1 (14-1/2-ounce) can sliced stewed tomatoes
1 (10-ounce) can cream of potato soup
1 (8-ounce) can pizza sauce
1 (6-ounce) can tomato paste
1 (10-ounce) package frozen broccoli cuts
1 (8-ounce) can green beans, undrained
4 cans (13 ounces each) chicken broth
2 ribs celery, chopped with leafy tops
1 envelope onion soup mix
Salt and pepper to taste

In a Dutch oven on top of the stove, fry bacon over medium heat until crispy. Remove bacon, leaving drippings in pan.

Cool bacon and crumble. Return to drippings with remaining ingredients and simmer gently 1 hour.

Serves 8 to 10.

Easy and so good — and it freezes fabulously.

## KANSAS CITY STEAK SOUP
### (From the Muehlebach Hotel)

1 cup onions, chopped
1 cup carrots, chopped
1 cup celery, chopped
2 pounds ground beef or round steak cut into cubes
1 stick margarine, melted
1 cup flour
2 quarts stock (may use water)
1 package (16-ounce) frozen mixed vegetables
1 (16-ounce) can tomatoes
1 tablespoon monosodium glutamate
2 tablespoons beef stock base
1 teaspoon pepper

Steam onions, carrots and celery al dente. Brown meat and set aside. Combine flour and melted margarine to make a paste. Combine in stock and boil until thickened slightly.

In a separate pan, combine frozen mixed vegetables, tomatoes, MSG, beef base and pepper. Bring to a boil and simmer until vegetables are cooked.

Now combine all ingredients into the stock pot. This soup freezes well and is a meal in itself. Serve with crusty rolls and a salad.

---

A good day never fails to make an even better tomorrow.

## SOPA DE LIMA

2 corn tortillas
Oil for frying
2 teaspoons vegetable oil
1/3 cup chopped onion
1 California chile, roasted, peeled, chopped or
    1/4 cup canned chopped green chiles
4 cups chicken broth
1 cup shredded cooked chicken
Salt
1 tomato, chopped
1 tablespoon lime juice
4 large lime slices

Cut tortillas into 2" x 1/2" strips. Pour oil for frying 1/2 inch deep into a small saucepan or skillet. Heat to 365 degrees. Fry tortilla strips in hot oil until browned and crisp. Drain on paper towels.

Heat 2 teaspoons vegetable oil in a large saucepan. Add onion and chile. Saute until onion is tender but not browned. Add broth, chicken and salt to taste. Cover and simmer 20 minutes. Add tomato; simmer 5 minutes longer. Stir in lime juice. Taste and add more lime juice if desired.

To serve, ladle soup into bowls and add some fried tortilla strips. Float a lime in the center of each serving. Makes 4 servings.

## EASY OLD-FASHIONED BEAN SOUP

6 cups stock
1 cup dried navy beans
8 ounces ham, cut into bite-sized pieces
1 large bay leaf
6 peppercorns
4 whole cloves
1-1/2 cups carrots, chopped
1-1/4 cups celery with tops, chopped
1 cup onion, chopped
Salt and pepper to taste

In a soup kettle bring stock and beans to a boil. Cook for 2 minutes. Turn off heat, cover and let stand 1 hour. Stir in ham, bay leaf, peppercorns and whole cloves. Simmer, covered, 1-1/2 hours. Discard seasonings from the soup. Add vegetables and cook 1/2 hour longer or until vegetables are tender. Season to taste.

Serves 4 to 6.

Great for any time of the year.

# CHICKEN SALAD SANDWICHES

1 (2-1/2 pound) fryer
1/2 cup celery, chopped
2 tablespoons chopped onion
Salt and pepper to taste
1 cup mayonnaise
1-1/2 loaves sliced bread

Cut chicken into serving pieces. Cover with water and poach until chicken is tender. Drain chicken, reserving about 2 tablespoons liquid. Remove meat from the bones and chop. Combine remaining ingredients and enough chicken broth to make mixture spreadable. Spread chicken on buttered bread. Cover with top slice. Cut each sandwich into 3 fingers.

Serves 20 to 25.

# SHRIMP SANDWICHES

1 pound shrimp, chopped and cooked
1 (8-ounce) package cream cheese
1/4 cup butter or margarine
2 tablespoons mayonnaise
2 tablespoons lemon juice
Dash of Worcestershire sauce
1/4 cup minced celery
1 small onion, chopped
Salt and pepper to taste
Garlic to taste
Unsliced bread

Soften cream cheese and butter. Combine cream cheese, butter, mayonnaise, lemon juice and Worcestershire sauce. Beat until smooth and fluffy. Stir in shrimp, celery, onion and seasonings. Slice bread lengthwise. Trim crust. Spread filling over bread. Roll bread as for a jelly roll, beginning at narrow end. Fasten with wooden picks. Cover with a damp towel and refrigerate for several hours. Remove picks and slice filled rolls into pinwheels to serve.

Serves 20 to 25.

# CHEESE-STUFFED ROLLS

8 French rolls
1 pound sharp cheddar cheese, grated
1 cup stuffed olives, sliced
1/2 pound bacon, cooked and crumbled
1/2 teaspoon Worcestershire sauce

Split rolls almost through. Mix remaining ingredients and spoon filling into rolls. Wrap securely in foil and heat in covered crock cooker for 2 to 3 hours at low.

Serves 6 to 8.

# BARBECUED BRISKET

8 - 10 pounds brisket (1st cut)
8 ounces bottled barbecue sauce
1 quart catsup
3/4 cup wine vinegar
3 ounces Worcestershire sauce
2 tablespoons liquid smoke
2 tablespoons prepared mustard
3 tablespoons lemon juice
6 bay leaves
1 clove garlic, mashed
12 peppercorns
1 cup beef consomme
16 sour dough rolls

Mix sauce. Pour over brisket. Bake 3-1/2 to 4 hours at 350°, basting often. Serve on sliced, toasted, buttered sourdough rolls.

Serves 16.

# BARBECUED HAMBURGERS FOR A LARGE PARTY

8 pounds lean ground beef
2 teaspoons salt
1/2 cup shortening or oil
1-1/2 cups chopped onion
1-1/2 cups chopped celery
1/2 cup brown sugar
2 tablespoons prepared mustard
1/2 cup vinegar
2 quarts tomato sauce

Brown beef in a heavy large Dutch oven. Stir to keep crumbly. Pour off fat, stir in salt. In a large skillet melt shortening and saute onion and celery until tender. Add to hamburger with remaining ingredients. Simmer for 15 minutes. Serve on warmed hamburger buns.

(I usually put this mixture in a large crock pot and let everyone help themselves.)

Serves 35 to 40.

# MONTE CRISTO SANDWICH

Double deck:
    1 layer cold sliced turkey or chicken breast
    1 layer Swiss cheese and ham

Cut in half, dip in batter of:
    2 eggs, well beaten
    1-1/2 tablespoons heavy cream
    Dash of salt

Saute in butter to golden brown.

Serve with strawberry jam.

# GYRO SANDWICH

## GYRO PATTIES

1-1/4 pounds lean ground beef
1-1/4 pounds lean ground lamb
1/4 cup oregano
1-1/2 tablespoons onion powder
1 tablespoon garlic powder
3/4 to 1-1/2 tablespoons freshly ground pepper
1 teaspoon thyme
3/4 teaspoon salt

## YOGURT SAUCE

1 cup plain yogurt
1/4 cup finely chopped cucumber
1/4 cup finely chopped onion
2 teaspoons olive oil, garlic powder, salt and
    freshly ground pepper
8 large pita bread rounds, cut in half
Thinly sliced onion rings (garnish)

For patties: Preheat broiler or prepare barbecue. Combine ingredients lightly but thoroughly in large bowl. Shape into 16 thin patties and broil, turning once, until done as desired.

For sauce: Combine first 4 ingredients in small bowl. Add garlic powder, salt and pepper to taste.

To assemble sandwich, place 1 meat patty in each pita half and top with yogurt sauce and onion slices.

# BURRITO DOG

4 weiners
4 large flour tortillas
3 green onions, chopped, including green tops
1/4 pound grated cheddar cheese
1 cup refried beans
Taco sauce

Lay out tortillas and spread each with equal portions of refried beans. Sprinkle each with onions and cheese. Top each with weiners and season to taste with Taco sauce.

Roll up one edge over hot dog and fold in the outside edges. Continue to roll up, forming an envelope.

Wrap each burrito in a double thickness of aluminum foil that has been brushed with melted butter. Place on grill and cook over medium coals 10 to 15 minutes, or until piping hot. Turn frequently.

Kids and guys love these...

Serves 4.

# SAUSAGE FILLED BAGUETTES

        1 loaf sourdough bread
        1 onion, minced
        1-1/2 pounds Italian sausage in bulk
        3 tablespoons heavy cream
        2 eggs, lightly beaten
        2 tablespoons imported Dijon mustard
        2 tablespoons chopped parsley
        2 tablespoons chopped chives
        Salt, if desired, and freshly ground pepper to taste
        2 to 3 tablespoons sweet butter
        3 large cloves garlic, crushed
        1 to 2 teaspoons fresh thyme leaves for garnish

With a long sharp knife, scoop out center of bread, leaving crust intact and about 1/4-inch or less of bread in place. It is easier to cut off ends before you start and use them for another purpose. Make bread crumbs from insides, and use 1-1/4 cups in the filling.

In a large saute pan, saute onion and sausage together until sausage is cooked. Pour off most of fat, and add cream, eggs, mustard, parsley, chives, pepper and bread crumbs. Stuff bread with filling.

Brush outside of loaf with melted butter and crushed garlic. Wrap in foil and bake at 450° for 15 minutes. Unwrap and crisp crust to serve. Sprinkle top with thyme leaves and slice.

# DEVILLED STEAK IN PITA ROLLS

        6 pita rolls (Arabic pocket bread)
        1 tablespoon oil
        1 pound lean ground top-round steak
        1 tablespoon Worcestershire sauce
        1 tablespoon Dijon mustard
        1 tablespoon prepared horseradish
        2 tablespoons capers
        2 teaspoons cornstarch dissolved in 2 tablespoons water
        1/4 cup beef broth

Heat pita rolls and open one side.

Heat oil in wok over high heat. Add beef and stir-fry until no longer pink. Stir in Worcestershire sauce, mustard, horseradish and capers. Stir dissolved corn-starch into beef broth. Add to meat and stir until liquid thickens.

Spoon into pita rolls and serve hot.

Makes 6 servings.

# HOMEMADE SLOPPY JOES

3 pounds ground beef
1-1/2 teaspoons salt
1/2 teaspoon pepper
1-1/2 cups chopped onion
1/2 cup chopped green pepper
1/2 cup chopped celery
2 (15-ounce) cans tomato sauce
1 cup water
1/2 cup ketchup
2 tablespoons Worcestershire sauce
1 tablespoon prepared mustard
2 tablespoons brown sugar, packed
20 hamburger buns

Cook beef in large skillet or Dutch oven until it loses redness. Drain excess fat.

Add salt, pepper, onion, green pepper and celery; cook, stirring occasionally, about 5 minutes to soften vegetables. Stir in remaining ingredients, except buns, and simmer 15 minutes, stirring occasionally.

Serve between buns.

# AVOCADO BURGERS

1-1/2 pounds very lean ground beef
1/3 cup fine dry bread crumbs
1-1/4 cups tomato juice
1 egg, beaten
1 small onion, chopped
3 teaspoons chili powder
1/2 teaspoon Mexican oregano
Salt
1-1/2 tablespoons Worcestershire sauce
1 small avocado, pitted and thinly sliced
3/4 cup jack cheese, grated
4 ounces chopped green chilies
Salt to taste

Mix together the meat, bread crumbs, 1/4 cup tomato juice, egg, onion, 2 teaspoons chili powder, oregano, salt and Worcestershire. Mix and pat into 8 equal patties.

In the center of 4 of the patties, place the avocado slices, grated cheese and 1 tablespoon of the chilies; reserve the rest.

Top each patty with a second patty and press the edges together to seal. May be chilled ahead at this point. May bake or barbecue.

Meanwhile, combine remaining tomato juice, salt, chili powder and chilies. Simmer 10 minutes. Serve each patty with sauce spooned over. Dynamite for any kind of gathering.

Serves 4.

# SUMMER PITA POCKET SANDWICHES

1 pound lean ground beef
1 medium onion, chopped
2 cloves garlic, crushed
2 tablespoons oil
2 medium tomatoes, chopped, or 1 cup canned tomatoes, chopped
1/2 cup raisins
1/4 cup slivered almonds
1 teaspoon salt
1 teaspoon vinegar
1/2 teaspoon cinnamon
1/8 teaspoon pepper
4 (4-inch) pita breads, halved crosswise

In a skillet cook beef, stirring to break up all the pieces. Remove from skillet and drain off fat.

In the same skillet, saute the onion and garlic 5 minutes. Stir in tomatoes and beef, stir well, and blend in the remaining ingredients. Simmer 20 minutes more or until the liquid is absorbed. Spoon into pita halves.

Serves 4.

If you like, use hamburger or hot dog buns instead of pita bread. Serve with fresh tomato soup for a complete summer dinner.

## Back to School Favorites
## HAM BISCUITS

Flour
4 teaspoons baking powder
1-1/2 teaspoons salt
4 tablespoons shortening
Milk
2 cups ground cooked ham
4 tablespoons melted butter
1 teaspoon Dijon mustard
1/2 cup cheddar cheese, grated

Sift 2 cups flour, baking powder and 1/2 teaspoon salt together. Cut in shortening. Add 2/3 cup milk to form a soft dough. Combine ham, 2 tablespoons butter and mustard. Roll dough out, spread with ham mixture. Roll up as for jelly roll, cut into 1-inch slices. Place on baking sheet. Bake at 425 degrees for 15 to 20 minutes. Blend remaining butter and 2 tablespoons flour in a saucepan. Stir in 1-1/2 cups milk, cook stirring constantly until thickened. Add remaining salt or to taste and cheese. Serve sauce over biscuits.

Makes 10 to 12 biscuits.

My kids being Irish always loved this recipe and it is so easy.

# Salads
# and
# Dressings

## HONEY MUSTARD DRESSING

1/2 cup honey
1/4 cup prepared mustard
1-1/2 cups salad oil
1 pint mayonnaise
1/4 cup cider vinegar
1/4 cup onions, chopped
Salt to taste
1 teaspoon Worcestershire sauce
Chopped parsley to taste

Combine all ingredients together with a whisk. Chill. Pour over mixed green or fruit salad. This dressing keeps well in the refrigerator.

Yields 2 pints.

## GRANDMA'S BOILED MUSTARD DRESSING

1 cup milk
2 egg yolks, beaten
3 teaspoons dry mustard
4 teaspoons sugar
2 teaspoons flour
1 teaspoon salt
1/4 teaspoon pepper
1 cup vinegar, heated
2 tablespoons butter or margarine
2 egg whites, stiffly beaten

Bring milk to the boiling point. Add dry mixed ingredients to the beaten egg yolks. Blend gently, stirring constantly with milk. Pour hot vinegar slowly into this, stirring constantly. Cook mixture until well thickened. Remove from heat and add butter and beat well. Then fold in stiffly beaten egg whites.

This is an old family recipe that has been used for generations. It is a little touchy to make, but so worth the effort. It is good for many dishes, especially for summer dishes. Use it hot on hot dishes and cold on cold foods. The flavor is tantalizing.

## RED RASPBERRY VINEGAR

Put in a large glass bowl or stainless steel bowl:

6 quarts red raspberries
1 quart wine vinegar

Let stand in a cool place for about 20 minutes. Strain. Measure the liquid into an enamel or stainless steel pan and add an equal amount of sugar. Bring to a boil and simmer 10 minutes. Cool and store in tightly-lidded sterile jars.

# MAGIC PAN OIL AND VINEGAR SALAD DRESSINGS

1 cup vegetable oil
1/2 cup tarragon wine vinegar
1 teaspoon tarragon leaves
1/2 teaspoon salt
1/8 teaspoon black pepper
1 teaspoon sugar
1/2 teaspoon Dijon mustard

Into a small mixing bowl place tarragon leaves, salt, pepper, sugar and Dijon mustard. Using a small wire whisk, beat vinegar into spices. Continue mixing until thoroughly mixed. Slowly add oil. Continue mixing until oil is completely blended and dressing has a light creamy color. Allow to sit 20 minutes in the refrigerator for flavors to blend.

To prepare Magic Pan Sweet and Sour Dressing, add 2 additional teaspoons of sugar.

# BASIL WINE VINEGAR

1 pint dry white wine
1 pint white vinegar
20 bunches fresh young basil

Place wine and vinegar in a saucepan over low heat. Bring to scalding but not a boil. Meanwhile, wash basil and place in a sterilized quart jar. Pour hot liquid slowly over basil. Seal tightly and store in a dark place for 3 weeks. Strain vinegar through a cheesecloth and pour into smaller sterilized bottles. Add a sprig of basil to each bottle if you wish.

Makes 1 quart.

# TARRAGON WINE VINEGAR

1 pint dry red wine
1 pint cider vinegar
20 to 30 bunches fresh tarragon

Place wine and vinegar in a saucepan over low heat. Bring to scalding but not a boil. Slowly pour hot liquid over tarragon in a sterilized quart jar. Seal tightly and store in a dark place for 3 weeks. Strain vinegar through cheesecloth and pour into smaller bottles if you wish. Add a bunch of tarragon to each sterilized bottle if you wish.

Makes 1 quart.

# DILL WINE VINEGAR

1 pint dry white wine
1 pint white vinegar
20 to 30 flowers of dill

Place wine and vinegar in a saucepan over low heat. Bring to scalding but do not boil. Meanwhile, wash and cut dill into 1-inch lengths. Place in a sterilized quart jar. Pour hot liquid slowly over dill. Seal tightly and store in a dark place for 3 weeks. Strain vinegar through cheesecloth and pour into smaller sterilized bottles.

Makes 1 quart.

# HAWAIIAN FRENCH DRESSING

1/4 cup white wine vinegar
3/4 cup salad oil
1 teaspoon salt
1/4 teaspoon monosodium glutamate
1/2 teaspoon dry mustard
1 teaspoon sugar
1/4 teaspoon ground pepper
1/4 cup fresh pineapple juice or
    crushed fresh pineapple
1/4 cup minced fresh mint

Blend vinegar with dry ingredients before mixing in oil, pineapple and mint. Shake in a closed jar and chill before using. Excellent on both green and fruit salads.

# TOMATO FRENCH DRESSING

1 (8-ounce) can whole tomatoes, drained
1/3 cup salad oil
1/4 cup chili sauce (bottled)
1/4 cup granulated sugar, or to taste
1/3 cup red wine vinegar
1 clove garlic, crushed
1/2 teaspoon celery seed
1/2 teaspoon salt
1/2 teaspoon instant minced onion
Dash dry mustard
Dash black pepper

Drain tomatoes; use liquid for another purpose. Remove seeds from tomatoes and set tomatoes aside.

Combine remaining ingredients in bowl of food processor, or in large bowl. Blend together. Add well-drained tomatoes, pulse on-off once or twice only, until tomatoes are chopped bite-size, or chop tomatoes by hand and add to liquid in bowl. Refrigerate.

Makes about 1 cup.

# SWEET AND SOUR DRESSING

Wonderful addition to a green salad and perhaps some orange and avocado slices, or for fruit salad.

1/2 cup sugar
1/4 cup wine vinegar
1-1/2 teaspoons lemon juice
1/4 cup oil
2 teaspoons chili sauce
1/2 teaspoon Worcestershire sauce
1/4 teaspoon dry mustard
1/4 teaspoon curry powder
Dash of Tabasco
1 clove garlic, chopped

Combine all ingredients in a glass jar and shake until well mixed. Chill several hours before serving. Will last about one month in the refrigerator.

# CREAM DRESSING IN THE FOOD PROCESSOR

1/4 cup firmly packed parsley leaves
1 small clove garlic, peeled
2 or 3 whole green onions, cut into 1-inch lengths
1 egg
1 tablespoon white wine vinegar
1 tablespoon fresh lemon juice
1 teaspoon white horseradish (optional)
1/4 teaspoon salt
Freshly ground pepper
1/2 cup vegetable or safflower oil
1 cup nonfat yogurt or sour cream

Insert the metal knife blade in processor. Process parsley leaves until finely minced; set aside. With machine running, drop garlic clove through food chute, scraping down container sides. Add green onions to container. Process and chop with 4 to 6 half-second pulses; set aside with parsley.

Place egg, vinegar, lemon juice, horseradish, salt and pepper in container. With machine running, add oil through the chute within 20 seconds. Add parsley, green onions and yogurt to container. Process 3 or 4 seconds. Cover and refrigerate.

VARIATIONS:

## Bleu Cheese Dressing

Omit horseradish and parsley. Remove rind from 3 ounces bleu cheese, cut into 1-inch chunks. After yogurt is added, add bleu cheese to container and process with 4 half-second pulses to chop and combine simultaneously.

## Green Goddess Dressing

Quarter 1 medium ripe avocado and, after oil is added, add avocado to container. Puree 30 seconds before adding remaining ingredients.

# MARIE CALLENDAR'S HOT BACON DRESSING

> 3 tablespoons cornstarch
> 1 tablespoon soy sauce
> 3 tablespoons wine vinegar
> 1/3 cup water
> 1/2 cup brown sugar
> 1-1/4 cups pineapple juice

Place in a saucepan and simmer until thick, stirring frequently.

Add: Bacon bits
     Chopped green onions
     Chopped red and green pepper

Serve warm.

# MOLDED CHICKEN CRANBERRY SALAD

LAYER 1:

> 1 envelope unflavored gelatin
> 1/4 cup cold water
> 1 can (2 cups) whole cranberry sauce
> 1/2 cup broken walnut meats
> 1 tablespoon lemon juice

Soften gelatin in cold water; dissolve over hot water. Add to cranberry sauce, nuts and lemon juice. Pour into a flat 10″ x 6″ x 2″ casserole and chill until firm.

LAYER 2:

> 1 envelope unflavored gelatin
> 1/4 cup cold water
> 1 cup mayonnaise
> 1/2 cup water
> 3 tablespoons lemon juice
> 3/4 teaspoon salt
> 2 cups chicken, cooked and diced
> 1/2 cup diced celery
> 2 tablespoons chopped parsley

Soften gelatin and dissolve, as above. Blend in mayonnaise, water, lemon juice and salt. Add chicken, celery and parsley. Pour over first layer and chill until firm. Cut in squares; invert each on salad greens. Top with mayonnaise and walnut halves.

---

Life can't give you joy
Unless you really will it.
Life just gives you time and space.
It's up to you to fill it.

## FRESH GREEN BEAN SALAD

2 pounds fresh green beans
1/2 medium red onion, chopped
1/2 cup salad dressing
3/4 cup sour cream
1-1/2 teaspoons sugar
1-1/2 teaspoons vinegar
Salt and pepper to taste
1/2 teaspoon dill weed

Snap ends off beans and cut in half. Steam until al dente. Cool. Add remaining ingredients and mix well. Cover and chill overnight or longer.

Serves 6 to 8.

## A Salute to Octoberfest
## OCTOBERFEST APPLESAUCE SALAD

1 small package lemon jello
1/4 cup cinnamon red hot candies
1 cup boiling water
1/4 cup sugar
1 cup applesauce

### Topping:

1 small package lemon jello
1 cup boiling water
7 to 10 ice cubes
1/2 cup heavy cream, whipped
1 (3-ounce) package cream cheese, softened

Dissolve jello and cinnamon candies in boiling water. Stir in sugar and apple-sauce. Put into mold or 8" x 8" pan and place in fridge to set. Topping: Dissolve jello in boiling water. Add ice cubes and stir until jello thickens. Whip jello and then add softened cream cheese. Stir, then fold in whipped cream. Spread on first layer.

Serves 8 to 10. Delightful for the fall holidays.

## SOUR CREAM BEAN SALAD

1/2 cup sour cream
1/3 cup mayonnaise
1 (16-ounce) can French-cut green beans
1 big cucumber, sliced and seeded
6 green onions
1 teaspoon dill weed
Dash of salt, pepper and garlic powder

Blend sour cream and mayonnaise together. Add drained beans and remaining ingredients. Toss well. Cover and chill several hours. Serve on lettuce or eat as is.

## MOLDED SPINACH SALAD

1 small package lime gelatin
1 cup boiling water
1/2 cup cold water
1 tablespoon vinegar
1/2 cup mayonnaise
1 cup spinach, cooked and well drained
3/4 cup cottage cheese
1/3 cup celery, chopped
1/3 cup onion, chopped
Bleu cheese salad dressing of your choice

Dissolve gelatin in the boiling water. Add cold water and vinegar. Cool. Add the mayonnaise and beat. Refrigerate until cool. Beat again and add the spinach, cottage cheese, celery and onion. Place in favorite ring mold. Chill until firm and serve with bleu cheese salad dressing.

Serves 8.

## DIFFERENT POTATO SALAD

1 cup sour cream
2 tablespoons wine vinegar
1 tablespoon prepared mustard
2 teaspoons granulated sugar
1-1/2 teaspoons salt
1/2 teaspoon pepper
1/2 teaspoon caraway seeds
4 cups diced, cooked potatoes (about 4 medium)
1/2 cucumber, chopped
2 small onions, chopped

In a large bowl, blend sour cream, vinegar, mustard, sugar, salt, pepper and caraway seeds. Add remaining ingredients and toss gently until well mixed. Refrigerate to develop flavors until serving. Serve on crisp greens. The caraway seeds and sour cream give new flavor to this potato salad recipe.

Serves 8.

## GRISWOLDS BEAN SPROUT SALAD

1 can bean sprouts, washed and drained
1 tablespoon sesame seeds, toasted
1/4 cup green onion, chopped
6 tablespoons soy sauce
1 teaspoon oil
1/4 teaspoon sugar
Dash of garlic salt and cayenne

Mix together all the ingredients and chill.

Serves 6 to 8.

# KATHY GALLAGHER'S
# SEAFOOD/PASTA SALAD

40 ounces (2-1/2 pounds) Angel Hair pasta,
    cooked al dente
2 tablespoons Tapenade (French olive paste)
1 tablespoon Dijon mustard
1 teaspoon salt
1/2 teaspoon black pepper
6-1/2 ounces oilve oil
3 ounces lemon juice
1-1/2 ounces sherry vinegar
2 tablespoons chopped fresh basil
2 tablespoons chopped fresh parsley
2 tablespoons Pommery mustard
1 tablespoon fresh garlic (crushed/minced)

Combine all ingredients except pasta. Toss pasta in dressing. Add chopped tomatoes, chopped avocados, sliced red and green bell peppers.

Place on plate and top with 15 chopped jumbo shrimp and 30 whole scallops (with roe, if available).

Serves 6.


# PAPAYA AND SHRIMP SALAD

1 head leaf lettuce, washed and separated
1/2 white cabbage, finely shredded
2 papayas, peeled, seeded and thinly sliced
2 firm medium tomatoes, sliced
1/2 pound cooked bay shrimp
2 tablespoons roasted peanuts, coarsely crushed
2 green Serrano chilies, seeded and cut into slivers
Juice of 3 limes
2 tablespoons fish sauce (Nam Pla)
2 tablespoons palm sugar
2 green onions, finely chopped

Arrange the lettuce leaves on a platter.

In a bowl, combine the shredded cabbage with the papaya slices and tomatoes, reserving a few slices for garnish. Place this mixture on the platter and sprinkle with shrimp and peanuts. Decorate with the remaining tomato and chilies.

Mix the lime juice, fish sauce, palm sugar and green onions together in a bowl until the sugar has dissolved. Pour this dressing over the salad and refrigerate until served.

Note: An equal amount of cooked pork cubes makes an interesting substitution for the shrimp.

Serves 6 to 8.

## SUMMER STEAK SALAD

2 pounds boneless sirloin, cut into 1/2-inch cubes
1/2 cup butter
3/4 pound mushrooms, sliced
1 (9-ounce) package frozen artichoke hearts, cooked and cooled
1 cup celery, diced
1 pint cherry tomatoes
2 tablespoons parsley, chopped
2 tablespoons chives, chopped
2 cups steak salad dressing (see below)
2 tablespoons Dijon mustad
Bibb lettuce

In a large skillet on high heat, saute meat cubes a few at a time in butter until brown on all sides. Do not overcook. Place in a large bowl and cool. Saute mushrooms quickly in skillet with remaining butter. Combine beef, mushrooms and remaining vegetables. Mix lightly. Mix the salad dressing with the mustard and pour over the beef/vegetable mixture. Toss, cover and marinate overnight. Serve on a bed of lettuce.

## STEAK SALAD DRESSING

2/1/2 cups saffron or olive oil
3/4 cup wine vinegar
6 green onions, finely chopped
1/3 cup parsley, chopped
1/3 cup dillweed, chopped
1/8 teaspoon Tabasco sauce
Salt and pepper to taste

Combine everything in a glass jar and shake well. Use about 2 cups of dressing. Save the remainder for other uses.

Serves 6.

## SEVEN-LAYER SALAD

1-1/2 heads iceberg lettuce
1/2 cup chopped celery
1/2 cup chopped green pepper
1/2 cup chopped red onion
1(10-ounce) package frozen peas, thawed
1 pint mayonnaise
2 tablespoons sugar
6 ounces shredded cheddar cheese
8 slices bacon, crisply cooked and crumbled

Tear lettuce in small pieces into a large salad bowl (a glass bowl shows off layers). Add, in layers, celery, green pepper, onion and peas. Cover with mayonnaise; sprinkle sugar evenly over mayonnaise. Top with cheese, then bacon. Cover with plastic wrap.

Refrigerate 8 hours before serving.

Yields 12 servings.

# FRESH FRUIT SALAD

2 cups boiling water
2 (3-ounce) packages apple jello
1 envelope unflavored gelatin
1/4 cup water
3/4 cup sugar
5 or 6 peaches, sliced and sweetened
1-1/2 cups sliced green grapes
4 oranges, sectioned
3 pears, diced
3 bananas, diced
1 cantaloupe, cut into balls
1 basket blueberries
Juice from the fresh fruits
1/2 pint whipping cream, whipped and sweetened
Mayonnaise to taste

Pour boiling water over packages of the apple jello. Add unflavored gelatin which has been softened in 1/4 cup water. Stir until dissolved.

Add sugar and fruit to gelatin. Add enough water to fruit juices to make 2 cups and stir into gelatin mixture. Pour into favorite molds and chill until set.

Combine the whipped cream and mayonnaise for dressing. When ready to serve, unmold salad and top with the dressing.

Serves 30.

This is fabulous for your 4th of July picnic. It serves the whole family and is wonderful with any type of barbecue.


# APRICOT-MARSHMALLOW DELIGHT

1 can apricots
1 can crushed pineapple
1 package orange gelatin
1 cup miniature marshmallows
1/4 cup sugar
1-1/2 teaspoons flour
1 tablespoon butter
1 egg, beaten
1 cup whipping cream
1/2 cup grated cheddar cheese
Lettuce

Drain apricots, reserving 1/2 cup syrup; chop apricots. Drain pineapple, reserving 1/2 cup syrup. Dissolve gelatin in 1 cup boiling water; stir in marshmallows. Add reserved apricot syrup and fruits; pour into pan. Chill until firm. Blend sugar and flour in saucepan; stir in reserved pineapple syrup. Add butter and egg; cook over low heat until thickened, stirring constantly. Cool custard. Whip cream; fold into custard. Spread whipped cream mixture over salad; sprinkle with cheese. Chill for several hours. Cut salad into squares; serve on lettuce.

Yields 12 servings.

## LOW CALORIE SHREDDED CHICKEN SALAD

Fresh cilantro is a must in this full meal salad as it gives just the right amount of zip. I don't mind counting calories when it tastes so good.

1 pound chicken breasts
1/2 cup chicken broth
1 medium-sized head iceberg lettuce, shredded
4 green onions, thinly sliced
1 small bunch cilantro
1 (4-ounce) can water chestnuts, very thinly sliced
1 stalk celery, very thinly sliced
1/2 cup petite peas (optional)
3 radishes, very thinly sliced
1/4 cup toasted sesame seeds
1 avocado, sliced, or 4 slices or spears fresh pineapple
Sesame oil dressing

Poach chicken breasts in broth for 15 minutes, or until cooked through. Let cool; then remove skin and bones and dice meat finely. Place chicken in a bowl with lettuce, onion, cilantro sprigs, water chestnuts, celery, peas and radishes. Pour sesame oil dressing over salad and mix well. Spoon into serving bowls and sprinkle with sesame seeds. Garnish with fresh avocado slices or fresh pineapple.

Serves 4.

Calories: 310 per serving.

## SESAME OIL DRESSING

Mix together in a small container 1 teaspoon salt, dash Tabasco, 1/2 teaspoon each dry mustard and grated lemon peel, 1-1/2 teaspoons white wine vinegar, 1 tablespoon each honey and soy sauce, and 2 tablespoons each sesame oil and lemon juice and safflower oil.

## FRESH CRANBERRY SALAD

2 (12-ounce) packages fresh cranberries
3 cups sugar
2 cups red seedless grapes, cut in halves
1/4 cup walnuts, chopped fine
2 cups whipping cream

Grind the fresh cranberries. Add the sugar and let stand at room temperature overnight. Drain cranberries. Add grapes and walnuts to cranberries. Whip cream and fold into cranberries. Refrigerate until ready to serve.

Serves 12.

A wonderful, Oregonian treat!

# PARTY SPINACH SALAD FOR GRADUATION

                    2 tablespoons white wine vinegar
                    1 tablespoon dry vermouth
                    2 teaspoons Dijon mustard
                    1 teaspoon soy sauce
                    1/2 teaspoon curry powder
                    1/2 teaspoon sugar
                    1/2 teaspoon salt
                    1/4 teaspoon pepper
                    1-1/4 pounds spinach

Combine all the ingredients except spinach in a jar and shake well. Pour into salad bowl. Wash and dry spinach. Tear into bite-sized pieces and place in a salad bowl on top of dressing. Cover with plastic wrap and chill thoroughly. Toss well just before serving and top with:

                    1 green apple, diced
                    1/3 cup dry roasted Spanish peanuts
                    1/4 cup golden raisins
                    1 bunch green onions, chopped
                    1 tablespoon sesame seeds, toasted

Toss and serve.

Serves 8.

This is fabulous with any meats you barbecue; you might add an ear of fresh corn for that perfect spring and summer party.


# HOLIDAY POTATO SALAD

                    8 medium-sized new potatoes
                    1 (10-1/2 ounce) can bouillon
                    1 large red onion, finely chopped
                    12 cherry tomatoes
                    1 (4-ounce) can artichoke hearts, drained and sliced
                    4 hard-cooked eggs, diced
                    Chopped parsley
                    Salt and pepper
                    1 cup mayonnaise

Boil the potatoes in their jackets until tender, about 25 minutes. Drain. When cool, peel and slice.

Marinate the potato slices in the bouillon for 1 hour.

Put chopped onion into a salad bowl or sealable plastic container with the cherry tomatoes, sliced artichoke hearts, diced eggs and a sprinkle of chopped parsley, salt and pepper to taste.

Just before serving, drain the potatoes and add to vegetables. Stir in mayonnaise at last minute.

If transporting the salad, keep it *cold*.

## HOT WEATHER GUACAMOLE SALAD

1/2 to 1 cup avocado
2 tablespoons lemon juice
1/2 cup sour cream
1/2 cup salad oil
1 clove garlic, mashed
1/2 teaspoon sugar
1/2 tablespoon chili powder
1/4 teaspoon salt
Few dashes Tabasco
1/2 head each romaine and iceberg lettuce
1/2 cup sliced pitted black olives
1/2 cup shredded cheddar cheese
1/4 cup chopped green onions, include green part
1 cup corn chips
1 (1-pound) can albacore or 1 pound of any
      leftover cooked meat
2 tomatoes, cut in wedges for garnish

Put first 9 ingredients in the blender; blend well and chill.

Just before serving, place remaining ingredients in a salad bowl and toss gently with the dressing.

Serves 6.

## HEAVENLY CHEESE SALAD MOLD

1 (3-ounce) package lemon flavored gelatin
1 cup boiling water
3/4 cup pineapple juice
1 tablespoon lemon juice
1-1/4 cups crushed pineapple, drained
1 cup (1/4 pound) sharp cheddar cheese, shredded
1 cup heavy cream, whipped
Lettuce

Dissolve gelatin in water; add juices. Chill until slightly thickened. Fold in crushed pineapple, cheese and whipped cream and pour into 1-1/2 quart mold. Chill. Unmold on lettuce.

Serves 8.

## WATERGATE SALAD

8 ounces instant pistachio pudding
8 ounces Cool Whip
8 ounces crushed pineapple, drained
8 ounces miniature marshmallows
8 ounces nuts, chopped

Make pudding according to package instructions. Add remaining ingredients and pour into favorite mold and chill.

Serves 8 to 10.

# CURRIED BUFFET SLAW

1 can consomme
1 cup water
1 bay leaf
3 cloves
3 pounds cabbage, shredded
1 onion, chopped
2 cloves garlic, crushed
4 tablespoons butter or margarine
2 tablespoons flour
1 tablespoon curry powder or to taste
Salt and pepper to taste
1-1/2 cups sour cream
1/2 cup bread crumbs
Paprika

In a large saucepan simmer consomme, water, bay leaf and cloves for 5 minutes. Remove bay leaf and cloves. Add cabbage, cover and simmer for 10 minutes. Drain cabbage, reserving 1/2 cup broth. In a small skillet, saute onion and garlic in the butter for 2 to 3 minutes. Blend in flour and seasonings. Stir and mix in sour cream and reserved broth. Stir over low heat until sauce simmers and thickens. Pour sauce over cabbage and mix well. Place cabbage in a 2-quart casserole. Sprinkle with crumbs and paprika. May be made ahead at this point. When ready to serve, bake at 425° for 15 to 20 minutes.

Serves 8 to 10.

Great for a different way to serve sauerkraut.
This is terrific with any pork or chicken product.

# JICAMA SALAD

1 medium-sized jicama
1/2 fresh pineapple, cut into (1-inch) square cubes
2 oranges, peeled and cut into small pieces
2 cucumbers, peeled and cut into (1-inch) squares
Juice of 2 fresh limes
1/2 teaspoon chili powder
1 teaspoon salt

Peel the jicama and cut into chunks, saving some large slices for decorative chunks for garnish. Put into cold water immediately and leave until it gets very white. Drain and place in bowl with pineapple, oranges and cucumbers. Squeeze lime juice over top and sprinkle with chili powder and salt. Toss well to combine. Serve in bowl with reserved slices of jicama jutting out like flower petals.

This is a recipe from Antonio's Restaurant, 7472 Melrose, Los Angeles.

# CEVICHE SACRAMENTO

1-1/2 pounds mild white fish (scallops, turbot, halibut, sole)
1 cup fresh lime juice
3 to 4 cans California green chilies, chopped
1 cup minced onion (green, red, white or yellow)
1 teaspoon salt
1/2 teaspoon crumbled oregano leaves (more if desired)
Dash white pepper
1/4 cup olive oil
2 to 3 large tomatoes, peeled, seeded and chopped
Lettuce leaves
8 large avocado halves
Chopped parsley or coriander
Sour cream
Chopped green onion

Cut fish into (1/2-inch) cubes. Place in a stainless steel bowl. Stir in lime juice. Place in refrigerator for 3 hours, or overnight. Just before serving, stir in chilies, onion, seasoning, oil and tomatoes.

To serve, place lettuce leaves on salad plates. Place avocado halves in center of each plate. With a slotted spoon, fill each avocado half with fish mixture. Garnish with chopped parsley or coriander leaves or sour cream and chopped green onion.

Makes 8 servings.


# NECTARINE CHICKEN SALAD

3 cups diced, cooked chicken
3 cups diced nectarines
1 cup thinly sliced celery
1 tablespoon green onion, minced
1/3 cup orange juice
Salt and pepper to taste
1/2 cup whipping cream, whipped
1/2 cup mayonnaise
Crisp salad greens
1/4 cup walnuts, finely chopped

In a large bowl combine chicken, nectarines, celery, onion, orange juice, salt and pepper; set aside.

Lightly combine the whipped cream and mayonnaise. Fold into the chicken mixture just to coat. Spoon into lettuce-lined salad bowls. Garnish with the walnuts. Chill if desired.

A great make-ahead for a luncheon or a shower. Serve with crescent rolls.

Makes 4 servings.

# ARTICHOKE GRAPEFRUIT SALAD

1 (15-ounce) can artichoke hearts, drained
1/4 cup salad oil
2 tablespoons vinegar
1 teaspoon Worcestershire sauce
1/4 teaspoon salt
1/8 teaspoon pepper
1 tablespoon parsley, chopped
3 cups iceberg lettuce
2 cups romaine
1 cup endive
2 pink grapefruits, sectioned.

Cut artichoke hearts in half. Combine next 6 ingredients and pour over artichokes and chill 3 to 4 hours. Combine cut-up greens in a salad bowl. Add artichoke mixture, grapefruit sections and toss lightly.

Serves 6.


# BEET JELLO SALAD

1 (15-ounce) can pickled beets
3/4 cup cold water
2 cups cranberry juice
1/4 teaspoon salt
1/8 teaspoon pepper
1 bay leaf
2 (3-ounce) packages lemon jello
2 tablespoons lemon juice
2 tablespoons minced celery
3 tablespoons minced green onion

Drain juice from beets and place juice in a pan. Dice beets and set aside. Add water to beet juice, cranberry juice, salt, pepper and bay leaf. Heat to boiling. Remove from heat. Add jello and stir until dissolved. Stir in lemon juice and bay leaf. Chill until mixture is syrupy. Stir in remaining ingredients. Put in 8-cup mold and chill until set. Serve with sour cream horseradish sauce (see below).


## Sour Cream Horseradish Sauce

1 cup sour cream
1 tablespoon horseradish
1/2 teaspoon sugar
Salt to taste
Cream to thin

Mix together and chill.

Serves 8.

# HOLIDAY GREEN SALAD

DRESSING:

1/2 cup lemon juice
1/2 cup catsup
1/2 cup chopped onion
1 teaspoon salt
3 tablespoons honey
1 cup salad oil

Combine all ingredients in a food processor with metal blade or in blender. Blend until well mixed. Dressing can be refrigerated for several weeks.

SALAD:

1 head iceberg lettuce
2 bunches romaine lettuce
1 large cucumber, peeled and coarsely chopped
1 pint cherry tomatoes, cut in half
2 avocados, peeled and diced
3/4 cup black olives, coarsely chopped
2 cups croutons

Tear lettuce into bite-size pieces. Store in plastic bags until ready to use. Before serving, place lettuce in large salad bowl, add remaining ingredients and toss with salad dressing.

Serves 12-14.

# MUSHROOM, CHEESE AND WATERCRESS SALAD

1 cup fresh mushrooms
1 cup diced Gruyere cheese
1/2 cup bias-sliced celery
2 cups washed fresh watercress
1/2 cup fresh alfalfa sprouts (optional)

DRESSING:

1/4 cup wine vinegar
1/2 cup olive oil
1 tablespoon Italian seasoning
Dash salt
Freshly ground pepper

Toss mushrooms, cheese, celery and watercress in a salad bowl. Just before serving, make dressing and pour over salad. Toss lightly again. Sprinkle top with sprouts, if desired.

Serves 4.

## HOLIDAY CRANBERRY SALAD

1 package Knox gelatin
1 large package cherry jello
1 large can crushed pineapple
1 can Royal Ann cherries
Juice from the canned fruit plus enough orange juice
    to make 4 cups
1/2 cup pecans, chopped
Juice from 1 lemon and 1 orange
Dash of salt
1-1/2 cups sugar
1 pound cranberries

Dissolve gelatin in 1/2 cup of canned fruit juice. Heat remaining liquid and pour over jello. Add dissolved gelatin. Grind cranberries in blender with lemon and orange juice. Cook cranberries with sugar and a dash of salt for 10 minutes. Add chopped pecans and mix all ingredients together. Pour into 4 foil Christmas tree molds or a large mold and chill until firm.

DRESSING:

2 egg yolks, beaten
1/2 cup sugar
1/2 teaspoon salt
1/4 cup lemon juice

1 teaspoon grated lemon rind
1 tablespoon vinegar
1 tablespoon butter or margarine
1 cup whipping cream, whipped

Cook egg yolks, sugar, salt, lemon juice, lemon rind and vinegar in a double boiler or heavy saucepan until thick. Add butter and cool. Fold in whipped cream.

Decorate top of salad with the dressing. If serving from a large dish, cut into squares and place on lettuce leaves and garnish.

Serves 12.

## APPLE WALNUT SALAD

1 (3-ounce) package lemon gelatin
1-1/2 cups boiling water
1-1/2 cups diced, unpeeled Delicious apples
2 tablespoons sugar
2 tablespoons lemon juice
1/2 cup sweet pickle relish
1/2 cup coarsely chopped walnuts
1 cup diced celery

Dissolve gelatin in boiling water. Cool until begins to gel. Add diced apple, lemon juice and sugar. Mix well to prevent darkening of apples. Add remaining ingredients. Fold into thickened gelatin. Pour into a 1-1/2-quart ring mold or an 8" x 8" pan and chill until firm. Serve with mayonnaise.

Serves 6 to 8.

From "Centennial Cookbook," Eagle Grove, Iowa.

# MANDARIN SALAD

1/2 cup sliced almonds
3 tablespoons sugar
1/2 head iceberg lettuce
1/2 head romaine lettuce
1 cup chopped celery
2 whole green onions, chopped
1 (11-ounce) can Mandarin oranges, drained

DRESSING:

1/3 teaspoon salt
Dash of pepper
1/4 cup vegetable oil
1 tablespoon chopped parsley
2 tablespoons sugar
2 tablespoons vinegar
Dash of Tabasco

In a small pan over medium heat, saute almonds in the 3 tablespoons sugar, stirring constantly until almonds are coated and browned. Cool; store in an airtight container.

Mix all dressing ingredients together and chill.

Mix vegetables together. Just before serving, add the almonds and Mandarin oranges; toss with the dressing.

Serves 4 to 6.

# APPLE CIDER SALAD MOLD

2 envelopes unflavored gelatin
3 tablespoons sugar
1/2 teaspoon salt
3-3/4 cups apple cider
3 tablespoons lemon juice
3-1/2 cups red Delicious apples, chopped but unpeeled
1 cup celery, finely chopped

In a 2-quart saucepan, stir gelatin, sugar and salt until well mixed. Stir in apple cider and lemon juice. Cook mixture over low heat, stirring until gelatin is dissolved. Refrigerate until mixture mounds slightly when dropped from a spoon.

Stir in apples and celery. Pour into a 6-cup mold and refrigerate. Unmold onto plate to serve.

Serves 12.

## TABOLUH SALAD

1 cup bulghar wheat
1 cup finely chopped parsley
1 cup chopped green onions
1 pound tomatoes, coarsely chopped
3/4 cup lemon juice
1/4 teaspoon black pepper
1 clove garlic, minced

Cover wheat with boiling water and let stand 2 hours. Drain. Add remaining ingredients and refrigerate overnight.

Serves 6 to 8.

## FREEZER COLESLAW

1 medium cabbage, shredded
1 teaspoon salt
1 carrot, grated
1 green pepper, chopped
1 cup white vinegar
1/2 cup cold water
1 teaspoon whole mustard seed
1 teaspoon celery seed
2 cups sugar

Mix cabbage with salt. Let stand 1 hour, then squeeze out excess moisture. Add carrot and green pepper. Set aside. Meanwhile, combine remaining ingredients and boil 1 minute. Cool to lukewarm, then pour over vegetable mixture and mix well. Pack into containers and freeze. Makes 4 to 5 cups. Unused coleslaw can be refrozen.

## BING CHERRY SALAD MOLD

3 (1-pound) cans Bing cherries
3 (3-ounce) packages black-cherry gelatin
2-1/4 cups hot water
1-1/2 cups dry sherry
2-1/4 cups cherry syrup
1-1/2 cups sour cream
1-1/2 cups thin sliced almonds, crumbled

Drain cherries, saving 2-1/4 cups syrup. Dissolve gelatin in hot water. Add sherry and cherry syrup. Chill until slightly thickened. Add cherries, sour cream and almonds. Pour into a large mold and chill. Unmold on a bed of lettuce.

Serves 16-18.

# SALAD OF ARUGULA AND CHERRY TOMATOES

Allow a small handful of arugula and 4 to 6 cherry tomatoes per person.

## Creamy Mustard Vinaigrette

1/3 cup tarragon vinegar
2/3 cup olive oil
1/3 cup crumbled Gorgonzola cheese
1 tablespoon lemon juice
Freshly ground black pepper

1. Wash arugula carefully and dry well. Cut tomatoes in half.

2. Put the arugula and the cherry tomatoes in a large salad bowl.

3. Combine all the ingredients for the vinaigrette (makes 1-1/3 cups). Pour over the salad, toss well, and serve immediately.

# GREENS WITH FRUIT AND POPPY SEED DRESSING

1 small head romaine lettuce
1 small bunch spinach
1 jar marinated artichoke hearts
1 can drained mandarin oranges
1 (4-ounce) package alfalfa sprouts
1 avocado, sliced
3/4 cup seedless grapes

Wash, dry and tear romaine and spinach leaves into bite sized pieces. Chop up artichoke hearts. Toss ingredients, saving 1/3 of the alfalfa sprouts for the garnish. Just before serving, add dressing to taste and garnish with the remaining alfalfa sprouts.

Serves 8.

## Poppy Seed Dressing

1 egg
1/4 cup sugar
1/4 cup lemon juice
1 tablespoon poppy seeds
1 teaspoon dry mustard
1 teaspoon paprika
1/2 teaspoon onion salt
1-1/2 cups oil
1/4 cup honey

Combine the first 7 ingredients, blending well. Add 1/4 cup oil, a few drops at a time, beating well. Add remaining oil slowly while continuing beating. Add honey and beat well. Chill.

Makes 2 cups.

---

Some women like to travel
While others like a book
But the woman who will get her man
Is the girl who likes to cook

# Sauces
# and
# Marinades

# BARBEQUE'S GALORE STEAK WITH SOUR CREAM HORSERADISH

## Marinade

1/2 cup wine vinegar
2 tablespoons olive oil
1 teaspoon Worcestershire
1 teaspoon Dijon mustard
3 cloves garlic, crushed
1/4 cup soy sauce
1/4 cup catsup
1/4 cup brown sugar
1/2 cup red wine
3 to 4 pounds top sirloin

Combine marinade ingredients in a jar and shake.

Place steak in a glass baking dish. Pour over marinade. Cover with plastic wrap and refrigerate overnight, turning steak with tongs several times.

## Sour Cream Horseradish Sauce

1 teaspoon pepper
1 cup sour cream
Salt to taste
4 green onions, chopped finely
1 tablespoon prepared horseradish
1 teaspoon Dijon mustard

Combine all ingredients together and chill overnight.

Barbeque steak over medium high heat for 20 minutes. Turn, brush steak with Sour Cream Horseradish Sauce and continue barbequing for 12 to 15 minutes for medium rare.

Serves 6 to 8.

# HONEY BASTED HAM

1/4 cup dark corn syrup
1 pound honey
2/3 cup butter or margarine

In small saucepan, combine the 3 ingredients. Bring to boil. Stir constantly over just enough heat to keep mixture at very gentle boil for 15 minutes.

For half of a semi-boneless, fully cooked ham (approximately 4 to 5 lbs.), place ham, cut-side down, in shallow baking pan. Score fatted sides of ham, inserting a whole clove in center of each of the scored sections of the fat.

Baste surface of ham with simmering glaze, using about 3 tablespoons of mixture every 10 minutes for 1 hour and 15 minutes at 350°, or until honey glaze becomes candied but not overly browned. It will harden while cooling.

Keep honey mixture warm over hot water in top of double boiler. At end of baking time, open oven door, turning on broiler heat just to candy honey coating of ham. Let ham stand 20 minutes before carving. Allow 1/2 pound per serving.

# CUMBERLAND SAUCE

1/2 cup port wine
1/2 cup lemon juice
1 cup currant jelly
1/2 cup onion, chopped
1-1/2 tablespoons cornstarch
1 tablespoon orange rind
1 tablespoon lemon rind
Few drops Tabasco
1/4 teaspoon ginger

Combine all ingredients except cornstarch in a saucepan and bring to a boil. Combine cornstarch with a little of the sauce and mix well. Heat over low heat until slightly thickened. Do not boil.

Wonderful served with holiday turkey, pork, lamb or goose and wild rice stuffing.

# SAUCE TARTARE

1 egg yolk
2 teaspoons mustard such as Dijon or Dusseldorf
2 teaspoons red wine vinegar
1 cup peanut or vegetable oil
Salt and freshly ground pepper
1/4 teaspoon Worcestershire sauce
2 tablespoons finely chopped onion
2 tablespoons finely chopped cornichons
        (imported French sour pickles)
1 tablespoon chopped capers

1. Put the yolk in a mixing bowl and add the mustard and vinegar.

2. Stir with a wire whisk and gradually add the oil. Beat briskly until all the oil is added.

3. Add salt and pepper to taste, Worcestershire sauce, onion, cornichons, and capers. Blend well.

Yield: About 1-1/4 cups.

# TERIYAKI SAUCE

1 tablespoon soy sauce
2 tablespoons sugar
4 teaspoons powdered ginger
1 clove garlic, minced
2 tablespoons sherry
2 tablespoons oil
1/2 cup consomme

Combine all ingredients and use as a marinade. An excellent baste for chicken, beef and turkey.

## SZECHUAN PEPPERCORN SAUCE

2 teaspoons black Szechuan peppercorns
2 tablespoons chopped scallions
2 teaspoons chopped ginger root
1/2 teaspoon salt
3 tablespoons soy sauce
2 tablespoons sesame oil
1 tablespoon chicken stock
1 teaspoon red wine vinegar
1 teaspoon sugar

Remove the seeds from the peppercorns (good quality peppercorns usually have no seeds or very tiny ones). Crush the peppercorns and mix with remaining ingredients. Serve over chicken breast poached in white wine and chicken broth.

## MR. MUELLER'S MARINADE FOR A CRUSTY ROAST

4 parts barbeque sauce
4 parts Italian dressing
1 part soy sauce
1/3 package dry chili mix

Marinate roast in this mixture for several hours. Now char the roast on all sides, about 12 to 15 minutes per side. Insert meat thermometer into roast. Roast in 400° oven until desired doneness.

## SALSA FRIA

4 tomatoes, peeled and finely chopped
1/2 cup minced onion
1/2 cup minced celery
1/4 cup minced green pepper
1/4 cup olive oil
3 tablespoons chopped mild green chilies
2 tablespoons red wine vinegar
1 teaspoon mustard seed
1 teaspoon ground coriander
1 teaspoon salt
Dash of pepper
Corn tortillias cut in quarters and crisply fried

Combine all ingredients except tortillas. Cover and chill for at least several hours. Serve as a dip for fried tortilla quarters, or as a mild sauce for other dishes.
Makes 6 cups.

---

Yogi is what you get from drinking too much yogurt

# LOW CALORIE BEARNAISE SAUCE

1-1/2 tablespoons white wine vinegar
1-1/2 tablespoons dry vermouth
Sprig parsley
1 teaspoon chopped green onion
1/4 teaspoon crumbled dried tarragon
2 egg yolks
1/2 teaspoon Dijon-style mustard
1/4 cup low-fat yogurt
2 tablespoons sour cream

Combine in a saucepan the vinegar, vermouth, parsley, onion and tarragon; cook down until reduced to 2 teaspoons. Let cool.

Beat egg yolks with a whisk in the top of a double boiler and beat in mustard. Place over barely simmering water and let warm slightly, beating. Beat in strained vinegar glaze and 1 tablespoon yogurt, beating until blended.

Add remaining yogurt and sour cream, 1 tablespoon at a time, beating until sauce is smooth and thick. Remove from heat.

Makes 3/4 cup sauce; about 18 calories per tablespoon.

# BRANDY SAUCE

1 cup sugar
1-1/2 cups boiling water
2 tablespoons arrowroot or cornstarch
1/8 teaspoon salt
1/2 cup brandy

Combine sugar, arrowroot (or cornstarch) and salt in a pan and gradually add boiling water, stirring constantly. Continue stirring and simmer over low heat until sauce is clear and thick. Remove from the heat and stir in the brandy. If a thicker sauce is desired, increase arrowroot or cornstarch to three tablespoons.

You may add nutmeg and cinnamon to taste if desired. A bit of powdered ginger will give extra flavor too!

# JACKIE'S WHITE SAUCE

1-1/3 cups powdered milk
3/4 cup whole wheat flour
1 teaspoon salt
1/2 cup margarine
Freshly ground black pepper to taste

Mix together the first 3 ingredients. With a pastry blender, cut in the margarine until the mixture resembles fine crumbs. Refrigerate in a tightly covered container.

To make 1 cup of sauce, pour 1 cup cold milk into a small heavy-duty pan. Thoroughly stir in 1/2 cup of the mix. Stir until the mixture is thick and bubbly. Grind in black pepper to taste.

Makes 6 cups.

## ELSIE'S CRANBERRY SAUCE

16 ounces cranberries
2 cups water

Cook until berries pop. Strain into another pan. Force through colander with 2 cups sugar. Boil, cook 4 minutes.
Chill in a glass dish. It takes a whole day to set. Make the day before.

## GLORIA PITZER'S MERRY CALL WHIP

4 raw egg yolks
1/4 cup lemon juice
3/4 cup and 1 tablespoon light vinegar
1 tablespoon salt
3/4 cup sugar
1/4 cup dairy creamer powder (Cremora)
4 teaspoons Dijon mustard
3/4 cup margarine cut into small pieces
1 (5-1/3-ounce) can evaporated milk
1/2 teaspoon paprika
2-1/4 cups corn oil

Place all ingredients except oil in a blender. Process on and off for 20 seconds. Add oil 1 tablespoon at a time and blend at high speed until smooth. Batter will be on the thin side. Place in a 6 cup container. Cover tightly and refrigerate overnight or 6 to 8 hours before using.

## GREEN-CHILI SALSA

10 fresh hot green peppers
        *or* 3 (4-ounce) cans chopped green chilies
8 pounds firm ripe tomatoes
3 cups chopped onions
1 cup chopped green bell pepper
1/4 cup lemon juice
6 tablespoons distilled white vinegar
2 teaspoons dried leaf oregano
1 tablespoon salt

Wash 8 pint jars in hot soapy water; rinse. Keep hot until needed. Prepare lids as manufacturer directs.
Peel fresh hot peppers if using. Discard seeds; chop peppers. Set aside.
Wash tomatoes. Immerse in boiling water for 30 seconds. Plunge into cold water. Slip off skins. Cut out cores; coarsely chop tomatoes.
In a (6-quart) pot, combine chopped hot peppers, tomatoes and remaining ingredients. Bring to a boil. Cover, simmer over low heat 5 minutes.
Ladle hot salsa into 1 hot jar at a time, leaving 1/4 inch headspace. Wipe rim of jar with a clean damp cloth. Attach lid. Place in canner. Fill and close remaining jars. Process in a boiling water bath, 45 minutes for pint jars.
Makes 8 pints.

## RICK ROYCE'S ORIGINAL BBQ SAUCE

1 tablespoon onion powder
2 cups tomato sauce
1 teaspoon garlic powder
1/2 cup cider vinegar
1 tablespoon Worcestershire sauce
1/2 cup dark brown sugar, packed
1 pinch allspice
1 pinch cloves
1 tablespoon black pepper
2 tablespoons honey
1 tablespoon lemon juice
1 cup red wine
1/2 teaspoon liquid smoke

In a 2-quart saucepan, combine ingredients and simmer over low heat until sauce thickens. Set sauce aside until needed. Sauce may be used for a quick marinade before cooking (5 minutes on each side). Also, use sauce on ribs during the last 10 minutes of cooking.

Yields 3 cups.

––––––––––––––––––––

A fine is a tax for doing wrong. A tax is a fine for doing all right.

––––––––––––––––––––

I used to burn, but now I smolder. That's how I learn I'm growing older.

## ORANGE HONEY SAUCE & GLAZE

1/3 cup undiluted frozen orange juice
1/3 cup honey
1/3 cup sherry wine

Brush mixture on meats and poultry during final 10 minutes of cooking, or heat and serve as a table sauce.

## JEZEBEL SAUCE

1 (18-ounce) jar pineapple preserves
1 large jar apple jelly
1 (2-ounce) can dry mustard
1 (8-ounce) jar horseradish

Mix all ingredients together and refrigerate in airtight jars. Keeps indefinitely. Serve as a side dish for relish on cooked meats. Excellent with ham or pork.

## HOLIDAY LAMB RUB

1/2 cup cranberry juice
2 tablespoons light corn syrup
1/2 cup port wine
2 cloves garlic, crushed
Salt and pepper

Combine all ingredients and marinate lamb in a dish for at least 2 hours—overnight is better. Roast lamb with marinade basting several times during cooking process. Wonderful served with wild rice stuffing and Cumberland Sauce.

## FOAMY HARD SAUCE

1 cup sugar
1/2 cup butter, softened
4 egg yolks, beaten
2 ounces sherry or brandy
Pinch of salt
1 cup heavy cream

In top of double boiler, with a whisk or electric beater, cream together sugar and butter. When light, add beaten yolks, brandy and salt, beating well.

Heat cream until hot but do not boil. Add slowly to rest of ingredients, continuing to beat well.

Place over boiling water, stirring with a whisk until the sauce is the thickness of cream, but do not allow it to boil.

This stores well in the refrigerator and may be carefully reheated over warm water. It is delightful served over gingerbread or Persimmon Steamed Pudding.

Yield: 3 cups.

## WESTERN HERB SAUCE

2 tablespoons finely chopped onion
1/4 cup olive oil
1/4 cup melted butter
1/4 cup steak sauce
1/4 cup chopped parsley
2 tablespoons chopped chives
Salt and pepper to taste

Saute onion in oil and butter until lightly browned. Add remaining ingredients and heat. Serve warm.

## BEEF PALACE MEAT MARINADE

1 cup dry red wine
3 tablespoons Worcestershire sauce
2 teaspoons salt
2 teaspoons pepper
Juice of 1/2 lemon
1/2 teaspoon garlic powder
1/4 cup oil

Combine all ingredients except oil. Whisk or shake until blended. Add oil. Shake marinade before using and pour over roasts or steaks. Turn often and marinate an hour or two for steaks, and overnight for large roasts.
Remaining marinade may be used for basting during cooking.

## CREAMED HORSERADISH SAUCE

1/4 cup whipping cream, whipped
1/4 cup horseradish
1/4 teaspoon seasoned salt
Few drops Tabasco sauce

Place horseradish in a strainer and allow it to drain thoroughly. Fold the horse-radish into the other ingredients. Serve with most red meats.

## SWEET AND SOUR BASTING SAUCE

1 cup crushed pineapple, undrained
2/3 cup white wine or chicken broth
2 tablespoons white wine vinegar
2 tablespoons soy sauce
1 teaspoon lemon juice
1 clove garlic, minced
1/2 teaspoon dry mustard
2 tablespoons brown sugar
2 tablespoons onion, chopped

Combine ingredients in a saucepan and simmer 10 to 15 minutes. Brush over fish, steaks, poultry, lamb, pork and ribs during cooking.

## CURRY SAUCE

1 cup sour cream
1/2 cup mayonnaise
2 tablespoons chopped parsley
2 teaspoons curry powder
1 teaspoon lemon juice
1/2 teaspoon Worcestershire sauce
1/4 teaspoon salt

Combine ingredients and chill.

## BLENDER HOLLANDAISE SAUCE

1/2 cup butter or margarine
3 egg yolks
2 tablespoons lemon juice
1/4 teaspoon salt
Dash white pepper
1/2 teaspoon prepared mustard

Heat butter in small saucepan until bubbly but not browned. Put egg yolks, lemon juice, salt, white pepper and mustard in blender container; cover and run on speed 2 (or low) about 5 seconds. While continuing to run on same speed, add butter in a slow, steady stream until blades are covered; turn to speed 6 (or high) and add remaining butter slowly. Serve immediately. Makes approximately 1 cup.

## BLENDER BEARNAISE SAUCE

2 tablespoons white wine
1 tablespoon tarragon vinegar
2 teaspoons dried tarragon
2 teaspoons chopped shallots or onion
1/4 teaspoon freshly ground black pepper
1/4 teaspoon sugar
3/4 cup Blender Hollandaise Sauce (see above)

Put all ingredients except Hollandaise Sauce in small saucepan. Cook rapidly over high heat until most of the liquid is gone. Pour mixture into Hollandaise Sauce in blender container; cover and run on speed 7 (or high) for 6 seconds. Makes approximately 1 cup.

## BLEU CHEESE SAUCE

1 cup mayonnaise
1/4 cup crumbled bleu cheese
1 teaspoon lemon juice
1 tablespoon chopped parsley

Combine ingredients and chill.

## LOW SODIUM B-B-Q SAUCE

3 cups tomato juice
3 cups orange juice
1/2 cup lemon juice
1 cup light brown sugar
1 cup honey
1 teaspoon onion salt or onion powder
1 teaspoon garlic salt or garlic powder
1/2 teaspoon liquid smoke
Tabasco to taste

Mix and simmer until reduced by half.

Refrigerate.

Will last a year.

## GRAND MARNIER SAUCE

5 egg yolks at room temperature
3/4 cup sugar
1/4 cup Grand Marnier
1 cup heavy cream
1 tablespoon sugar

Beat egg yolks until light in the top of a double boiler. Beat in 3/4 cup sugar and place over simmering water, stirring constantly, until thickened, about 20 minutes. Remove from heat and beat until cool. Add Grand Marnier and refrigerate until chilled.

Whip cream just until it begins to thicken, then add 1 tablespoon sugar. Continue beating until cream is medium thick but will still pour. Fold into egg sauce and pour into a serving dish. Chill until serving time, or freeze. Serve over fresh fruit.

Serves 8.

## LEMON MUSTARD SAUCE

3/4 cup mayonnaise
3 tablespoons fresh lemon juice
1-1/2 tablespoons Dijon mustard
1/2 cup heavy cream, whipped

Mix together the mayonnaise, lemon juice and mustard. Fold in the whipped cream.

Delicious on hot steamed broccoli, asparagus spears or green beans.

Makes 2 cups.

# SAUCE PROVENCALE
## (Microwave)

1 cup dry red wine
1 (8-ounce) can tomato sauce
1 cup beef bouillon
1 teaspoon wine vinegar
2 cloves garlic, minced
1 cup chopped onion
1/2 cup chopped carrot
1/2 cup chopped green pepper
1/4 cup chopped parsley
1 cup chopped mushrooms
1/4 teaspoon dried thyme leaves
1/4 teaspoon dried basil leaves
1 bay leaf
Salt and pepper to taste

Put all the ingredients together in a large covered casserole. Cook, covered, in the microwave, stirring occasionally, for 40 minutes. Remove the cover and continue cooking until the sauce is thick, stirring occasionally, if needed.

Use this sauce with just about any fish, poultry or meat dish, or even with an omelet. If, after trying the recipe once, you wish to make it in bulk, double, triple or quadruple the amounts. Naturally, more cooking time will be needed. Bring the mixture to a boil and cook, covered, until the vegetables are well cooked, remove the lid and cook until the sauce is thick. Freeze in one-cup lots and defrost just what you need.

# PLUM SAUCE

1 (12-ounce) jar plum preserves
2 tablespoons vinegar
1 tablespoon brown sugar
1 tablespoon finely chopped onion
1 teaspoon seeded and finely chopped dried red chili
        pepper or 1 teaspoon crushed red pepper
1 clove garlic, minced
1/2 teaspoon ground ginger

In a small saucepan combine plum preserves, vinegar, brown sugar, onion, red chili pepper or crushed red pepper, garlic and ground ginger. Bring mixture to boiling, stirring constantly. Remove from heat, cool slightly. Refrigerate in a covered container overnight to blend seasonings. Makes 1-1/4 cups.

# ORANGE BUTTER

4 tablespoons undiluted frozen orange juice concentrate
1 pound butter, softened
1 tablespoon grated orange rind
1/2 pound powdered sugar, sifted

Thaw orange juice concentrate. Add together softened butter, juice, rind and sugar. Blend thoroughly. Place in a mold and refrigerate.

## FRESH PEACH OR PLUM CHUTNEY

            2 tablespoons salt
            7 cups sliced fresh peaches or plums
            3 cups sugar
            1-1/2 cups cider vinegar
            2 large cloves garlic
            1 cup chopped onion
            1 teaspoon ground ginger
            1/4 teaspoon crushed red pepper
            3/4 cup lime juice
            1 cup raisins
            1/4 to 1/2 cup chopped candied or preserved ginger

Add the salt to a quart of water and pour over the peaches or plums. Let stand one day. Drain. Mix one quarter cup water, sugar, vinegar and garlic. Bring to a boil, add peaches or plums and cook until they are clear, about 45 minutes. Remove peaches. Add onions, spices, lime juice and raisins to syrup. Cook until thickened, 12 to 15 minutes. Add peaches or plums and candied ginger; bring to boiling point. Ladle into hot, sterilized half-pint jars. Seal.

Yield: 4 jars.

## HOT FUDGE TOPPING FOR SUNDAE BAR

            2 (13-ounce) cans evaporated milk
            2 cups sugar
            Dash of salt
            1 pound butter (do not use margarine)
            1/3 cup dark corn syrup
            1 (12-ounce) package chocolate chips
            1 (1-pound) bag light caramels
            1 teaspoon vanilla

Put all the ingredients except the vanilla in the top of a large double boiler over simmering water, cooking and stirring until mixture is melted and smooth (this takes about 30 minutes). Using a portable mixer, beat as it cooks over water. Add the vanilla and blend another minute or two. This makes 2 quarts of Hot Fudge and keeps in the fridge for about 6 weeks, or freeze if desired. This is so good you will never use another store-bought product.

## CHOCOLATE SYRUP FOR SUNDAES

            1 cup cocoa
            1 cup hot water
            1 cup honey
            1/2 cup brown sugar, firmly packed
            Dash of salt
            1 tablespoon vanilla

Place all ingredients in a heavy saucepan over medium-low heat, stirring until melted. Use portable mixer to beat mixture while it continues to cook, until it has a satiny texture. Refrigerate it, covered, for several weeks or you can freeze it as well. Makes about 2-1/2 cups.

# IMPROVISED GRAVY

When you don't have enough natural pan juices and drippings to make a gravy or you need gravy to create a tasty dish out of leftover meat, here is a basic recipe that will serve well. You can add compatible seasonings like fresh herbs or a little duxelles. Use beef bouillon for red meat and chicken for poultry.

> 2 tablespoons minced shallots, scallions or onion
> 3 tablespoons butter
> 3 tablespoons flour
> 1/4 cup red wine or dry vermouth (optional)
> 1-1/2 cups beef or chicken broth
> Leftover drippings or additional tablespoon butter
> Salt
> Freshly ground pepper

Saute the minced shallots or onion in the butter until translucent. Stir in the flour and, cooking slowly, stir until it turns light brown. Remove the pan from the fire, add the wine if you are using it, and an equal amount of broth. Stir until smooth; return to the fire and slowly add the remaining broth, stirring constantly. Continue to cook, stirring often, for another 5 minutes. Stir in leftover drippings or butter, salt and pepper to taste.

# THE SORCERY OF SAUCERY
## Bechamel Sauce

> 2 tablespoons butter
> 2 tablespoons flour
> 2 cups scalded milk
> 1 tablespoon butter (additional)
> 1 tablespoon finely chopped onion
> 2 tablespoons ground ham
> 1/4 teaspoon nutmeg

Saute the onion and ham in the 1 tablespoon of butter until the onion is soft and transparent and the ham brown. Add the scalded milk and let it stand 15 minutes. Bring the 2 tablespoons of butter to the bubbly stage and add the flour. Let it cook a few minutes, stirring constantly. Strain the milk and stir it into the butter-flour mixture. Cook until glassy and smooth.

This is the base. Great with tuna, chicken, etc.

### For a Cream Sauce

Add a cup of cream to the bechamel.

### For a Mornay Sauce

Melt in a cup of grated parmesan cheese.

### For a Cheese Sauce

Melt in a cup of aged, grated cheddar cheese.
A little mustard, Worcestershire and sherry wine give it added pizzazz.

# Eggs, Cheese, Pasta, Pizza, etc.

# BACK TO SCHOOL MACARONI CASSEROLE

1 (12-ounce) package macaroni
1 large onion, chopped
1 bell pepper, chopped
1 (1-pound) can stewed tomatoes
2 tablespoons olive oil
Salt and pepper to taste
1 cup cheddar cheese, grated
1 cup leftover cooked meat
Cilantro or parsley, chopped

Preheat oven to 350 degrees. Cook macaroni according to package instructions. In a skillet saute onion and pepper in olive oil, add tomatoes, reduce heat and stir until sauce reduces. Salt and pepper to taste. Drain macaroni and place in a buttered casserole dish. Add a layer of sauce, meat (optional), a sprinkle of cilantro or parsley, then the grated cheese. Repeat layers. Bake 20 minutes until bubbly and cheese begins to brown.

Serves 4. This is a great way to feed youngsters and use up leftover meats of any kind.

## SUPER BOWL ONION PIE

3 eggs
1 cup milk
2 cups herb seasoned croutons
1 teaspoon Worcestershire sauce
1 tablespoon green onion, sliced
1-1/2 teaspoons salt
1 pound ground beef
1 tablespoon butter
2 cups green onions, sliced
1 (8-ounce) package cream cheese
Tabasco
Paprika

Beat one egg until foamy and stir in 1/2 cup milk. Add stuffing and let stand until liquid is absorbed. Combine with the next 4 ingredients; mix well.

Press meat mixture into the bottom and up sides of a 9-inch pie plate. Melt butter in a skillet and add the 2 cups of sliced green onions. Cook over low heat just until the onions are wilted. Pour over meat mixture.

Beat cream cheese until fluffy; add 2 eggs, Tabasco to taste, and 1/2 cup milk. Beat until smooth. Pour over onion mixture. Sprinkle top of pie with paprika.

Bake at 350° for 40 minutes, or until a knife inserted in center comes out clean. Let stand 5 minutes before cutting.

This serves 4 to 6, but one pie is never enough!

## CHILI-GHETTI

2 tablespoons butter
1 garlic clove, minced
3/4 cup chopped onion
1 pound ground beef
2-1/2 cups tomatoes (1 pound-3 ounce can)
3 (15-ounce) cans chili with beans
1 (8-ounce) package spaghetti
3 cups shredded cheddar cheese
1 cup sour cream
1/2 cup grated Parmesan cheese

In a large skillet, melt butter. Brown garlic, onion and ground beef. Drain off excess fat and add tomatoes and chili. Simmer 45 minutes.

Meanwhile, cook spaghetti and drain. Remove skillet with chili mixture from heat and stir in cheddar cheese until melted. Fold in sour cream. Combine chili mixture and spaghetti, mixing well. Place in buttered baking dish and top with Parmesan cheese. Bake for 45 minutes in 350° oven.

Serves 8.

## APPLE HARVEST DRESSING

2 cups chopped, peeled, tart apples
1/2 cup chopped cooked prunes
1/2 cup seedless raisins
5 cups toasted bread cubes
1/4 cup melted butter or margarine
1/4 cup firmly packed light brown sugar
Grated rind of 1 lemon
1/2 teaspoon paprika
1/2 teaspoon ground cinnamon
1 teaspoon salt
3/4 cup apple juice or cider

Mix all ingredients. Use as a stuffing for chicken, duck or pork.

Makes about 8 cups.

## BEER BATTER FOR VEGETABLES

1-1/4 cups presifted flour
1 teaspoon salt
2 tablespoons shortening
1 egg, lightly beaten
1 cup stale beer

Sift flour and salt together into a mixing bowl. Cut in shortening until mixture resembles fine crumbs.

Add egg and beer; beat until smooth.

Makes about 2 cups.

# BAKED HUNGARIAN NOODLES

1 pound fine noodles
4 cups cream-style cottage cheese
4 cups sour cream
1 cup minced onion
3 to 4 cloves garlic, minced
4 tablespoons Worcestershire sauce
4 dashes Tabasco sauce
4 tablespoons poppy seeds
2 teaspoons salt
Freshly ground pepper to taste
Paprika
Freshly ground Parmesan cheese

Cook noodles in boiling, salted water until tender. Drain. Combine noodles with the remaining ingredients except the paprika and Parmesan cheese. Approximately 30 minutes before serving, bake in buttered casseroles at 350° until hot. Sprinkle with paprika and serve with Parmesan cheese.

Serves 24, but can easily be divided by 4 to serve 6. Can be made well in advance of the party and baked just before serving.

# SPEEDY SPINACH LASAGNE

1 package spaghetti sauce mix
1 (6-ounce) can tomato paste
1 (8-ounce) can tomato sauce
1-3/4 cups cold water
2 eggs
1 (15-ounce) container Ricotta or
    1 pound creamed cottage cheese
1/2 teaspoon salt
1 (10-ounce) package frozen chopped spinach,
    thawed and drained
1/2 cup grated Parmesan cheese
1/2 pound sliced mozzarella cheese
1/2 pound uncooked lasagne noodles, broken in half

Empty spaghetti sauce mix into saucepan; add tomato paste, tomato sauce and water. Heat, stirring, until well blended. Remove from heat.

Beat eggs in a large bowl and add Ricotta or cottage cheese, spinach, salt and 1/4 cup Parmesan cheese.

Lightly grease bottom of a 13 x 9 x 2-inch baking dish; cover with a little sauce. Layer noodles, half of the cheese-spinach mixture, half the mozzarella cheese and half the tomato sauce. Sprinkle with 1/4 cup Parmesan cheese. Cover dish with a lightly greased sheet of aluminum foil and bake in a preheated 350° oven for 60 minutes or until noodles are tender. Let stand 10 minutes before cutting in squares and serving.

Serves 8.

## WILD RICE DRESSING

2 medium onions, minced
2 medium carrots, minced
2 cups diced celery
1/2 cup minced parsley
1 cup butter or margarine
2 to 2-1/2 quarts fluffy bread cubes (about 10-12 slices)
1 tablespoon salt
1/2 teaspoon pepper
1/2 teaspoon sage (or more)
1/2 teaspoon thyme
1/2 teaspoon marjoram
1/4 pound wild rice, cooked (follow directions on package)
Broth from giblets (about 1 cup, more or less)

Saute onion, carrot, celery and parsley in butter over low heat for 5 minutes.

Mix bread cubes with seasonings. Add hot onion mixture and toss lightly. Add cooked wild rice and mix well. Add just enough hot broth to moisten the mixture lightly. It should still be fluffy.

Pack lightly into breast and body cavities. Makes enough for a 14-16 pound turkey.

## KROPPE KAKER

5 pounds potatoes (White Rose or new)
2 cups flour, plus
1 teaspoon salt per each quart of water (optional)
1/2 pound salt pork
1 onion
1/2 teaspoon allspice
2 to 3 tablespoons ground beef

Cut rind off salt pork and save.

Peel potatoes. Boil half of the potatoes, reserving the other half in cold water. Mash the cooked potatoes; grate the remaining fresh potatoes.

Grind the salt pork with the onion and fry. If pork is very fat, add the ground beef. Add the allspice and set this mixture aside.

Add the grated potatoes to the mashed potatoes and add enough flour to make the mixture hold together. With moistened hands, mold small ball-size patties, making a depression in the center, into which you add a portion of the pork mixture, closing the patty into a ball and enclosing the meat mix.

Using a large pot, rub insides with pork rinds; fill half full of water (include the pork rind) and bring to a full boil. Drop in the potato balls and cook 15 to 20 minutes, until the balls float to the surface. Spoon potato balls onto a platter.

Using some of the water in the pot, add sufficient butter, milk and allspice to make a sauce. May be thickened if desired.

# EGGS FLORENTINE
## WITH CHEESE SOUFFLE SAUCE

3 (9-ounce) packages frozen creamed spinach
8 hard-cooked eggs, peeled and halved
1 medium onion, chopped
6 tablespoons butter
6 tablespoons flour
1/2 teaspoon salt
1 teaspoon dry mustard
1-1/2 cups milk
1/8 teaspoon bottled red-pepper seasoning
6 eggs, separated
1-1/2 cups shredded Swiss or Muenster cheese

Cook spinach, following package directions; pour into greased 3-quart glass souffle dish. Arrange cut surfaces of hard-cooked egg halves against side of dish.

In a small saucepan, saute onion in butter until soft. Blend in flour, salt and mustard; cook, stirring constantly, just until bubbly. Stir in milk and red-pepper seasoning; continue cooking and stirring until sauce thickens and bubbles 1 minute.

Remove from heat. Sauce will be thick. Beat egg yolks into sauce, one at a time, beating well after each addition.

Beat egg whites just until they form soft peaks in a large bowl. Stir about 1/4 of the egg whites into sauce; stir in cheese; fold into remaining egg whites. Carefully pour on top of spinach. Bake at 350° for 45 minutes or until puffed and golden brown. Serve at once.

Serves 10-12.


## CHESTNUT & SAUSAGE DRESSING

2 dozen Italian chestnuts
2 tablespoons butter or margarine
1 onion, chopped
1/2 pound Italian sausage
2 teaspoons salt
1/4 teaspoon pepper
1/4 teaspoon poultry seasoning
2 tablespoons chopped parsley
1 cup bread crumbs
1/2 cup chicken broth

Simmer chestnuts 15 minutes or until tender. Peel and skin. Chop chestnuts into small bits. Melt butter in saucepan and saute onion 5 minutes. Add crumbled sausage meat and cook 5 minutes, stirring often. Add chestnuts, crumbs and seasonings, stirring until mixed. Stir in broth. Use to stuff chickens, turkey or game birds.

# OYSTER DRESSING

*Sufficient to stuff a 4-pound turkey.*
*Triple quantity to stuff a 10 to 16-pound turkey.*

1/2 cup butter
4 tablespoons parsley, chopped
1/2 cup onion, chopped
4 cups crustless white or corn bread crumbs
1/4 teaspoon poultry seasoning
3/4 teaspoon salt
1/4 teaspoon pepper
1/2 teaspoon paprika
2 cups chicken broth or oyster liquor
1/4 cup dry white wine
3 eggs, lightly beaten
1 pint oysters, freshly shucked and chopped

Melt butter in saucepan, saute parsley and onion for 5 minutes, or until onions are transparent. Add crumbs and seasonings and mix thoroughly.

Add broth, wine and eggs. Cook 3 minutes, stirring occasionally. Add oysters, cook for 2 to 3 minutes longer, stirring constantly.

# MUSHROOM PIE MADEIRA

2 pounds mushrooms
4 tablespoons butter
Salt and pepper
Juice of 1/2 lemon
2 tablespoons butter
3 tablespoons flour
1-1/2 cups chicken stock
1/2 cup Madeira wine
1/2 cup heavy cream
Pastry for 1 pie crust
1 egg, beaten

Wash and dry mushrooms. Heat 4 tablespoons butter in a skillet. Add mushrooms, salt, pepper and lemon juice. Cover and cook for 10 minutes over medium heat, shaking pan. Arrange mushrooms in a buttered baking dish.

To pan juices, add 2 tablespoons butter, flour and chicken stock. Cook until smooth and thickened. Add Madeira wine and cream. Season to taste.

Pour sauce over mushrooms. Cover with pastry, making 2 slits on top. Brush with beaten egg. Bake at 450° for 15 minutes, then reduce heat to 350° and bake 10-15 minutes longer, or until crust is golden brown.

Serves 6 to 8.

# BACON AND EGGS SUPREME

1/4 cup butter
1/4 cup flour
1 cup cream
1/4 cup milk
1/4 teaspoon each: thyme, marjoram, basil
1/4 cup chopped parsley
1 pound sharp cheddar cheese, grated
1-1/2 dozen hard-cooked eggs, sliced in half lengthwise
1 pound bacon, cooked and crumbled
2 cups bread crumbs
1/2 cup butter

Melt 1/4 cup butter in a medium-size saucepan. Add flour, milk and cream, stirring until sauce thickens. Stir in herbs and cheese. Mix well, making sure cheese has melted. Arrange eggs in a greased large pottery baking dish (about 3-quart size). If your dish is deep, you can slice your eggs vertically with an egg slicer so you will have more pieces. Layer bacon, sauce and buttered bread crumbs on top. Refrigerate. Bake uncovered for 30 minutes at 350°.

This can be prepared a day or two in advance and it will serve 12 people.

# FRENCH BREAD PIZZA

1 (8-ounce) can tomato sauce
1 (6-ounce) can tomato paste
1 teaspoon Italian herb seasoning
1/3 pound mozzarella cheese
1/3 pound cheddar cheese
1/3 pound Monterey Jack cheese
1 bunch green onions
1/2 green pepper
1/4-1/2 pound salami or pepperoni
1/4-1/2 pound mushrooms (optional)
1 loaf country-style French bread

Preheat oven to 450°. In a saucepan, combine tomato sauce, tomato paste and seasoning. Simmer a few minutes.

In the meantime, grate or shred the cheeses. Thinly slice the green onions, pepper, salami and mushrooms. Split a wide loaf of French bread in half, lengthwise. Place, split side up, on foil-lined cookie sheet. You may have to slice off a portion of crust so that pieces balance.

Spread each half with tomato mixture. Top with cheeses, vegetables and meats. Bake for 15 minutes or until cheeses are melted and bubbly.

Serves 4.

## TANGY RICE CASSEROLE

3/4 pound jack cheese
3 cups sour cream
Salt and pepper to taste
2 (4-ounce) cans chopped green chilies
3 cups cooked rice
1/2 cup grated cheddar cheese

Cut jack cheese in strips. Mix sour cream and chilies. Season rice with salt and pepper. In a 1-1/2 quart casserole layer one-half the rice. Top with sour cream mixture and cheese strips. Top with last half of rice. Bake at 350 degrees for 30 minutes. During last few minutes of baking, sprinkle with grated cheddar cheese. Heat until cheese melts. Can be prepared ahead of time.

Serves 6.

## SPAGHETTI MIZITHRA (Greek-Style)
### From The Spaghetti Factory

1 pound spaghetti
1 cup butter or margarine
1/2 pound Kasseri cheese, grated
1/4 pound Romano cheese, grated
1/4 cup chopped parsley

Cook spaghetti until tender but firm to the bite; drain. Melt butter in large skillet and cook just until it turns brown. Meanwhile, combine cheeses. Place spaghetti on warm platter, sprinkle with mixed cheeses, then drizzle with browned butter. Sprinkle with parsley.

Makes 6 servings.

## APPLE PANCAKES

4 tablespoons butter
1/2 cup brown sugar
1 teaspoon cinnamon
1/2 teaspoon nutmeg
3 apples, peeled and cored
1/2 teaspoon salt
3 eggs
3/4 cup milk
3/4 cup flour

Melt butter in large ovenproof round pan. Add brown sugar, cinnamon and nutmeg. Add sliced apples. Make a batter of the salt, eggs, milk and flour. Pour over apple mixture. Bake at 425° about 25 minutes.

Serves 4.

## CHEESE PANCAKES

3 cups flour
2 teaspoons salt
4 teaspoons baking powder
1 teaspoon baking soda
2 tablespoons sugar
8 eggs
2-2/3 cups milk
2 cups cheddar cheese, grated
2 cups cottage cheese
1 cup sliced fresh mushrooms
1/2 cup green onion, chopped

Mix all the dry ingredients together in a bowl. Beat eggs and milk together. Add to the dry ingredients. Mix until smooth. Fold in the cheese, mushrooms and onions. Bake on a hot greased griddle until browned on all sides.

Serves 8-10.

## FRESH STRAWBERRY PUFF PANCAKE

1/4 cup butter
3 eggs
1-1/2 cups milk
1/2 cup sugar
3/4 cup unsifted all-purpose flour
1/4 teaspoon salt
3 cups strawberries, halved
Sour cream
Brown sugar

Put butter in a 9-inch ovenproof frying pan or other baking dish. Place dish in a 425°oven until butter melts and bubbles, about 10 minutes.

Meanwhile, beat together the eggs, milk, 6 tablespoons sugar, flour, salt until smooth.

Remove pan from the oven and immediately pour mixture into the hot pan all at once. Return pan to the oven and bake at 425° for 30 minutes or until edges are puffed and browned.

Combine strawberries with remaining 2 tablespoons sugar. When pancake is done, remove from oven and immediately spoon strawberries into the center. Cut into wedges and pass sour cream and brown sugar.

Serves 4.

---

We live by the clock today. A man spends eight hours earning money, eight hours spending 150 percent of what he has earned, and most of the remaining eight hours wondering why he can't sleep.

# ANNE BANCROFT'S LASAGNA

Olive oil
1 or 2 pieces, plus 1-2 cloves, garlic
2 (24-ounce) cans large tomatoes, pureed
1 (6-ounce) can tomato paste
2 fresh basil leaves
2 pounds chopped meat
1/2 to 1 cup bread crumbs
1/4 cup water
1 bunch parsley, chopped
Salt and pepper to taste
1 pound lasagna noodles
3 pounds ricotta cheese
2 medium-sized mozzarella cheeseballs, sliced
1/2 pound Parmesan cheese, grated

First, prepare sauce. It can be done the night before. In the bottom of a large pot, put a touch of olive oil. Add garlic and tomatoes. Stir in the tomato paste and basil leaves. Simmer 4 to 5 hours, adding a little water if necessary.

While sauce is cooking, prepare the meatballs. Mix well the chopped meat, breadcrumbs, water, parsley, salt and pepper. Roll into tiny meatballs. Put a drop of olive oil in a skillet and add 1 to 2 cloves of garlic. Fry meatballs until lightly browned, then put into sauce.

Cook lasagna noodles and drain. Then spread a couple of spoonsful of sauce in the bottom of a large baking pan. On top of sauce, place a layer of noodles, half the ricotta cheese, sauce with meatballs, then slices of mozzarella. Repeat layer. Sprinkle Parmesan over all. Cover with foil and bake at 350° for 20-30 minutes. Take foil off and bake an additional 15 minutes.

Serves 10.

# LINGUINE WITH ZUCCHINI AND TOMATOES

1/3 cup butter or margarine
1/3 cup onion, chopped
1 green pepper, seeded and cut into strips
4 ounces linguine, cooked and drained
2-3 cups sliced zucchini
4 medium tomatoes, peeled, seeded
    and cut into strips
1/4 cup parsley, chopped
1/2 cup shredded Gruyere or other Swiss cheese
1/2 cup freshly grated Parmesan cheese

Melt butter in a skillet and saute onion for about 5 minutes. Add green pepper and cook a few minutes more. Combine with remaining ingredients reserving a few tablespoons Parmesan cheese for top. Place in buttered 2-quart casserole and top with Parmesan. Bake covered at 350° for 30-40 minutes, or until cheese is bubbling. Do not overcook.

Serves 4 to 6.

# SANTA BARBARA LINGUINE

3 ounces prosciutto
1/4 pound Oriental pea pods
1/2 pound mushrooms,
   canned and sliced
Butter
1 large shallot, minced
2 cloves garlic, minced
6 tablespoons vermouth

1/3 cup canned double strength
   chicken broth
1 tablespoon lemon juice
6 tablespoons whipping cream
1 small egg yolk
Salt, pepper, dash of cayenne
3/4 pound linguine
2 tablespoons olive oil
Freshly grated Parmesan cheese

Have prosciutto cut slightly thick rather than paper thin. Cut into strips 1/2-inch long by 1/8-inch wide. Snip off stem ends of each pea pod, pull down to remove string, pinch off other end. Slice pea pods in thirds. Blanch in simmering water 3 minutes, drain and set aside.

Saute mushrooms in 2 tablespoons butter for 5 minutes. Strain liquid from mushrooms and reserve. Keep mushrooms warm.

Combine shallot, garlic, vermouth, chicken broth, lemon juice and reserved mushroom liquid in saucepan. Cook over high heat until reduced by 3/4. Cut 3/4 cup butter into 6 pieces and whisk in one chunk at a time, waiting until each is dissolved before adding more. Whisk in cream in slow stream. Whisk in egg yolk. Cook, stirring constantly, until sauce thickens slightly. Season to taste with salt, pepper and cayenne. Set aside.

Cook linguine in boiling salted water until firm-tender. Drain and rinse with tepid water. Toss with olive oil. Add prosciutto, mushrooms and pea pods to cream sauce; reheat gently. Pour over linguine and toss. Serve with Parmesan cheese on the side. Makes 4 main dish servings.


# RAGOUT OF EGGS AND MUSHROOMS

2 tablespoons olive oil
1 tablespoon minced onion
1 tablespoon chopped parsley
1 pound mushrooms, sliced
1 tablespoon all-purpose flour
1/2 cup dry white wine
Salt and pepper to taste
6 hard-cooked eggs, coarsely chopped

Heat olive oil over medium heat and cook onion and parsley for 2 minutes. Add mushrooms; cover and cook over low heat for 10 minutes.

Stir in flour and wine. Cover and simmer for 5 minutes. Season with salt and pepper.

Add eggs and simmer, covered, for 5 more minutes, stirring occasionally.

Serve as an entree with hot garlic bread, or with broiled ham or sausages. Makes 6 servings.

# SEAFOOD FETTUCINI WITH GARLIC AND MUSHROOMS
## Mama Mia, Is This Good!

1 pound fettucini noodles
1/2 cup olive oil
1/2 cup garlic, minced
1/4 cup green onions, chopped
1/2 cup parsley, chopped
1/2 cup fresh basil, chopped (don't fudge, get fresh)
1 pound fresh mushrooms, sliced
1/2 cup dry white wine (I love vermouth)
Dash of Tabasco
1/2 tablespoon chicken stock base
1/2 tablespoon beef stock base
1 cup Italian tomatoes, chopped
    (use canned, they're better)
1 cup cooked lobster, chopped
1 cup cooked shrimp
1 cup cooked crab, chopped
1/4 pound sweet butter
1/2 cup parsley, finely chopped

In a large skillet, add olive oil and saute the garlic, green onions, parsley and basil. Add the mushrooms, saute for a few minutes, then add the wine, Tabasco and the tomatoes. Bring to a boil, add the chicken and beef stocks. Let simmer gently. Add seafood, simmering until just heated through. Boil fettucini until al dente. Drain. Add butter, then sauce and top with parsley. Serve immediately.

Serves 8. This is so good it should be against the law. The marriage of fresh basil, garlic and mushrooms make this a memorable occasion, then add the seafood—now you have a fabulous dinner.

Serve with a Cabernet, crusty bread and a green salad. For dessert a little sherbet with liqueur over the top and Italian cookies.

# FITZIE'S FAMOUS FRENCH TOAST

5 eggs
3 tablespoons sugar
2/3 cup milk
1 tablespoon vanilla
1/4 teaspoon cinnamon
Butter
8 slices of bread

Heat your skillet to medium-high. Mix together the first five ingredients. Coat skillet with a light coating of butter. Thoroughly soak bread in batter, then cook to a light golden brown.

Serves 4.

# TEX-MEX STUFFING

2 medium size onions, finely chopped
1/4 cup (1/2 stick) butter
1 large green pepper, seeded and finely chopped
3 medium size ribs of celery, finely chopped (1 cup)
Turkey giblets and/or liver, finely chopped (optional)
2 canned hot jalapeno peppers, seeded and finely chopped
1 clove garlic, finely chopped
8 cups crumbled cornbread
2 hard cooked eggs, coarsely chopped
2 (8-ounce) cans niblets corn (drained)
1 cup turkey or chicken broth
2 teaspoons chili powder
1/2 teaspoon salt
1/4 teaspoon pepper

Saute onion in butter in large skillet until softened, about 3 minutes. Stir in green pepper and celery; saute 3 minutes. Stir in turkey giblets and/or liver, if using, jalapeno peppers and garlic.

Combine cornbread, hard-cooked eggs and corn in large bowl. Drizzle in broth, tossing to moisten. Add sauteed vegetables, chili powder, salt and pepper. Toss again.

Stuff turkey (or whatever you're going to stuff) and roast according to your favorite recipe. Or spoon dressing into greased, shallow 3-quart baking dish. Bake, covered, in pre-heated moderate oven (350°) for 45 minutes. Uncover last 10 minutes for crusty top.

Makes 10 cups (enough for a 12-pound turkey or 5 whole chicken breasts).

466 calories per cup, 20 gm. fat, 825 mg. sodium, 128 mg. cholesterol.


# IMPOSSIBLE PIE

12 slices bacon fried crisp and crumbled
1 cup Swiss cheese, grated
1/3 cup green onion, chopped with some green parts
2 cups milk
1-1/4 cups Bisquick
4 eggs
1/4 teaspoon salt
1/8 teaspoon pepper

Preheat oven to 400°. Place bacon and cheese in a 10-inch pie plate.

Combine remaining ingredients and beat for 1 minute. Pour into pie plate. Bake 30 minutes at 400°.

MICROWAVE: 12 to 14 minutes at high, turning plate halfway through the cooking time.

Serves 6.

# TEMPURA
## (Batter-Fried Food)

**Tempura Sauce:** 3/4 cup dashi (fish stock) or 3/4 cup clam juice
1/4 cup soy sauce
1/4 cup sake
3-1/2 teaspoons sugar
3 tablespoons grated white radish
1 teaspoon powdered ginger

Mix together the fish stock, soy sauce, sake and sugar. Divide among 6 small bowls. Just before serving, place a little radish and ginger in each bowl.

## Tempura

Any combination of raw foods may be used, but here are a few typical suggestions: 18 shrimp, 2 fillet of flounder, 6 scallops, 1 lobster tail, 1 carrot, 1 green pepper, 18 string beans.

Remove shell from shrimp but leave tail. Slit, and discard vein. Cut across underside to straighten shrimp. Cut flounder in 3-inch pieces. Cut scallops in slices. Remove meat of lobster and cut into bite-size pieces. Cut carrots in lengthwise slices and then into squares. Cut green peppers in squares. Leave string beans whole. Dry all ingredients thoroughly. No moisture should remain.

**Tempura Batter:** 2-1/2 cups sifted flour     2 cups cold water
3 egg yolks     1 quart vegetable oil

Sift the flour 3 times. Beat the egg yolks and water together. Gradually add the flour, stirring lightly from the bottom with chopsticks or a spoon. Don't overstir — flour should be visible on top.

Heat the oil to 325° — a constant temperature is important for good tempura. Hold shrimp by the tail and dip in the batter; drop into the oil and fry until lightly browned. Dip other ingredients into batter on a spoon and gently drop into oil. Serve foods as soon as they are cooked, with the tempura sauce or coarse salt.

# WELSH RAREBIT
## (Microwave)

1 (10-3/4 ounce) can cream of celery soup
1/4 cup dry white wine
1/2 teaspoon Worcestershire sauce
1/2 teaspoon dry mustard
1-1/2 cups sharp cheddar cheese, grated
1 egg, lightly beaten

Combine soup, wine, Worcestershire and mustard in a 2-quart glass cassserole. Cook on medium 4 minutes, stirring twice. Slowly stir in cheese and egg. Cook on medium 4 to 5 minutes, or until the mixture is hot and bubbly, stirring twice.

Serve over toast points or crackers. This is lovely with a nice green salad...a great easy dinner when it is hot outside.

Serves 4.

# EGGPLANT CELERY PIZZA

2 cups whole wheat flour
1 tablespoon dry yeast
1 cup warm water (about 85°)
2 tablespoons safflower oil
1 teaspoon honey
1 clove garlic, minced
1 cup sliced mushrooms
1/4 cup chopped onion
1-1/2 cups (15-ounce can)
   tomato puree

1/2 teaspoon dried oregano
1/2 teaspoon dried basil
1/4 teaspoon pepper
1 cup cubed eggplant
1/2 cup chopped celery
1/2 cup chopped green pepper
1/4 cup sliced almonds
2 tablespoons olive oil
1-1/2 cups mozzarella cheese
   shredded (6 ounces)

1 teaspoon chopped fresh parsley

To make the crust: Combine the flour and yeast in a large bowl. In a cup, combine the water, 1 tablespoon of the oil, and the honey. Pour into the flour mixture and beat vigorously until well mixed. Cover the bowl with plastic wrap and set in a warm place to rise for 10-15 minutes.

Meanwhile, oil a 14-inch pizza pan and preheat oven to 425.°

Punch down the dough and place in the prepared pan. Press with fingers to cover the bottom of the pan and pinch up the sides to the rim. Bake for 8 minutes.

To make the sauce: Heat the remaining oil in a medium-size saucepan; saute the garlic, mushrooms and onion until tender. Stir in the tomato puree, parsley, oregano, basil and pepper. Bring mixture to a boil; reduce heat and simmer, uncovered for 15 to 20 minutes to reduce the sauce slightly and to combine flavors.

Spread the sauce evenly over the partially baked crust. Arrange the eggplant, celery, green pepper and almonds evenly over the top. Sprinkle on the olive oil; top with the cheese.

Bake until the crust is browned and the cheese is melted.

Serves 8.

# JACKIE'S FAVORITE BUFFET SOUFFLE

*This warms up beautifully the second day and it serves a bunch.*

2 (10-ounce) packages chopped spinach, thawed and drained
1/2 pound sharp cheddar cheese
4 tablespoons flour
1/4 pound butter or margarine
1 large onion, minced
2 (16-ounce) cartons creamed cottage cheese
Salt and pepper to taste
Worcestershire sauce to taste
6 eggs, beaten

Mix together all the ingredients except the eggs. Mix well. Fold in beaten eggs. Bake in a greased casserole at 350° for 1 hour, or until done.

Serves 8 to 10.

# CANNELONI

### Filling

4 tablespoons olive oil
2 cloves garlic, minced
2 medium onions, chopped
2 pounds ground beef
2 cups cooked spinach, drained
    and chopped (frozen)
1/4 teaspoon dry oregano or
    1 teaspoon fresh
Salt and pepper
12 chicken livers
1 tablespoon butter

### Sauce

2 large onions, chopped
2 cloves garlic, chopped
4 tablespoons olive oil
6 cups fresh tomatoes, chopped
    or canned Italian tomatoes
2 cups tomato paste
2 cups dry red wine
2 cups condensed beef bouillon
2 cups Parmesan cheese,
    freshly grated
Salt and pepper to taste

To make filling: Heat olive oil and saute garlic and onion for 5 minutes. Add ground beef and cook until brown. Drain. Add spinach, oregano, salt and pepper. Cook the chicken livers in the 2 tablespoons of butter and then add them to the beef mixture. Mix well.

To make the sauce: Saute garlic and onion in olive oil until golden. Add the tomatoes and tomato paste and simmer 5 minutes. Add the dry red wine, beef bouillon, 1 cup of the Parmesan cheese, and salt and pepper to taste.

The large canneloni shells can be found in an Italian deli. Cook in 2 quarts boiling water 5 minutes and drain.

To assemble: Stuff the canneloni shells with part of the filling. Place in a large shallow pan and spoon any remaining filling over the shells. Pour the sauce over the shells and sprinkle with the remaining Parmesan cheese. Bake at 400° for 20 minutes. (You can use crepes instead, but bake at 350° for 20 minutes.)


## EASY PARTY PIZZA
### (No Knead Crust)

1 cup self-rising flour
3 tablespoons cornstarch
1 tablespoon Parmesan cheese
2/3 cup beer or club soda
1 tablespoon oil

In a mixing bowl using a large spoon, mix the first 3 ingredients. Pour in beer or soda and oil; mix until smooth and thick like a biscuit dough. Dump into the center of a Pam-sprayed pizza tin. Wet the back of a large spoon and spread the dough evenly over the surface of the pan. Bake at 375° 15 minutes.

Top with 8 ounces of pizza sauce, 2 cups of shredded cheese, mushrooms and sliced pepperoni. Return to a 375° oven and bake 20 minutes longer.

Easy and so good — your kids will love you for this one.

Serves 6.

# ELEGANT LASAGNA
## FOR A SPECIAL OCCASION

1/2 pound lasagna noodles
1 pound lean ground beef
1 onion, chopped
3 cloves garlic, minced
1 tablespoon olive oil
3 pounds (6-7 large) tomatoes,
    peeled, seeded, chopped

1-1/2 teaspoons seasoned salt
    (or to taste)
2 tablespoons chopped parsley
    (or 1 tablespoon dried)
1 teaspoon basil
1/2 teaspoon oregano
1/4 teaspoon freshly ground pepper

1/4 cup dry red wine

Cook lasagna noodles in boiling water until "al dente" — still firm to the bite. Drain and keep them in cold water until ready to use. Saute ground beef, onion and garlic in olive oil until meat is no longer pink. Add remaining ingredients and cook at a fast simmer until sauce is quite thick (about 30-40 minutes). Skim fat. Preheat oven to 400°.

## Bechamel

1/2 cup butter
4 tablespoons flour
1 cup milk

1 cup chicken broth
1 chicken bouillon cube (optional)
1/8 teaspoon salt

Melt butter. Add flour and cook, stirring with a whisk, for one minute. Slowly add milk and chicken broth and bring to a boil, still using the whisk. Taste and add chicken bouillon cube, if needed. Add salt.

## Ricotta Filling

1 egg
1/2 pound ricotta cheese

1/16 to 1/8 teaspoon nutmeg
1/2 teaspoon salt

1/4 cup grated Parmesan cheese

Beat egg in a bowl. Add remaining ingredients and stir well with fork.

## Cheeses

1-1/2 cups grated Parmesan cheese
4 ounces mozzarella cheese, sliced

4 ounces teleme cheese
Butter

In the following order, layer in a lightly-greased 13″ x 9″ baking dish: a little meat sauce, half of the noodles, half of the remaining meat sauce, 1/2 cup Bechamel, 1/2 cup Parmesan, half of mozzarella, teleme and ricotta mixture, the remaining noodles and meat sauce. 1/2 cup Bechamel, 1/2 cup Parmesan, remaining mozzarella, teleme, ricotta, Bechamel and Parmesan. Dot with butter. Bake at 400°, uncovered, for 30 minutes, or more, until bubbly.

---

If you were another person, would you like to be a friend of yours?

# CALIFORNIA MEXICAN LASAGNA

2 tablespoons cooking oil
1 clove garlic, pressed
1 onion, chopped fine
3/4 pound ground beef
3 medium tomatoes or 1 (1-pound) can stewed
    tomatoes, chopped coarse
1 cup chicken stock
1 (7-ounce) can tomato sauce
Salt and pepper to taste
1/4 teaspoon ground cinnamon
1/4 cup raisins, or prunes, or dates
    or even grapes
1 (8-ounce) carton small-curd cottage cheese
    or ricotta
1 egg
1/4 pound jack cheese, shredded
4 corn tortillas
1 (7-ounce) can green chiles or 6 Anaheim
    or Poblano chiles, seeded and deveined

Preheat oven to 350°. In a 10" skillet, saute garlic and onion in oil until onion is translucent. Add ground beef and cook over medium-high heat until all pink color has disappeared. Remove excess grease. Add tomatoes, chicken stock, tomato sauce, salt, pepper, cinnamon and raisins. Simmer uncovered for about 20 to 30 minutes, or until the sauce has a thick catsup-like consistency.

While the sauce is simmering, combine cottage cheese with egg in a small bowl. Shred jack cheese onto a piece of waxed paper. Grease a 10" x 6" x 1-3/4" casserole dish.

Heat tortillas in a hot dry skillet about 15 seconds to the side. Place two tortillas on the bottom of greased casserole dish. Cover with half the green chiles, half the cottage cheese mixture, then half the meat sauce. Cover with the other two tortillas and the rest of the green chiles, cottage cheese, and meat sauce. Top with the shredded cheese.

Heat in preheated oven until bubbly and cheese is beginning to brown (about 25 minutes). Allow this to cool 10 minutes before cutting into squares.

Delicious with a simple green salad.

Serves 4.

---

If you keep your mouth shut you will get credit
for knowing what you aren't talking about.

The prudence of the best of minds is often
overcome by the tenderness of the best of hearts.

# DEEP DISH ZUCCHINI PIZZA

            4 cups shredded zucchini, well-squeezed
            3/4 cup shredded Monterey Jack cheese
            3/4 cup shredded sharp cheddar cheese
            2 eggs, lightly beaten

Preheat oven to 400°. Zucchini must be squeezed of all excess moisture. Combine with cheeses and lightly beaten eggs. Press into a buttered, shallow 9-1/2" x 13-1/2" roasting pan (a glass baking dish would not be deep enough).

            3/4 to 1 pound bulk sausage (or thinly sliced hot dogs)
            1 medium onion, chopped
            2 cloves garlic, minced
            1 (6-ounce) can tomato paste
            1/2 can water
            2 tablespoons chopped oregano (or 2 teaspoons dried oregano)
            2 tablespoons chopped basil leaves (or 2 teaspoons dried basil)

In skillet, lightly brown sausage or hot dog slices, using no fat if possible. Add onion and garlic, cooking until soft. Pour off any fat. Stir in tomato paste and water, then herbs. Simmer for a minute or so, then spoon over zucchini.

            1 green pepper, seeded and cut in thin strips
            1/4 pound mushrooms, sliced
            1/2 cup grated Parmesan cheese
            3/4 cup shredded Monterey Jack cheese
            3/4 cup shredded sharp cheddar cheese

Arrange green pepper strips and mushroom slices on top. Sprinkle with cheeses. Bake, uncovered, at 400° for 30 minutes until cheeses are bubbly.

Serves 4 to 6.


# POTATO DUMPLINGS

Potatoes should be cooked in their jackets one or two days before preparation. They can be stored, cooled and unpeeled, in the refrigerator.

            2 pounds potatoes
            1 or 2 eggs
            1 teaspoon salt
            2/3 cup flour

Boil potatoes until cooked; cool. Refrigerate for one day. Peel and press potatoes through a food mill or grater.

Beat egg slightly and add to potatoes. Season to taste with salt and, if desired, a few caraway seeds. Add flour and knead mixture together thoroughly.

With floured hands, shape potato mixture into large dumplings. Chill. Drop dumplings into boiling salt water and simmer for 15 to 20 minutes; cover with a lid while cooking.

Serve with sauerbraten or any meat gravy. Serves 4.

# Vegetables

# BAKED SWEET POTATOES AND PIPPINS

                6 medium-size sweet potatoes or yams
                4 tart apples, peeled and cored
                1/2 cup dark brown sugar
                1/4 teaspoon mace
                1/4 teaspoon nutmeg
                1/4 cup butter
                1/2 cup apple cider or apple juice

Cook potatoes in jackets in boiling salted water to cover until tender. Peel, cut into 1/2-inch slices. Cut apples into 1/4-inch slices. Place potatoes and apples in alternate layers in a buttered 2-quart baking dish. Sprinkle with sugar, mace, and nutmeg. Dot with butter. Pour in apple cider or juice. Bake in a 350-degree oven for 1 hour or until the apples are tender.

Serves 6 to 8.

# LEMON BASIL CARROTS

                1 pound baby carrots or medium carrots
                    cut into 2-1/2 inch pieces
                2 tablespoons butter or margarine
                1 tablespoon lemon juice
                1 clove garlic, minced
                Salt
                1/2 bunch fresh basil, chopped
                Pepper to taste

Cook carrots in a small amount of water until tender crisp. In another saucepan, melt butter. Stir in remaining ingredients. Add carrots and toss. This is so good you don't have to be Bugs Bunny to appreciate it.

Serves 4.

# GREEN BEANS VINAIGRETTE

                3 pounds fresh green beans
                1 tablespoon onion, grated
                1-1/4 teaspoons salt
                3/4 teaspoon pepper
                1 tablespoon Dijon mustard
                3 tablespoons wine vinegar
                12 tablespoons olive oil
                1/2 teaspoon lemon juice

Steam the beans 10 to 15 minutes. They should be crispy tender. Rinse in cold water and chill. Combine all remaining ingredients except olive oil and lemon juice. Gradually whisk in the olive oil and lemon juice. Pour dressing over beans and marinate in refrigerator until ready to serve.

Serves 12.

# STUFFED ARTICHOKES

6 to 8 artichokes
1 can Italian-style seasoned bread crumbs
1 cup freshly grated Romano cheese
3 cloves garlic, crushed
2 cups finely chopped parsley
1-1/2 teaspoons salt
1 teaspoon black pepper
1/4 pound butter
1 lemon, thinly sliced
1 cup cooking oil

Remove stems of artichokes and trim the tips of leaves. Pound each artichoke on a board until the leaves open and discard the choke.

Combine bread crumbs, cheese, garlic, parsley, salt and pepper. Stuff each leaf and the center of the artichoke. Top each artichoke with a large pat of butter and a thin slice of lemon.

Pour the cooking oil over all the artichokes, then place them in a large pot and add lightly salted water that reaches about 1/2 inch high on the artichokes, or use a steamer. Cover and cook over medium heat, being sure that the water stays at the same level by adding additional hot water as necessary.

Artichokes should cook in about 1 hour, but the best test is to pull a large bottom leaf; when it pulls easily, the artichokes are done.

May be served cold, but best hot.

Makes 6 to 8 servings.

# TOMATO RINGS WITH SPINACH

| | |
|---|---|
| 3 pounds spinach | Salt and pepper to taste |
| 3 tablespoons margarine, melted | 1 tablespoon vinegar |
| 6 eggs, lightly beaten | 1/4 teaspoon savory |
| 1-1/3 cups milk | 8 tomato slices |
| 2 medium-sized onions, chopped | Salt and pepper |

Cook spinach several minutes. Squeeze out all water, then chop. In a bowl, combine spinach, margarine, eggs, milk, onions and seasonings.

Grease eight 5-ounce custard cups. Divide the spinach mixture equally between the cups. Place cups in a shallow roasting pan in 1" hot water. Bake at 350° for 35 to 40 minutes, or until custard is set.

To serve, season tomato slices with salt and pepper. Loosen custard from sides with a knife. Lay tomato slices over top of custard cup and invert. Place on a platter garnished with parsley or watercress.

Serves 8.

## MARINATED GREEN BEANS

2 pounds fresh green beans
2 quarts boiling water
1-1/2 tablespoons coarse salt
2 teaspoons mustard seed
2 teaspoons dill weed
1 teaspoon dried hot chilies, crushed
1 teaspoon dill seed
3 garlic cloves, whole
2 cups water
2 cups white vinegar
2/3 cup sugar

Wash beans and cut off ends. Add beans to boiling water and 1 tablespoon of the salt. Boil 5 minutes and drain. Put beans in a 2-quart container and add mustard seed, dill weed, chilies, dill seed and garlic.

Combine 2 cups water, vinegar, sugar and 1/2 tablespoon of salt in a saucepan and bring to a boil. Pour over beans. Let cool and place in a covered container in the refrigerator for 8 hours.

These beans are just wonderful and low in calories. Also you can use this same process to marinate raw carrots, cauliflower, broccoli or a combination.

## BARBECUED POTATOES

2 pounds new potatoes
1/4 cup finely chopped onions
1/2 green pepper, diced
2 tablespoons chopped parsley
1 cup finely shredded sharp cheese
1-1/2 cups tomato juice
1 tablespoon vinegar
1/2 teaspoon sugar
1 teaspoon Worcestershire sauce
3 drops Tabasco
1/2 teaspoon dry mustard
1 teaspon salt
1/4 teaspoon pepper

Peel and dice potatoes in 1/2-inch cubes.

Combine onions, green peppers, parsley and cheese. Place alternate layers of potatoes and cheese mixture in a buttered casserole (or use individual casseroles). Combine remaining ingredients and pour over the casserole. Bake covered at 350° for 30 minutes. Uncover and bake another 15 minutes.

Serves 4 to 6.

## STUFFED VEGETABLES
### (Microwave)

2 tablespoons olive oil
2 tablespoons pine nuts
1 finely-chopped medium-sized onion
1/2 cup raw rice
1-1/4 cups water
1/4 cup currants
1 tablespoon chopped mint
   (or 1 teaspoon dried mint)
1-1/2 teaspoons salt

1/2 teaspoon ground cinnamon
1 teaspoon dried orange peel
1/8 teaspoon pepper
2 teaspoons sugar
1 cup tomatoes, chopped finely
1/2 cup tomato paste
1/2 cup water
Hollowed-out tomatoes, zucchini
   green peppers or large onions

Put the oil and pine nuts in a casserole and cook for several minutes in the microwave oven until the nuts are toasted, stirring occasionally. Remove and reserve the nuts. Add the onion to the oil, cover and cook in the microwave oven 4 minutes, stirring once. Add the nuts and all other ingredients except the tomato paste, the 1/2 cup water, and the hollowed-out vegetables. Stir. Cook, covered, in the microwave oven for 14 minutes, stirring several times.

Stuff the vegetables and arrange in a covered casserole. Mix the tomato paste with the water and pour over and around the vegetables. Cook, covered, until the vegetables are tender. Cooking time varies with the vegetables being used. Do not overcook.

Tip: If you stuff onions, peel and cut down 1/3 of the way from the top in two cuts at right angles to each other. Partially cook, covered, in the microwave oven and then the centers can be removed easily.

This is one of the best stuffings you will ever taste. Try it another time as a stuffing for a chicken or a duck. Or try it as a rice dish to be served with any meat. It's heavenly.

Serves 6.


## BAKED CORN FOR THE HOLIDAYS

2 cans cream-style corn
1 can sweetened condensed milk
1/2 cup finely chopped green pepper
4 tablespoons pimientos, chopped
2 tablespoons finely chopped onion or onion bits
2 teaspoons salt
4 eggs, beaten,

Mix together everything and pour into a buttered casserole. Bake in a 350° oven 45 to 55 minutes. Terrific with baked ham, chicken or turkey.

Serves 8.

---

Bad luck is often a synonym for bad judgement

## MUSHROOM PIE MADEIRA

2 pounds mushrooms
4 tablespoons butter
Salt and pepper
Juice of 1/2 lemon
2 tablespoons butter
3 tablespoons flour
1-1/2 cups chicken stock
1/2 cup Madeira wine
1/2 cup heavy cream
Pastry for 1 pie crust
1 egg, beaten

Wash and dry mushrooms. Heat 4 tablespoons butter in a skillet. Add mushrooms, salt, pepper and lemon juice. Cover and cook 10 minutes over medium heat, shaking pan. Arrange mushrooms in a buttered baking dish.

To pan juices, add 2 tablespoons butter, flour and chicken stock. Cook until smooth and thickened. Add Madeira wine and cream. Season to taste.

Pour sauce over mushroms. Cover with pastry, making 2 slits on top. Brush with beaten egg. Bake at 450° for 15 minutes, then reduce heat to 350° and bake 10-15 minutes longer, or until crust is golden brown.

Serves 6 to 8.

## BOURBON BAKED BEANS

4 (1-pound) cans baked beans
1 teaspoon dry mustard
1/2 cup chili sauce
1 tablespoon molasses
1/2 cup bourbon
1/2 cup strong coffee
Sliced canned pineapple
Brown sugar

Place all ingredients except pineapple and brown sugar in a buttered baking dish; cover and let stand at room temperature at least 3 hours. Place in a pre-heated 375° oven for 40 minutes, covered. Arrange pineapple on top and sprinkle with brown sugar and bake uncovered another 40 minutes.

Serves 12-16.

## BARBECUED CORN

1/4 cup barbecue sauce
1/2 cup butter
8 ears corn, unhusked

Blend barbecue sauce and butter together. Spread mixture generously over the corn. Wrap each ear securely in heavy duty foil. Cook over hot coals for 15 to 20 minutes, turning several times.

Serves 8.

## JACKIE'S MEATLESS MEAL FOR LENT

1 cup raw rice
3 medium-sized zucchini, thinly sliced
1 (4-ounce) can green chilies, chopped
12 ounces Monterey Jack cheese, shredded
1 large tomato, thinly sliced
Salt to taste
2 cups sour cream
1 teaspoon oregano
1 to 2 cloves garlic, crushed
1/4 cup green pepper, chopped
1/4 cup green onion, chopped
2 tablespoons parsley, chopped

Cook rice according to package instructions. Cook zucchini until barely tender; drain. Set both aside.

In a 3-quart casserole that has been buttered, put a layer of cooked rice, cover with chilies, and sprinkle with half the cheese. Add zucchini, tomato slices and salt to taste. Combine the remaining ingredients, except the parsley, and spoon over the tomato layer. Bake in a 350° oven for 45 minutes. Remove from oven and sprinkle with chopped parsley.

Serves 6 to 8.     A nice meatless dish, high in protein and terrific tasting.

## CHEESE CRUNCH SPUDS

6 medium potatoes
1 cup sour cream
2 teaspoons salt
Pepper to taste
1 tablespoon chopped chives
1/2 cup milk
1 cup grated cheese
1/2 cup crushed corn flakes

Pare and slice potatoes 1/4-inch thick. Place in shallow, buttered pan. Combine sour cream, salt, pepper, chives and milk and pour over. Top with cheese and corn flakes. Bake in 350-degree oven 50 minutes to an hour.

## WONDERFUL BAKED BEANS

Cut 1 onion into rings, then cut rings into smaller pieces. Saute in 2 tablespoons butter. Put 1 tablespoon vinegar in a measuring cup and add half-and-half to make 1 cup; add to 1/3 cup brown sugar, 1/4 cup sifted flour, 1 teaspoon dry mustard and 1 teaspoon salt. Blend in 1 tablespoon molasses, 1/4 teaspoon Worcestershire sauce, 3 drops of Tabasco. Add the sauteed onions and 2 (1-pound) cans molasses-style baked beans. Place in a lightly buttered casserole; garnish with 1 slice of hickory smoked bacon cut in small pieces. Bake at 350° for 1 hour.

Serves 6 to 8.     Great for a picnic!

## RABBI YALE BUTLER'S
## VEGETABLE KUGEL FOR PASSOVER

2 tablespoons margarine ("Mother's Passover" brand)
3 carrots, grated
1/2 cup chopped celery
1/2 cup chopped parsley
1 onion, chopped
1/2 cup chopped green pepper
1/3 cup water
1 package frozen chopped spinach
3 eggs, beaten thick
1/2 teaspoon garlic powder
1/4 teaspoon pepper
1/2 teaspoon salt (optional)
3/4 cup matzo meal

Melt margarine in large frying pan. Add all vegetables and water; cook over low heat until vegetables are tender — approximately 10-12 minutes. Place vegetables in large bowl, add beaten eggs, salt, garlic powder, pepper and matzo meal.

Using 1/2 teaspoon oil on waxed paper, lightly grease 10-inch pie plate or 9 x 9-inch square pan. Pour in mixture. Bake in a preheated 350° oven for 45-50 minutes, until firm.

Cut into 10 equal servings.

1 serving equals 105 calories; 1/2 fat exchange, 1/2 bread exchange, 2 vegetable exchanges.

### Summer Vegetable Magic
## PESTO STUFFED TOMATOES

3 medium tomatoes
2 tablespoons margarine
1/2 cup bread crumbs
3 to 4 tablespoons pesto
4 tablespoons parsley, chopped
1/4 cup sharp cheddar cheese

### Pesto

2 cups fresh basil
1 teaspoon salt (or to taste)
1/2 teaspoon pepper
2 teaspoons walnuts or pine nuts
1-1/2 cups olive oil
2 teaspoons garlic

Cut the tomatoes in half, scoop out centers. Season and drain. Mix together the bread crumbs, pesto, parsley and butter in a small saucepan. Cook over low heat 3 minutes. Add cheese. Fill tomato cups with mixture and bake at 350 degrees for 20 minutes. To make pesto sauce blend all ingredients in a blender or food processor until smooth.

Serves 6. This is wonderful for any barbecue party.

# FRENCH FRIED ONION RINGS

 2 large white onions
 1 cup flour
 1 teaspoon baking powder
 1 cup prepared cracker meal (from the grocery store;
     rolled cracker crumbs cause onions to wilt)
 1/2 cup milk
 Fat for deep frying

Cut onions into 1/3-inch slices; separate and drop into cold water. Sift flour and baking powder together. Dip each slice into flour, then into milk, and last into meal. Let dry a little. May be done ahead and kept in a cool place. Fry lightly in deep hot fat, turning once. Drain on brown paper.

Serves 6.

# BEST BUFFET POTATOES

 6 medium potatoes
 1/4 cup butter, melted
 1 can cream of chicken soup
 1/3 cup chopped green onions, tops included
 1-1/2 cups cheddar cheese, grated
 1 pint sour cream
 2 cups crushed corn flakes (optional)

Cook potatoes until tender; peel and grate.

Mix butter and soup. Stir in onions, cheese and sour cream.

Butter a 2 1/2 quart casserole. Combine potatoes and soup mixture. Top with corn flakes or additional cheddar cheese. Bake at 350° F. 45 minutes or until brown on top.

Serves 6 to 8.

# CZECH POTATO PUDDING

 3 large potatoes, peeled and grated
 2 medium-size onions, grated
 2 eggs, whole
 1/8 teaspoon pepper, freshly grated
 1-1/2 teapoons of salt, or according to taste
 Parsley, chopped

Mix ingredients thoroughly. Using a ring form, pour two tablespoons of vegetable oil on bottom of pan to grease thoroughly. Also pour two tablespoons of oil on top of the ingredients.

Bake for one hour in 400° oven until the top forms a crust. Invert pudding, fill center with creamed chopped spinach or creamed mushrooms.

Serves 8.

# FRESH VEGETABLE CASSEROLE

1-1/2 pounds mushrooms, sliced*
1 onion, sliced
1 tomato, sliced
1 tablespoon butter
1 tablespoon flour
1/2 cup sour cream
Juice from 1/2 lemon
1/2 teaspoon salt
1/8 teaspoon pepper
1-1/2 ounces brandy
1 tablespoon cut parsley

Layer mushrooms, carrots* (use half the portion of mushrooms and use sliced carrots for remaining half), onion and tomato.

Make a white sauce with the butter, flour and sour cream. Add lemon juice and brandy to the sour cream mixture. Pour over vegetables. Add salt and pepper. Sprinkle parsley over all. Cover. Bake about 45 minutes at 350°.

# CARROTS AND PARSNIPS

4 medium carrots
4 medium parsnips
Butter
Salt and pepper
Tarragon

Shred equal amounts of carrots and parsnips with shredding blade of food processor or by hand. Poach very briefly in salted water and drain. Quickly saute in butter and season to taste with salt, pepper and tarragon.

Quick and wonderful. A nice accompaniment to Filo Wrapped Filets.

# SPINACH SOUFFLE

1 tablespoon butter
1 tablespoon onion, chopped
2 tablespoons cheese, grated
1-1/2 tablespoons flour
1 cup milk
4 egg yolks
4 egg whites, beaten
Salt and pepper to taste
2 cups spinach, cooked and chopped

Brown onions in butter. Stir in flour; add milk slowly. Add spinach, cheese and seasonings. Heat and remove from fire.

Mix in unbeaten egg yolks and cool. Fold in egg whites. Pour into greased souffle dish and set dish in pan of water. Bake at 350° until mixture rises and sets, approximately 30 minutes.

Serves 8.

# CREAMY PARTY POTATOES

4 baking potatoes (about 10-ounces each)
1 (8-ounce) package cream cheese at room, temperature
    cut in cubes
1 medium onion, finely chopped
3 eggs
3 tablespoons flour
1 teaspoon salt
1/4 teaspoon white pepper
1 (3-ounce) can French fried onions
4 tablespoons dry sherry

Bake potatoes. Scoop out insides and put in large mixing bowl. (Save the potato skins for deep frying for appetizer.)

Mash potatoes or put through a ricer. Add cream cheese and beat until smooth. Add onion, eggs, flour, salt and pepper and beat until light and fluffy. Spoon into an ungreased 1-1/2 or 2-quart casserole. You may use a souffle dish.

Sprinkle onion rings over the top. Cover with foil. May be refrigerated for a couple of days or you can freeze it at this point.

Before serving, bring casserole to room temperature. Drizzle top with sherry. Bake, covered, at 325° for 30 minutes. Remove foil and bake 20 more minutes or until casserole is hot and bubbly and top is golden and crusty.

Serves 8.

# DOWN HOME BAKED BEANS

1 pound dried beans
1/2 teaspoon soda
1/2 cup sugar
1 teaspoon ground ginger
1-1/4 teaspoons dry mustard
Dash of pepper
1/4 cup butter
1/4 teaspoon parsley flakes
1/4 teaspoon thyme
2 teaspoons salt
3 tablespoons molasses
1 tablespoon maple syrup

Cover beans with water in a 6-quart kettle. Bring to a boil. Cook for 2 minutes. Remove from heat and let stand 30 minutes. Bring to a boil again. Add soda and boil for 1 hour (you may have to add more water). Drain beans and place in a large casserole or beanpot.

Combine remaining ingredients. Pour one quart boiling water over mixture. Stir until butter melts. Pour mixture over beans and stir. Bake covered at 275° for 6 to 8 hours or overnight.

Serves 6 to 8.

# MARDI GRAS SPINACH STRUDEL

2 (10-ounce) packages frozen chopped spinach
1 large onion, finely chopped
2 tablespoons butter
8 ounces feta cheese
6 ounces ricotta cheese
3 eggs, beaten
1 green onion, chopped with some green
1/4 cup parsley, chopped
1 teaspoon dill weed
1/4 teaspoon nutmeg
Salt and pepper to taste
1/2 pound filo leaves
1/2 pound butter
1 cup soft bread crumbs

Thaw spinach and press out moisture. Saute onion in butter until limp. Add spinach. Remove pan from heat. Stir in the cheeses, eggs, green onion, dill and nutmeg. Season to taste. Set mixture aside to cool.

Open package of filo dough and remove one sheet carefully. Cover remaining sheets with a damp dishtowel. Place the single sheet of dough on a slightly damp towel. Brush well with butter, then sprinkle with some of the bread crumbs. Place another sheet of dough on top and repeat procedure. Continue until you have used 6 to 8 sheets in the package.

Place the cooled spinach mixture along one side of the prepared dough and roll up like a jelly roll. Lift carefully with spatulas and place seam side down on a cookie sheet. Bake at 375° for 15 minutes. Remove and cut 10 one-inch slices in each side of the roll, using scissors. Return to oven and continue baking 20 minutes more, or until golden. Serve immediately, cutting into it where the slashes were made. Serves 10.

Can be made and baked in advance and simply reheated at 375° for 15 minutes.

# HOLIDAY PEAS

1 package frozen peas
1 large cucumber, peeled and sliced very thin
2 tablespoons water
1 teaspoon tarragon
1 teaspoon salt
1/2 cup sour cream
1/2 cup mayonnaise
1 tablespoon lemon juice

Combine peas, cucumber, water, tarragon and salt in a heavy saucepan. Cover and cook 5 to 8 minutes. Drain. Combine sour cream, mayonnaise and lemon juice. Warm over low heat, stirring constantly. Stir vegetables into sauce and serve at once. This is great with green beans as well.!

Serves 4 to 6.

## EASTER ORANGE MASHED POTATOES

3 pounds potatoes
2 cups finely chopped onions
4 tablespoons sweet butter
1/2 cup heavy cream
3/4 cup fresh orange juice
Grated fresh orange zest (garnish)

Peel and quarter potatoes. Drop into a large pot of cold salted water. Bring to a boil and cook until potatoes are tender, about 30 minutes.

Meanwhile, in another pan cook the onions in the butter, covered, until very tender and lightly colored, about 25 minutes.

Drain and mash the potatoes, stir in the onions and their butter. Stir in cream and orange juice. Beat again with a wire whisk until fluffy. Turn into a heated serving dish and garnish the top with orange zest. Season to taste. Serve immediately.

This is supposed to serve 6, but at my house I can never depend on this so I make a huge batch. It is terrific with ham or pork roast.

## SUN-DRIED TOMATOES

Small tomatoes or cherry tomatoes
Coarse salt
Vinegar
Olive oil
Fresh rosemary, basil or thyme leaves (optional)

Cut the small tomatoes into quarters or cherry tomatoes in half. Arrange the tomato pieces, cut-side up, on a baking sheet. Salt them. Place the baking sheet in a preheated 200° oven for about 7 hours. Watch tomatoes carefully to make sure they do not burn. When done, they should have a dried, shriveled appearance.

As individual pieces dry completely, remove them, dip each in vinegar, and layer in a sterile glass jar. Cover the tomatoes completely with olive oil. Add the optional herbs. These tomatoes will last for months in or out of the refrigerator.

Can be used in many ways — in assorted antipasti, with cheeses, and in salads.

## CHARCOALED ONIONS

6 medium onions peeled          3 teaspoons butter
6 bouillon cubes                Salt and pepper to taste

Scoop out a small hole in the top of each onion. Place a bouillon cube, butter and salt and pepper to taste in each. Wrap each onion separately and tightly in aluminum foil. Place on hot coals for 30 minutes, turning frequently. Unwrap and serve. So easy and terrific with anything you barbecue. We love onions at our house and this is just a favorite.

Serves 6.

# YAM AND APPLE CASSEROLE

            6 to 8 yams (may use canned)
            2 to 3 oranges
            5 to 6 cooking apples
            Maraschino cherries
            2 cups boiling water
            1 cup sugar
            4 tablespoons cornstarch
            1 teaspoon salt
            1/4 pound butter

Parboil yams, cool, peel and slice. Peel and core apples. Slice. Peel and slice oranges. Layer yams, apples and oranges in a buttered baking dish. Arrange cherries on top to add color. Prepare sauce by pouring boiling water over the dry ingredients, stir, add butter. Cook until sauce thickens. Pour sauce over yams and bake in a 325° oven for 35 to 45 minutes.

Serves 6 to 8.      Super for the holidays and a pretty dish for a holiday table.


# NEBRASKA CARROTS

            2 bunches carrots, sliced
            1 large onion, diced
            1 (10-1/2 ounce) can condensed tomato soup, undiluted
            3/4 cup vinegar
            1 teaspoon dry mustard
            1/2 cup salad oil
            1 cup sugar

Cook carrots and onion in salted water until tender; drain and cool. Cover and refrigerate.

Place remaining ingredients in a saucepan, bring to a boil, stirring constantly. Simmer for 5 minutes. Add carrots and onions, toss to mix. Cool, cover and refrigerate at least overnight.

NOTE: This will keep in the refrigerator for several weeks. Good for buffets, pot-luck dinners. . . men love them.

Makes 1 quart.


# PICKLED MAUI ONIONS

            1 quart white vinegar
            1 quart water
            1/2 cup sugar
            1/3 cup Hawaii Rock salt (can be purchased in Oriental store)
            4 pounds onions (quartered)

Bring first 4 ingredients to a boil and pour over  onions; let cool. Refrigerate for one month.

Yield: 1 gallon.

## Summer Vegetable Magic
# HEAVENLY CORN

3 slices bacon
1 package Jiffy corn bread muffin mix
1 small bunch green onions, chopped
1 cup corn kernels (If you like you can
      use canned, just drain well)
1 (8-ounce) can tomato sauce
4 eggs
1-1/2 cups grated Jack cheese

Fry bacon until crisp, crumble. Using bacon grease, coat sides and bottom of a 2-quart baking dish. Beat one egg with 1/3 cup cold water and add muffin mix. Add bacon and onions. Spread in bottom of dish. Beat 3 eggs and add corn. Cover the muffin mixture with egg mixture. Spoon tomato sauce over all and top with cheese. Bake at 350 degrees for 30 minutes. Cut into squares to serve.

This is so good you will use this recipe again and again.

Serves 6.

# BROCCOLI CASSEROLE

1 (10-3/4 ounce) can cream of mushroom soup
1 cup mayonnaise
1 small onion, chopped, or a few onion flakes to taste
1 cup grated American cheese
2 eggs, beaten
2 (10-ounce) packages chopped broccoli,
      cooked 5 minutes and drained
Ritz cracker crumbs
Margarine

Mix soup, mayonnaise, onion, cheese and eggs together. Then add broccoli and mix very well. Put in buttered casserole. Top with Ritz cracker crumbs. Dot with margarine. Preheat oven to 350° and bake for 45 minutes.

Serves 6 to 8.

# FROZEN CUCUMBERS

2 quarts cucumbers, peeled and sliced thin
1 large onion, sliced
2 tablespoons pickling salt
1-1/2 cups sugar
1/2 cup white vinegar

Refrigerate the first three ingredients, covered, for 24 hours. The next day, drain ingredients. Blend in sugar and white vinegar and refrigerate for 24 hours.

After refrigeration, pack in freezer bags and freeze.

## MOM'S SUPER POTATO CASSEROLE

6 potatoes
2 cups cheddar cheese, shredded
1/4 cup butter, melted
1/3 cup green onion, chopped
1 teaspoon salt
1/4 teaspoon pepper
2 cups sour cream, room temperature
2 tablespoons butter

Peel cooked potatoes and coarsely shred them. Add cheese and melted butter. Mix lightly. Add onion, salt, pepper and sour cream. Mix lightly. Dot with butter. Bake for 25 minutes at 350.°

Serves 8.　　This is a lovely Holiday Buffet Dish.

## SWEET POTATO SURPRISE

1 or 2 large cans sweet potatoes, halved lengthwise
1-1/4 cups brown sugar
1-1/2 tablespoons cornstarch
1/4 teaspoon salt
1/8 teaspoon cinnamon
1 teaspoon shredded orange peel
1 (1-pound) can (2 cups) peeled apricot halves
1 cup apricot juice
2 tablespoons butter
1/2 cup seedless raisins
1/2 cup chopped pecans (put pecans on after mixture
　　has been poured over sweet potatoes)

Combine brown sugar, cornstarch, salt, cinnamon, orange peel, apricots and apricot juice, butter and raisins. Bring to a boil. Simmer until it thickens a bit. Place sweet potatoes in a greased baking dish. Pour mixture over potatoes and top with the pecans. Bake at 375° for 25 minutes. Makes about ten servings. This recipe can be fixed ahead and kept in refrigerator before baking.

## ONION CASSEROLE

2 pounds small onions
1 can cream of mushroom soup
1/2 cup cheddar cheese, grated
1/2 cup walnuts, chopped
1/2 cup cream
1 tablespoon butter
Salt and pepper to taste

Peel and boil onions until tender. Place in 2-quart casserole. Mix together soup, walnuts, cream and seasonings to taste. Pour over onions. Top with cheese and dot with butter. Bake in a 350-degree oven for 30 minutes.

Serves 6.

# WONDERFUL BAKED BEANS

1 onion, chopped
2 tablespoons butter
1 tablespoon vinegar
Light cream
1/3 cup brown sugar, packed
1/4 cup flour
1 teaspoon dry mustard
1 teaspoon salt
1 tablespoon molasses
1/4 teaspoon Worcestershire sauce
3 to 6 drops Tabasco
2 (1-pound) cans molasses-style baked beans
Hickory smoked bacon pieces (for topping)

Saute onions in butter. Add vinegar and enough light cream to make one cup. Combine remaining ingredients and pour all into a buttered casserole. Top with bacon pieces. Bake at 350° for 1 hour.

Serves 8.

## End of Summer Barbecue
# PICNIC POTATOES

3 to 4 large russets
Salt and pepper to taste
7 slices bacon
Chopped onion to taste
1 medium green pepper, chopped
1/2 pound American cheese, sliced
1/2 cup butter (you may use less
    or you may use margarine)

Pare and slice potatoes. Place on a large piece of foil. Sprinkle with salt and pepper. Fry bacon until crisp, drain and crumble. Sprinkle bacon over potatoes, add onion, green pepper and cheese slices. Dot with butter. Wrap foil securely. Place over hot coals, grill for 1 hour and 30 minutes, or until potatoes are tender, turning packet every now and then.

Serves 4 to 6. Super.

---

Send me not on Valentines Day
Mere affectionate display
Or fervent vows that Cupid's dart
Has whistled its way to the depths of your heart.
No, my darling, if your love runs deep,
In the morning just let me sleep.

# MASHED POTATOES
## WITH CRATER GRAVY

6 russet potatoes
6 tablespoons sweet butter
Salt and pepper to taste
3/4 cup warmed milk

Peel potatoes and boil until tender, about 20-25 minutes. Drain, then return to pot over medium heat, tossing and stirring the potatoes to thoroughly expel all moisture. Mash potatoes with a masher, adding butter and salt when they are clear of lumps. While mixing vigorously with a heavy whisk, add the warm milk. At this point, the more you beat, the fluffier the potatoes. Serve immediately, garnished with pepper and pats of butter.

### Crater Gravy

3 tablespoons butter
3 tablespoons flour
1 (10-ounce) can beef broth
3/4 cup water
1 (10-ounce) can condensed
  cream of mushroom soup

Melt butter and blend in flour. Add broth and water and cook until thickened, about 10 to 15 minutes. Add mushroom soup, stirring constantly until fully blended. Cook another 15 minutes, stirring constantly.

Makes 3 cups.


# BEANS FOR THE LABOR DAY PICNIC

This is an ideal dish for picnic and tailgate parties. Serve with thin slices of French bread and cold rare roast beef with horseradish sauce, and sliced beefsteak tomatoes.

2 pounds small white navy beans
2 cups olive oil
1-1/4 cups lemon juice
1/2 cup white vinegar
3 cups finely chopped celery
1/2 cup plus 1 tablespoon finely
  chopped green bell pepper
1/2 cup finely chopped parsley
2 tablespoons finely chopped onion
4-1/2 teaspoons salt
1/4 teaspoon thyme

Soak and cook beans according to package directions, but do not overcook. They should retain their shape. Marinate in the remaining ingredients, tightly covered, 8 hours or more.

Serves 24.

# Meats

## EASY BEEF BRISKET
## WITH MUSTARD RING

4 to 5 pounds beef brisket
    (remove as much fat as possible)
1 cup catsup
1/4 cup onion, chopped
1 tablespoon Dijon mustard
1/4 teaspoon pepper
2 tablespoons vinegar
1 tablespoon horseradish

Place meat in a shallow baking pan. Combine remaining ingredients. Pour this sauce over meat and allow to stand overnight or at least several hours. Season with salt to taste. Cover tightly with foil and bake at 300° for 1 hour per pound or until very tender. Pour off drippings, skim off fat and thicken drippings with a little cornstarch. Serve with Mustard Ring (see below).

### Mustard Ring

4 eggs, beaten
3/4 cup sugar
1-1/2 teaspoons dry mustard
1 cup water
1-1/2 envelopes unflavored gelatin
1/4 teaspoon salt
1/2 cup cider vinegar
1 cup heavy cream

Place eggs in top of double boiler. Add sugar and gelatin moistened in 1/4 cup water, mustard and salt. Blend well. Add remaining water and vinegar. Cook over hot water until slightly thickened. Whip cream and fold into cooled mixture. Turn into a 1-1/2 quart mold and chill.

Serves 8.

## CHEESEBURGER PIE

1 pound ground round
1/2 cup milk
1/2 cup catsup
1/3 cup bread crumbs
1/4 cup onion, chopped
1 teaspoon Worcestershire sauce
Salt to taste
1/2 teaspoon oregano
1/8 teaspoon pepper
1 (8" or 9") pie crust, unbaked
1 cup cheddar cheese, grated

Combine the first 8 ingredients and spread into the unbaked pie shell. Bake in a 350° oven for 35 minutes. Toss together the cheese and the Worcestershire sauce. Sprinkle over top of pie and bake 10 minutes more. Garnish with pickle slices. Slice and serve.

Serves 4.

# EVERYBODY LOVES THIS BEEF STEW

    4 tablespoons oil
    1 clove garlic, split
    2 large onions, sliced
    1/3 cup flour
    1-1/2 teaspoons salt
    1/4 teaspoon pepper
    2-1/2 pounds stew beef cut into 1-1/2 inch cubes
    1/2 teaspoon dill weed
    1 cup dry red wine
    1 can beef consomme
    1 (10-ounce) package frozen artichoke hearts
    18 mushrooms halved
    2 (8-ounce) packages refrigerated biscuits
    Melted butter
    Parmesan cheese

Saute garlic and onions in oil 'til golden. Remove. Dredge meat in flour, salt and pepper. Brown well in same oil, adding more if needed. Return onion. Add dill weed, wine, consomme.

Simmer 1-1/2 hours or until tender. Cook artichoke hearts 1 minute less than package directs. Add to meat. Saute mushrooms in melted butter 5 minutes. Add to meat. Mix and correct seasonings. Turn into a 2-1/2 quart baking dish. Top with biscuits and bake 400 degrees for 15 minutes.

Brush biscuits with butter and sprinkle with cheese. Bake 5 minutes more.

Serves 6.


# PORKRAUT ROLLUPS

    3/4 cup bread crumbs
    2 eggs, beaten
    1/3 cup milk
    1-1/2 teaspoons salt
    1/4 teaspoon pepper
    1 teaspoon thyme
    1 tablespoon Worcestershire sauce
    2 pounds lean ground pork
    1 (1-pound) can sauerkraut, rinsed, drained and chopped fine
    1/4 cup onion, chopped
    3 tablespoons pimiento, chopped
    1 tablespoon sugar
    5 slices bacon

Combine bread crumbs, eggs, milk, salt, pepper, thyme and Worcestershire sauce. Mix in pork. On waxed paper, pat pork mixture into a 9″ x 12″ rectangle. Combine sauerkraut, onions, pimiento and sugar. Spread evenly over the meat. Roll up from the narrow end, and place loaf in a greased, shallow baking pan. Lay bacon over the top. Bake at 375° for 1 hour and 15 minutes.

Serves 8.

## TULSA RIBS

6 pounds meaty beef ribs, cut into 4- to 5-inch long pieces

### Barbecue Sauce

2 tablespoons unsalted butter
1 cup chopped onion (1 large)
1 clove garlic, finely chopped
1 (16-ounce) can tomato sauce
1 cup cider vinegar
1 cup tomato-vegetable juice
1/2 cup prune juice
1 generous tablespoon slivered lemon peel (1/2 lemon)
3 tablespoons lemon juice (1 large)
1 bay leaf
6 crushed juniper berries (optional)
1/2 teaspoon cayenne pepper
2 tablespoons brown sugar *or* honey

Prepare charcoal for grilling or preheat gas unit.

To precook ribs, divide ribs up and wrap in 3 heavy-duty aluminum foil packets. Place on grid. Cover with dome. Cook over high heat for 1 hour. (If cooking over coals, replenish with new charcoal as needed.)

Meanwhile, prepare Barbecue Sauce: Melt butter in large saucepan over medium heat. Stir in onion; cook 2 minutes. Add garlic; cook 1 minute longer. Add tomato sauce, vinegar, tomato-vegetable juice, prune juice, lemon peel, lemon juice, bay leaf, juniper berries, if using, cayenne and brown sugar. Bring to boiling. Lower heat and simmer until sauce has thickened, about 30 minutes.

Remove rib packets from grid. Carefully open and place ribs back on grid. Place hood on grill. Cook until tender, 30 minutes to 1 hour, basting with barbecue sauce, and turning, if necessary. Pass extra barbecue sauce.

## LEG OF LAMB IN A BROWN PAPER BAG

1 (5-pound) leg of lamb
1 teaspoon seasoned salt
1 teaspoon rosemary
1 tablespoon paprika
2 cloves garlic, crushed
1/3 cup oil
1/2 teaspoon marjoram
1 large brown paper bag

Pierce lamb with a small knife in several places. Mix remaining ingredients and brush over lamb. Let stand overnight in refrigerator.

Place lamb in paper bag and twist end closed tightly. Place in a large roasting dish and cook 2-1/2 hours at 325 degrees (medium rare).

Tear open the bag and remove the meat to a platter. Pour juices into a sauce pan and skim off excess fat. Serve juices as table sauce.

# BARBECUED COUNTRY STYLE SPARERIBS

3 to 4 pounds country-style spareribs
1/2 cup firmly packed brown sugar
3 tablespoons dry mustard
1 teaspoon salt
1/8 teaspoon pepper
1 teaspoon ground ginger
1/2 cup tomato juice
1/2 cup orange juice
1 tablespoon grated onion
1/2 teaspoon garlic powder
1 tablespoon Worcestershire sauce
Fresh pineapple slices

Simmer ribs in water to cover in a large kettle for 30 minutes. Drain and arrange in a shallow glass baking dish.

Combine remaining ingredients except pineapple and let stand 15 minutes; then pour over the ribs, turning ribs to coat over all. Marinate in the refrigerator for at least 3 hours.

Barbecue ribs over hot coals 10 to 15 minutes per side, brushing with marinade sauce during the whole cooking time. A few minutes before the ribs are done, dip the pineapple slices in the remaining sauce, place on the grill and brown; serve with the ribs. Scrumptious . . . .

Serves 4.

Serve with corn on the cob, sliced beefsteak tomatoes and Picnic Potato Salad. Chilled watermelon for dessert and you will have a memorable Memorial Day get-together.


# BAKED HAM WITH RAISIN SAUCE

1 (3- to 5-pound) ham or picnic
1/2 cup raisins
1-3/4 cups sherry or apple juice
1 tablespoon corn starch
1 teaspoon dry mustard

1/3 cup brown sugar
1/4 teaspoon salt
1/8 teaspoon pepper
2 tablespoons lemon juice
2 tablespoons vinegar

Have butcher slice ham or picnic into 1/2-inch slices and tie. Roast ham 1 hour at 350 degrees or until hot. Meanwhile, prepare sauce. Combine raisins and sherry or apple juice and simmer 10 minutes. Stir together corn-starch, mustard, brown sugar, salt and pepper. Blend mixture with lemon juice and vinegar. Stir into wines/juice and raisins and cook 3 minutes or until sauce thickens and clears. Untie ham or picnic slices and arrange in a deep serving dish. Pour hot sauce over slices and serve immediately.

Variation: Sauce may be served separately with whole ham or picnic which is sliced at the table.

# PARTY STEAKS

8 (6- to 8-ounce) filet mignon steaks
    cut 1-inch thick
1 large clove garlic, crushed
1/2 teaspoon seasoned salt
1/4 teaspoon seasoned pepper
1/2 stick plus 1 tablespoon butter
2 tablespoons brandy
3 tablespoons flour

2 teaspoons tomato paste
1/2 teaspoon crushed garlic
3/4 cup dry red wine
1 cup chicken broth and
    1/2 cup beef broth
1/4 teaspoon Worcestershire sauce
2 tablespoons currant jelly
1/2 pound mushrooms, sliced

Place steaks on a work surface in a single layer. In a small bowl, make a paste of the garlic, seasoned salt and pepper. With hands, rub seasonings on both sides of steaks.

Heat 1 tablespoon butter in a large, heavy skillet (*not* non-stick) until very hot. Saute steaks over moderately high heat until brown on each side but still raw in the middle. Do not crowd. If butter begins to burn, reduce heat slightly.

Place steaks in a 9 x 13-inch casserole. Leave a little space between each steak.

Add brandy to skillet. Cook over moderate heat, stirring constantly, scraping all the goodies from the bottom of the pan. Add 1/2 stick butter; when melted and foamy, stir in flour. Reduce heat; cook and stir until mixture is golden. Stir in tomato paste and garlic (mixture will be thick and grainy). Remove pan from heat and whisk in wine and both broths. Bring to a boil and simmer for 10 minutes, stirring occasionally, or until reduced by a third. Stir in Worcestershire and jelly. When jelly has melted, stir in mushrooms. Adjust seasonings. Sauce should be coating consistency; if too thick, thin with water or wine. Cool completely. Pour over steaks in casserole; sauce should not come more than halfway up steaks. Cover; refrigerate overnight. Bring to room temperature. Preheat oven to 400.° Bake uncovered 15-20 minutes for medium rare, 20-25 minutes for medium to medium well. When serving, spoon sauce from pan over steaks.

# SAUSAGE-STUFFED APPLES

6 red or green cooking apples
1/2 pound sausage (bulk, sage, pork or Italian)
2 tablespoons currants or raisins (optional)
1 cup sherry, Madeira or marsala wine

Core apples and cut a slit around sides about 1/3 of the way down from top to prevent bursting. Blend currants or raisins with sausage and stuff apples, leaving a mound of sausage atop each.

Place in baking pan and bake 30 to 45 minutes at 350° or until apples are done and sausage is browned on top. During cooking, baste with wine every 10 minutes. Spoon cooking juices over apples at serving time.

## CURRIED PORK CHOPS AND APRICOTS

2 tablespoons oil
6 pork loin chops, 1" thick
1 pound apricots, cut in half
1 medium onion, chopped
1/4 cup butter
1/4 cup flour
1 teaspoon salt
1 teaspoon curry powder
2 cups milk
1/2 pound mushrooms, sliced

Heat oil and brown chops on both sides. Place in a 9" x 13" baking dish. Arrange apricot halves on meat, cut side down.

Using same skillet, stir in onion and butter until tender. Stir in flour, salt and curry powder. Cook over low heat, stirring until mixture is bubbly. Remove from heat. Stir in milk gradually, mixing ingredients with a whisk. Heat to boiling, stirring constantly. Boil mixture one minute. Stir in mushrooms.

Pour mixture over chops. Cover tightly with aluminum foil. Bake covered for 45 minutes at 350°. Uncover and bake 15 minutes longer.

Serves 6.

## CARNE ASADA

1 (1-pound, 4-ounce) top sirloin steak
2 tablespoons vegetable oil
1/2 teaspoon dried leaf oregano, crushed
1/2 teaspoon salt
1/4 teaspoon coarsely ground pepper
1/4 cup orange juice
1 tablespoon lime juice
2 teaspoons cider vinegar
2 orange slices, cut 1/2-inch thick

Place steak in a shallow glass baking dish. Rub oil on each side of steak. Sprinkle with oregano, salt and pepper. Sprinkle orange juice, lime juice and vinegar over steak. Cover and refrigerate overnight for best flavor — or several hours turning occasionally.

To cook, bring meat to room temperature. Prepare and pre-heat charcoal grill. Drain meat, reserving marinade. Place steak on grill over hot coals. Top with orange slices. Occasionally spoon reserved marinade over steaks as they cook. Grill 3 to 4 minutes on each side, or until medium-rare. Cook longer, if desired. Remove orange slices to turn steak. Replace orange slices on top of steak. Serve with beans and rice or cut into thin slices and use as a taco filling.

Makes 4 servings.

# COMMON SENSE COOKING

How would you like to pass off a chuck roast as expensive eye of round, sirloin tip or even standing rib roast? Here's how:

Buy a rolled chuck roast. It doesn't matter how much it weighs, the results will be the same.

Season with salt and pepper and rub with garlic clove if desired. Place in greased pan and bake for 8-10 hours at 150,° uncovered. When ready to be served, it will be bright pink in color and very juicy. If your oven is set at 150,° there is no way that the internal temperature of the meat can be any higher, no matter how long you roast it.

During this slow cooking, the tissues break down so that after 8-10 hours of cooking, the meat will be fork-tender, yet still rare, and it won't shrink. If you like your meat a little more well done, just set your oven so it corresponds with the degree of doneness indicated on your meat thermometer.

Rare beef registers at about 150,° medium at 160° and well done at 170.° It's important to use a meat thermometer, and if you have any doubt about your oven's accuracy, test it with an oven thermometer. At any rate, be sure to keep oven temperature well under 200° for this.

Another good tip: When you forget to defrost a roast and you need it for a meal, it is possible to take a big 6 to 8 pound roast, leg of lamb, pork loin roast, smoked ham or any other roast from the freezer, frozen hard as a rock, and have it as tender, juicy and good as if it had just come from the butcher the morning of the serving. All you have to do is put it in a pan, season it and put it in a preheated 450° oven for 25 minutes only.

Then lower the oven temperature to the degree at which you would normally cook that cut of meat, and continue cooking it in the regular way for the normal cooking time. Be sure to set your timer so you won't forget to lower the temperature after 25 minutes at 450.° This 25 minutes is in addition to normal cooking time.

# DINNER MEAT LOAF

| | |
|---|---|
| 1-1/4 pounds ground beef | 1/2 cup tomato juice |
| 1/2 pound ground pork | 1 onion, minced |
| 3/4 cup instant oatmeal | 1 tablespoon Worcestershire sauce |
| 2 eggs, beaten | 1 teaspoon salt |
| 1/2 cup milk | 1/4 teaspoon pepper |

Preheat oven to 350.° Mix beef, pork, oatmeal and eggs. Blend in milk, tomato juice, onion, Worcestershire sauce and seasonings. Pack firmly into 9" x 5" loaf pan, shaping a rounded top.

Bake for 1-1/2 hours. Let stand for 10 minutes before slicing. Drain off any excess juice at bottom of pan.

Serves 8.

## FAJITAS

1 (1-1/4 to 1-1/2-pound) skirt steak
Half can of beer
1/2 cup cooking oil
1 thinly sliced onion
Juice of a lime
1 dried red pepper, crushed
1 clove garlic, pressed
Fresh cracked pepper to taste

Make a marinade of all the ingredients and marinate the steak, covered, in the refrigerator about 1 hour.

Meanwhile, start the barbecue. Or you can use a cast iron skillet heated very hot.

When meat is ready to be cooked, slice it into about 6-inch pieces and grill quickly, turning once, not more than 3 to 4 minutes to the side.

Cut on the diagonal into thin strips and fold into a warm flour tortilla with sour cream, guacamole and salsa.

Serves 4.

The skirt is beef diaphragm muscle. For many years it was considered by butchers as a sort of throwaway, but the flavor of the skirt far surpasses that of the beef tenderloin and now, of course, with the new hot trend in Tex Mex cuisine, it has suddenly become very trendy.


## DELMONICO'S BEEF ROLLS

2 pounds round steak cut 1-inch thick
1/2 cup flour
8 slices bacon, cooked and crumbled
3/4 cup chopped parsley
3 tablespoons bacon fat
2 cups beef stock
1 tablespoon vinegar
1 tablespoon catsup
2 teaspoons Worcestershire sauce

Dredge steak with flour, pound until flattened. Cut the meat in strips 2 inches by 4 inches. Spread each strip with crumbled bacon and parsley. Roll up tightly with bacon and parsley inside; fasten with picks.

Sear in bacon fat; remove meat to roasting pan. Add beef stock, vinegar, catsup, and Worcestershire sauce to bacon drippings. Pour over meat; cover and bake at 350° F. for 2 hours until meat is tender. Remove meat to platter.

Continue cooking sauce, stirring until smooth and thickened. Pour sauce over meat.

Makes 6 to 8 servings.

# CHORIZO

1 pound Farmer John unseasoned pork sausage
1 pound lean ground beef
1 teaspoon oregano
1 teaspoon cumino
1 teaspoon garlic
1 teaspoon salt
1 teaspoon pepper
1/2 bottle Gebhardts chili powder
1/2 cup tarragon vinegar

Mix well. Place in a large bowl, cover and chill overnight. Next day, make patties and fry (or can be frozen).


# PUMPKIN AND PORK CHOP CASSEROLE

1 (3-pound) pumpkin,
    pared and coarsely chopped
1/4 cup brown sugar
1/4 teaspoon pumpkin spice
1/4 teaspoon mace
1/4 teaspoon cinnamon
1/4 teaspoon nutmeg
1/4 cup water
2 tablespoons molasses
1 tablespoon butter
4 pork chops
Salt and pepper, to taste

Preheat oven to 325° F.

In an oblong casserole dish arrange pumpkin. Sprinkle pumpkin with brown sugar, pumpkin spice, mace, cinnamon, nutmeg, water and molasses. Set aside.

Melt butter in a frying pan and brown pork chops. Arrange chops in casserole over pumpkin. Season with salt and pepper. Bake for 45 minutes, or until pork is tender.


# EASY BAKED STEW

2 pounds lean beef stew meat
Salt, pepper and paprika
2 tablespoons dry onion soup mix
6 medium size potatoes
8 white boiling onions
3 carrots, quartered
1 (10-1/2 ounce) can cream of celery soup
1/2 cup water
1/2 cup sherry

Season meat with salt, pepper, paprika and onion soup mix. Place meat in Dutch oven, add whole potatoes and onions and quartered carrots. Blend celery soup with water and wine and pour over meat. Cover and bake in slow oven (250-300 degrees) for 5 hours.

Serves 6 to 8.

## SCRUMPTUOUS STROGANOFF

1-1/2 pounds lean ground beef
4 tablespoons butter
1 cup chopped onion
1 garlic clove, chopped
1-1/2 pounds fresh mushrooms, sliced
3 tablespoons flour
2 teaspoons instant beef bouillon
1 tablespoon ketchup
1 tablespoon A-1 Sauce
1/2 teaspoon salt
1/8 teaspoon pepper
1 (10-1/2 ounce) can beef consomme or bouillon
1/2 cup white wine
1/4 teaspoon dill
1-1/2 cups sour cream

Brown meat in 1 tablespoon butter, then add remaining butter and saute onion, garlic, and mushroom until onion is clear, 3-4 minutes. Remove pan from heat and remove meat and onions from pan, set aside. Mix flour, instant bouillon, ketchup, A-1 sauce, salt, and pepper in fry pan. Gradually add beef consomme, return to heat, and bring to boil. Put meat back in pan, reduce heat, and simmer 5 minutes. Stir in wine, dill, and sour cream. Heat thoroughly. Serves 4.

## STUFFED CABBAGE LEAVES

8 large cabbage leaves
1 pound ground beef
1 beaten egg
1/2 teaspoon salt
1/4 teaspoon pepper
1-1/2 cups finely chopped celery
1 tablespoon chopped onion
1 cup bread crumbs
1 large tomato, peeled and chopped, or
    3/4 cup canned tomatoes
1 tablespoon brown sugar
3 tablespoons lemon juice
1 cup beef broth or bouillon
1/4 teaspoon salt

Cook cabbage leaves in a large kettle of slightly salted water just until cabbage is limp (about 3 minutes). Drain.

Combine ground beef, egg, salt, pepper, celery, onion and bread crumbs. Place about 1/3 cup of the meat mixture in center of each cabbage leaf. Fold the sides over the filling, then fold over the ends. Place in a large skillet with the seam side down.

Mix the remaining ingredients and pour over the rolls. Cover and simmer 45 minutes, occasionally spooning the sauce over the rolls.

# STUFFED LEG OF LAMB FOR EASTER

Have your butcher debone a 6-pound leg of lamb and insert a pork tenderloin in its place, tying all together well. With a sharp pointed knife, insert slivers of garlic into the meat at random on all sides (I use 8 to 10 cloves of garlic).

Mix together the following for your marinade:

| | |
|---|---|
| 1/2 cup chili sauce | 1 cup hot water |
| 2 tablespoons | 1 teaspoon salt |
|    Worcestershire sauce | 1/2 teaspoon pepper |
| 1/4 cup dry sherry | 1 teaspoon ginger, ground |
| 2 tablespoons oil | 1 onion, diced finely |

Place leg of lamb in a glass baking dish, pour the marinade over all and let marinate in the refrigerator 12 to 16 hours, turning occasionally.

Bake the meat uncovered in the marinade at 300,° allowing 35 minutes per pound. Your meat thermometer should register 180° when the meat is done. Baste the meat from time to time during the roasting. Garlic should be removed before serving.

Serves 8 to 10.

This is such a dynamic combination of two old favorites — just wonderful for that something different for the Easter holidays.

# BOLICHI
## (Stuffed Round Steak) (Microwave)

2 to 3 pounds round steak
Salt and pepper
1 medium onion, chopped
1/2 green pepper, chopped
1/2 cup cooked ham or bacon, diced
1 clove garlic, minced
1 stalk celery, chopped
1 tablespoon Worcestershire sauce
1/4 teaspoon basil
1 (10-ounce) can prepared brown or mushroom gravy

Pound steaks on both sides to tenderize. Season with salt and pepper.

Combine all ingredients except gravy. Spread mixture across center of meat and roll up. Secure with 3 pieces of string. Place seam side down on a glass roasting platter. Cover with plastic wrap. Cook on MEDIUM 5 minutes. Turn meat over. Pour gravy over all. Cook and cover on MEDIUM 15 minutes, or until steak is fork tender.

To serve, cut into rounds.

Serves 6.

## SPARERIBS, KRAUT AND DUMPLINGS

3 pounds meaty spareribs
1 teaspoon salt
1 onion, minced
1 large can or jar of sauerkraut
1 teaspoon caraway seeds
1 raw potato, grated
1 apple, peeled and grated

Cook ribs in water with salt and onion until almost done. Wash sauerkraut under running water, drain and add to ribs with the caraway seeds. Simmer for another 15 to 20 minutes. Add apple and potato and simmer 15 minutes. Now place dumplings (see below) on top of sauerkraut, and cover and steam 5 to 8 minutes, or until done.

### Dumplings:

2 eggs, beaten
1 cup milk
1 cup flake evaporated potatoes
1/2 teaspoon salt
2 cups flour
2 heaping teaspoons baking powder

Add milk to eggs, salt, flour and baking powder. Mix to form a soft dough. Divide into 8 balls and place on sauerkraut. Cover and steam.

Serves 6 to 8.

## SAVORY SUPER BOWL SAUSAGES

3 packages smoked sausage links

### Sauce:

12 ounces beer
1/2 cup honey
1 tablespoon lemon juice
1 tablespoon Worcestershire sauce
Tabasco
1 teaspoon salt
1 teaspoon dry mustard
16 ounces tomato sauce
1 cup brown sugar
1/2 teaspoon onion powder
2 cloves garlic, crushed
1/2 teaspoon savory
1/2 teaspoon mixed herbs

Combine all sauce ingredients and simmer over low heat 10 minutes.

Cut each sausage link into quarters and heat with sauce. Serve in a chafing dish.

This will be a favorite any time of the year...so easy and it is just fabulous.

# CAMPFIRE SAUSAGE AND BEANS

1 medium-sized onion, thinly sliced
1 medium-sized green pepper, cut into 1/2-inch squares
1 or 2 tablespoons vegetable oil
1 (15-ounce) can baked pork and beans
1 (15-ounce) can butter beans, drained
1 small can sliced mushrooms, drained
5 ounces ready-to-eat smoked sausage
1/2 cup catsup
1/4 cup mustard
2/3 cup maple syrup
1 teaspoon oregano
5 whole cloves
2 small bay leaves

Heat the oil in a large saucepan over a low fire and gently saute the onion slices and pepper squares until the onion is slightly transparent, about 3 or 4 minutes.

Add the baked beans, butter beans and sliced mushrooms and stir well. Cut the sausage into bite-size pieces and add to the beans, together with the catsup, mustard, maple syrup, oregano, cloves and bay leaves.

Cook the beans, stirring occasionally, until all the ingredients are piping hot. Serve immediately.

Serves 4.

# FLANK STEAK

1 cup fine dry bread crumbs
1/2 cup grated Romano or Parmesan cheese
2 tablespoons finely chopped parsley
3/4 teaspoon salt
1/8 teaspoon pepper
2 eggs, beaten
2 tablespoons milk
1-1/2 pounds flank steak, tenderized and cut into 4 pieces
1 clove garlic, finely chopped or 1/4 teaspoon garlic salt
1/4 cup olive oil
1/2 cup sherry or marsala

Combine bread crumbs, cheese, parsley, salt and pepper; mix well. Combine beaten eggs with milk. Dip meat in egg mixture, then in bread crumb mixture; repeat until all eggs and crumbs are used. Cook garlic in oil. Brown meat slowly in seasoned oil. When well browned, lower heat and add wine. Cover and simmer 30 minutes, or until tender.

## STUFFED PORK TENDERLOIN

2 pork tenderloins (3/4 to 1 pound each)
1 cup pitted dates
Zest of 2 oranges
Zest of 1 lemon
6 garlic cloves
Salt

Make a cavity the length of each tenderloin with the help of a wooden spoon handle. Combine the dates and the zests. Stuff each cavity with this mixture.

Make a paste with the garlic and salt using a mortar and pestle. Spread the paste over the tenderloin. Place the meat in a roasting pan and roast at 350° for about 40 minutes or 170° interior temperature.

Serves 6.

## LEG OF PORK WITH RED CABBAGE

2 pounds leg of pork (boneless fresh pork leg is best)
2 pounds red cabbage
4 tablespoons pork fat
Salt and pepper to taste
3 to 4 tart apples, chopped
1 tablespoon red currant jelly
Nutmeg and caraway to taste (optional)
1 large onion, sliced
3 cloves
2 bay leaves
1 tablespoon brown sugar
2 tablespoons vinegar
1 onion stuck with 2 cloves

Chop cabbage. Heat fat in a large heavy skillet and fry onion until slightly browned. Add the cabbage, cloves, 1 bay leaf, salt, sugar, vinegar, apples and water to cover the bottom of the pan. Stir and cook over a very low heat for about 2 hours (you may have to add a little more liquid). Add jelly just before serving.

Rub leg of pork with salt and pepper. Place the leg skin side down in a roasting pan with 1/2-inch hot water and bake in a 375° oven until the skin has softened, about 35 minutes. Cut the skin in a diamond pattern, add the onion with the cloves, and 1 bay leave, nutmeg and caraway seeds.

Continue roasting the joint until the meat is tender, basting often. Take the meat from the pan, keep hot, strain gravy and serve with the cabbage.

Serves 4 to 6.

# FILO WRAPPED FILET MIGNONS
## WITH MADEIRA SAUCE

4 (6-ounce) tenderloin filets cut 1-1/4″ thick, trimmed
Salt and pepper to taste
1/4 pound fresh mushrooms, minced
2 ounces cooked ham, ground
3 shallots, minced
2 tablespoons butter
1 teaspoon Dijon mustard
1 tablespoon dry sherry
8 sheets filo dough
6 tablespoons butter, melted

### Madeira Sauce:

1/2 cup beef broth
1/2 cup Madeira            Juice of 1/2 lemon
1 teaspoon Bovril          2 tablespoons butter,
                               softened

Oil a heavy skillet and in it sear the filets over high heat for 1 minute per side. Season with the salt and pepper and set aside.

In the same skillet, saute the mushrooms, ham and shallots in 2 tablespoons of the butter for about 5 minutes. Add the mustard and sherry. Cook and stir a few more minutes to form a moist paste. Set aside.

Brush 1 sheet of filo dough with butter and place another sheet on top. Repeat this 3 more times. On each stack of filo place 2 tablespoons of the mushroom mixture in the center and top with 1 filet. Wrap the filo around the filets and place seam side down on a greased baking sheet. Brush with melted butter and bake at 450° for 12 minutes or until lightly browned. Meat will be medium rare.

For the sauce, blend the pan juices from meat with broth, Madeira and Bovril. Bring to a boil, reduce heat and let simmer 5 minutes. Spoon 2 tablespoons of sauce over each filet and serve. Pour remaining sauce in a sauce boat. Serves 4.

# ELEGANT RACK OF LAMB

2 (3-pound) racks of lamb
1 cup honey
1/2 cup dry vermouth
4 tablespoons crushed sesame seeds
3 tablespoons soy sauce
2 cloves garlic, crushed
1 tablespoon ground ginger

Place rack of lamb, bone side down, in a shallow baking pan. Bake in a preheated 325° oven for 1-1/2 hours.

Combine marinade ingredients in a saucepan and simmer for 10 minutes. Baste lamb during baking process to give it a beautiful glaze and succulent flavor.

Serves 6.

## TORTILLA FLATS

1-1/2 pounds ground beef
1 package spaghetti sauce mix
1 teaspoon salt
1 clove garlic, crushed
1 (1-pound) can tomatoes, cut up
1 (8-ounce) can tomato sauce
1/2 cup red wine
1 (4-ounce) can diced green chilies
1 pound ricotta cheese
2 eggs, lightly beaten
8 corn tortillas
1 pound Monterey Jack cheese, grated

Preheat oven to 350°. Brown beef in a heavy skillet, add spaghetti sauce mix, salt, tomatoes, tomato sauce, garlic, wine and chilies. Blend thoroughly and simmer 10 minutes.

In a bowl combine the ricotta cheese with the eggs.

In a flat baking dish (8" x 12") place about 1 cup of the meat mixture. Place 2 tortillas over the meat, side by side, then spoon some of the ricotta mixture on top of each. Then layer with more meat and sprinkle with grated cheese. Repeat until each of the 2 stacks has 4 tortillas, ending with the grated cheese.

Bake for 30 minutes. Let stand 5 minutes before cutting into pie-shaped wedges.

This is so easy to prepare and so good. Great for supper or luncheon.

Serves 8.

## MOTHER'S DAY STEAKS

1-1/2 pounds top sirloin steak
3 tablespoons butter or margarine
1 tablespoon Worcestershire
1 teaspoon dried basil
1/2 teaspoon dried tarragon
3 cups sliced fresh mushrooms
1/2 cup dry white wine
1/4 teaspoon salt
1/8 teaspoon pepper
1 cup Monterey Jack cheese, shredded
1 tablespoon flour

Cut beef into 4 serving pieces. In a large skillet, melt butter or margarine. Add Worcestershire, basil and tarragon. Place beef in skillet, cook 5 minutes on each side for medium rare. Remove to a warm platter, cover with foil to keep warm.

Place mushrooms in skillet. Add wine, salt and pepper. Saute until mushrooms are cooked.

In a small bowl toss cheese with flour, stir into mushrooms. Cook until cheese is melted. Pour mushroom sauce over the steaks, serve immediately.

Serves 4.

## SUPER BOWL MEXICAN PIE

| | |
|---|---|
| 1 pound ground beef | 1/2 cup sliced ripe olives |
| 2 medium onions, chopped | 3/4 cup mayonnaise |
| 1 tablespoon chili powder | 1 (8-ounce) can refrigerated |
| Dash of salt |    crescent rolls |
| 2 garlic cloves, crushed | 2 medium tomatoes, thinly sliced |
| 1-1/4 cups sour cream | 1/3 cup chopped green chilies |

2 cups cheddar cheese, grated

In a skillet brown the onions until nicely browned. Add beef, chili powder, garlic and salt. Cook until meat loses its pink color. Drain off grease.

In a small bowl, combine sour cream, olives and mayonnaise. Separate dough into 8 triangles and put into the bottom of a 9 or 10-inch square baking pan. Press over bottom to form a crust.

Spoon meat mixture evenly over crust. Arrange tomato slices, slightly over-lapping, to cover meat. Sprinkle with chilies, 1 cup of the cheese. Now cover with sour cream mixture and sprinkle with remaining cheddar cheese.

Bake at 375° for 25 to 30 minutes, or until crust is golden brown and cheese is melted. Cool 5 minutes. Cut into wedges and stand back! Better make two just to be on the safe side.

I think this serves 6, but I never can count since they eat it so fast!

## CHILI-MEX CASSEROLE FOR CINCO DE MAYO

1-1/2 pounds lean ground beef
1 (16-ounce) can kidney beans, drained
1 (15-ounce) can mild enchilada sauce
1 (8-ounce) can tomato sauce
1 tablespoon dried minced onion
1 (6-ounce) package corn chips
1-1/2 cups sour cream
2 cups shredded cheddar cheese

In a skillet brown the ground beef; drain off fat.

Combine the beans, enchilada sauce and tomato sauce in a bowl with the minced onion.

Set aside 1 cup corn chips and 1/2 cup cheese. Add the remaining corn chips and cheese with the meat to the bean mixture. Blend well and pour into a buttered 2-quart casserole.

Bake, uncovered, at 375° for 20 to 25 minutes. Spread the top with the sour cream and sprinkle with the reserved cheese. Ring the remaining corn chips around the edge.

Return to the oven 3 to 4 minutes or until the cheese melts. This will double or triple and can be made the day before.

Serves 4.

## A Touch of France
## MUSHROOMS WITH VEAL

16 to 18 large fresh mushrooms
   (go to produce shop to find)
2 pounds ground veal
4 tablespoons clarified butter
2 onions, chopped finely
3 cloves garlic, crushed
Salt and pepper to taste

### Sauce:

2 tablespoons butter
2 cloves garlic, crushed
2 cups sour cream
Fresh dill, chopped (may use dried)
Lemon juice to taste
Parsley sprigs
Lemon wedges

Preheat oven to 400.° Remove stems from mushrooms (save for soups, etc.) Wipe caps clean and brush with butter. Bake 10 minutes, cut side down. Remove from pan and let cool.

Brown onions and garlic in butter 3 to 4 minutes. Add veal and brown. Cool. Mound a generous portion of meat mixture onto the mushroom cavity. Place on baking pan and bake at 350° 15 minutes.

Make sauce. Simmer garlic in butter 2 minutes. Stir in sour cream slowly, do not boil. Stir in lemon juice and sprinkle with dill. Keep sauce warm.

Place mushrooms on serving platter. Pour sauce over all. Garnish with parsley and lemon wedges.

Serves 4 to 6.


## ONE DISH BEEF AND ZUCCHINI

1-1/2 pounds lean ground beef
1 onion, chopped
2 cloves garlic, crushed
1/2 bell pepper, chopped
Salt and pepper to taste
3 medium zucchini, sliced thin
3 tomatoes, peeled and sliced
1 cup sharp cheddar cheese, grated

Brown meat, onions, pepper and garlic in a skillet. Drain off fat. Season to taste. Spread zucchini slices over meat, then cover with tomato slices. Cover and simmer slowly until vegetables are al dente. Uncover and sprinkle cheese over all. Cover and cook slowly until cheese melts. Serve with a fruit salad.

Serves 4.

This is a great one skillet meal that just takes a few minutes to make and the taste is just great after a hard day in school or at the office.

# PINEAPPLE PORK CHOP PILAU

6 pork chops

1 onion, sliced thin

2 tablespoons butter or margarine

8 cloves

1/2 teaspoon salt

1 teaspoon crushed coriander seeds

1 medium pineapple

1 cup sugar

1/2 cup lemon juice

1/2 teaspoon ground ginger

1 cup uncooked rice

1/2 teaspoon cinnamon

Brown pork chops on both sides; remove from skillet. Cook onion in butter with cloves, salt and coriander. Add chops and 1-1/2 cups water; simmer for 20 minutes.

Remove chops, strain gravy, adding water if necessary to make 1 cup.

Cut peeled pineapple into 1/2-inch slices. Boil sugar, lemon juice and ginger for 5 minutes. Add pineapple and cook until just tender, adding water if necessary to keep it from sticking.

Cook and drain rice. Cut half the pineapple into pieces and add to rice. Put rice in casserole, arrange chops over it and top with pineapple slices. Sprinkle with cinnamon and pour gravy over all. Bake, uncovered, in a preheated 300° oven for 35 to 40 minutes.

Serves 6.

# "JAMES BEARD'S PORK WITH SAUERKRAUT NOODLES"

2 tablespoons butter

1 tablespoon oil

2 to 2-1/2 cups thinly sliced cooked pork, or
    1-1/2 to 2 pounds fresh pork

2 tablespoons hot Hungarian paprika

1-1/2 cups white wine

3 cups sauerkraut, rinsed and drained

1 teaspoon caraway seeds

1 pound egg noodles

Salt and freshly ground black pepper

1/2 cup heavy cream

Heat 2 tablespoons butter with the oil in a heavy skillet. Brown the pork slices on each side over fairly high heat, about 3 minutes to a side. Remove the meat, add the paprika and cook in the fat for 1 minute. Pour in the wine and bring to a boil, stirring up the flavorful bits on the bottom of the pan. Cook until the wine is reduced slightly, then return the meat to the pan with the drained sauerkraut and caraway seeds. Simmer 10 to 12 minutes.

Cook and drain the noodles. Stir them into the pork-and-sauerkraut mixture and turn gently over medium heat, adding the heavy cream as you do so.

6 servings.

# BEEF BOURGUIGNONNE IN THE CROCK COOKER

6 strips bacon, cut into 1/2-inch pieces
3 pounds rump or chuck, cut into 1-1/2 inch cubes
1 large onion, sliced
1 large carrot, peeled and sliced
3 tablespoons flour
1 (10-ounce) can beef broth
1-1/2 cups burgundy
1 tablespoon tomato paste
2 cloves garlic, minced
1/4 teaspoon whole thyme
1 bay leaf
1/2 pound white onions, peeled (boiling)
    (may use canned if you like)
1 pound mushrooms, sliced

Cook bacon until crisp, remove with a slotted spoon. Brown meat in bacon fat, put meat into crock. Brown carrot and onion. Season with 1-1/2 teaspoons salt, 1/8 teaspoon pepper, stir in flour. Add broth and mix thoroughly. Pour ingredients over meat in crock cooker. Add cooked bacon, wine, tomato paste, garlic, bay leaf, thyme and 1/2 pound white onions. Cover crock and cook on low 8 to 10 hours. (Remember don't lift the lid during cooking time.)

Saute mushrooms in 2 tablespoons butter, add to crock cooker 1 hour before serving. If desired, turn cooker to high to tighten gravy and add 1/4 cup flour mixed with 2 tablespoons butter, combine and roll into balls the size of peas and drop into cooker.

This is Tina St. Onge's and my daughter Terry's favorite party time adventure. Delicious and no work.

Terry says she thinks it will serve 5 but the way everyone enjoys this dish she's never sure.

# CHILI-GHETTI

2 tablespoons butter
1 garlic clove, minced
3/4 cup chopped onion
1 pound ground beef
2-1/2 cups tomatoes
    (1 pound 3-ounce can)

3 (15-ounce) cans chili with meat
1 (8-ounce) package spaghetti
3 cups shredded cheddar cheese
1 cup sour cream
1/2 cup grated Parmesan cheese

In large skillet, melt butter. Brown garlic, onion and ground beef. Drain off excess fat and add tomatoes and chili. Simmer 45 minutes.

Meanwhile, cook spaghetti and drain. Remove skillet with chili mixture from heat and stir in cheddar cheese until melted. Fold in sour cream. Combine chili mixture and spaghetti, mixing well. Place in buttered baking dish and top with Parmesan cheese. Bake for 45 minutes in 350° oven.

Serves 8.

## CURING CORNED BEEF

Use the tougher cuts and those with considerable fat. Bone and cut them to uniform thickness and size. To cure 25 pounds of beef, pack it first in pickling salt, allowing 2 to 3 pounds of salt (3 to 4-1/2 cups) for the 25 pounds of meat. Spread a generous layer of coarse pickling salt in the bottom of a clean, sterilized crock or barrel. Pack in it a layer of meat that you've rubbed well with the salt; sprinkle more salt over the meat. Repeat the layers of meat and salt until all the meat is used or the crock is filled to within a couple inches below the top. Let the packed meat stand in the salt for 24 hours, then cover it with a solution of 1 gallon of water in which you've dissolved 1 pound (2 cups) of sugar, 1/2 ounce (c. 1 tablespoon) of baking soda, and 1 ounce (c. 2 tablespoons) of optional saltpeter or 1-1/4 teaspoons of pure crystalline ascorbic acid (also optional). Put a weighted plate on the meat to hold every speck of it below the surface of the brine; cover the crock/barrel; and in a cool place — not more than 38 degrees F. Let the meat cure in the brine from 4 to 6 weeks. The brine can become stringy and gummy if the temperature rises above 38 F. and the sugar ferments. The baking soda helps retard the fermentation. But watch it — if the brine starts to get ropy, take out the meat and wash it well in warm water. Clean and sterilize the container. Repack the meat with fresh sugar-water solution (above), to which you now add 1-1/2 pounds (2-1/4 cups) of pickling salt; this salt replaces the original 2 pounds of dry salt used to pack the meat. To store it, keep it refrigerated in the brine; or remove it from the brine, wash away the salt from the surface and can or freeze it.

## JACKIE'S TORTILLA CASSEROLE

1-1/2 pounds ground beef
1 onion, chopped
1 package dry taco seasoning
1 cup water
Garlic salt, salt and pepper to taste
1 cup medium hot red taco sauce
10 corn tortillas
2 (10-ounce) packages frozen chopped spinach
3 cups shredded Monterey Jack cheese
1/2 pound cooked ham, diced
1 cup sour cream

Cook ground beef with onion until meat is crumbly. Add taco seasoning and water. Cover and cook 10 minutes. Add salt, pepper and garlic salt.

In a 9" x 13" casserole, pour 1/2 cup taco sauce. Turn 5 tortillas in it to coat and spread in bottom of dish.

Press water out of spinach. Add half to the beef mixture. Spoon mixture over tortillas. Sprinkle with half of the cheese. Cover with remaining tortillas. Pour taco sauce over. Sprinkle with diced ham on top. Spoon sour cream over and top with remaining spinach and cheese.

Cover and bake at 375° for 25 minutes. Uncover and bake 25 minutes longer. Serves 10.

# ENCHILADAS CINCO DE MAYO
## Sauce:
2 (15-ounce) cans enchilada sauce
2 (16-ounce) cans tomato sauce
1 can water
2 cloves garlic, crushed
1 tablespoon sugar
1 teaspoon salt
1/2 teaspoon pepper
1 tablespoon cilantro, chopped
1/2 cup flour

In a large pan, combine the sauce ingredients except flour and heat. Place flour in skillet and brown; blend in a little water until smooth, then add to sauce. Simmer half hour and cool.

## Filling:
3 pounds lean ground beef
1 pound sharp cheddar cheese, grated
1 pound jack cheese, grated
1 large onion, chopped
3 small cans minced ripe olives
1 cup ripe olives, sliced
3 dozen corn tortillas

Fry ground beef until crumbly; pour off fat and season to taste. Place in bowl with chopped onion and minced olives. Mix and set aside.

Heat oil in a small skillet and fry tortillas on both sides until they just begin to crisp. Drain on paper towels. Dip a tortilla into the sauce; place a dab of the meat mixture and some cheese in the tortilla; fold in half and put into a large baking pan. (Use your broiler pan as it will hold a lot.)

When your pans are filled, pour the remaining sauce over the tortillas, sprinkle with both kinds of cheese and sliced olives. Bake at 350° for about 25 minutes. When serving, top each pan with spoonfuls of sour cream and chopped green onions.

Serves 16.

# CROCK POT HAM FOR RICE
3 pounds diced cooked ham
1 cup light raisins
1/4 cup water
2 tablespoons lemon juice
Cinnamon to taste
2 cans apple pie filling
1 cup orange juice

Mix all ingredients together and cook on low heat for 6 hours. Ham tastes better the next day. Serve over rice.

Serves 8 to 10.

# DRIED FRUIT CURRY

1 cup dried apples
1/2 cup dried pitted prunes
1/2 cup seedless raisins
1-1/2 cups water
1-1/2 pounds boneless lamb shoulder
      or 1-1/2 pounds beef chuck, trimmed
      of excess fat and cut into 1-inch cubes
1 teaspoon salt
2 tablespoons vegetable oil
1 cup finely chopped onions
2 tablespoons curry powder, preferably Madras-type
2 tablespoons red wine vinegar
1 tablespoon strained fresh lemon juice
1/4 cup salted peanuts, coarsely chopped
2 medium-sized bananas

Combine the apples, prunes and raisins in a bowl, pour the water over them and let them soak for at least 1 hour, turning the fruit occasionally.

Pat the cubes of lamb or beef completely dry with paper towels and sprinkle them with the salt. In a heavy 10- to 12-inch skillet, heat the oil over moderate heat until a light haze forms above it. Brown the meat in the hot oil in 2 or 3 batches, turning the cubes frequently with kitchen tongs or a slotted spoon and regulating the heat so that they color richly and evenly without burning. As they brown, transfer the cubes to a plate. Set aside.

Pour off all but about 2 tablespoons of the fat from the skillet and drop in the onions. Stirring constantly and scraping up the browned bits clinging to the bottom of the pan, cook the onions 3 or 4 minutes, or until soft.

Reduce the heat to low, add the curry powder, and stir for 2 minutes or so. Then return the meat, along with any liquid that has accumulated around it, to the skillet. Stir in the apples, prunes and raisins and the soaking water, the vinegar and the lemon juice. Bring to a boil over high heat, then reduce the heat to low.

Partially cover the skillet and simmer for about 1 hour, or until the meat is tender and shows no resistance when pierced with the point of a small sharp knife. Check the pan from time to time and, if the mixture looks too dry, add up to 1/4 cup water, a few tablespoons at a time. When the curry is done, however, most of the liquid in it should have cooked away.

Taste for seasoning and mound the curry on a heated platter. Just before serving, sprinkle the peanuts over the curry. Peel the bananas, cut them into 1/8-inch thick slices and arrange the slices around the curry. Dried fruit curry is traditionally accompanied by hot boiled rice.

Serves 4.

---

Big talkers are like leaky pitchers — Everything runs out of them.

# FATHER'S DAY BRISKET WITH BARBECUE SAUCE

1-1/2 teaspoons salt
1-1/2 teaspoons pepper
2 tablespoons chili powder
1 teaspoon crushed bay leaves
2 tablespoons liquid smoke
4 pounds beef brisket

Combine first 4 ingredients. Rub meat completely with liquid smoke. Place meat, fat side up, in a large roasting pan. Sprinkle dry seasoning mixture on top. Cover tightly and bake 4 hours at 275° or until tender. Scrape seasoning off and cut meat in very thin slices across the grain. Serve with Barbecue Sauce.

## Barbecue Sauce:

3 tablespoons brown sugar
1 (14-ounce) bottle catsup
1/2 cup water
2 tablespoons liquid smoke
Salt and pepper to taste
4 tablespoons Worcestershire sauce
3 teaspoons dry mustard
2 teaspoons celery seed
6 tablespoons butter
1/4 teaspoon cayenne pepper

Combine all ingredients. Bring to a boil, stirring occasionally. Cook for 10 minutes. Serve with sliced brisket.

Serves 6. This is absolutely dynamite served on onion rolls.

# HAWAIIAN POTPOURRI

1 fresh pineapple cut into spears
6 bananas
1 (1-1/2 inch thick) ham steak
1 teaspoon prepared mustard
1 tablespoon brown sugar
Butter
Juice of 1/2 lemon

Place pineapple spears around the sides of an oblong baking dish. Place peeled bananas in the center of the dish, inside the pineapple ring.

Place ham steak over fruit. Spread mustard over ham. Then sprinkle with brown sugar. Dot surface with butter and sprinkle with lemon juice.

Bake in a 350° oven for 20 minutes. Turn steak and cook 20 minutes on other side. Serve the ham steak sliced diagonally with the baked fruit.

I serve this with fresh creamed spinach and rice. It's so good you'll really feel a touch of the Islands in this dish.

Serves 4.

# TACO PIZZA PIE

1 pound lean ground beef
1 clove garlic, minced
1/4 teaspooon salt
1/4 teaspoon ground cumin
1/2 teaspoon chili powder
1 (4-ounce) can chopped green chilies
1 (8-1/2 ounce) can refried beans
2 medium tomatoes, chopped
3 green onions, chopped
1/3 cup chopped green bell pepper
1 cup shredded Monterey Jack cheese
1 cup (4 ounces) shredded cheddar cheese
Dairy sour cream
Bottled taco sauce or guacamole

## Cornmeal Crust:

1-1/2 cups all-purpose flour
1/2 cup yellow cornmeal
1 tablespoon baking powder
1 teaspoon salt
1/2 cup shortening or margarine
1/2 cup milk

Prepare dough for Cornmeal Crust. Preheat oven to 400.° In a large skillet, combine ground beef, garlic, salt, cumin and chili powder. Saute over medium heat until beef is browned, 4 to 5 minutes. Stir in the green chilies.

Spread refried beans over pizza dough. Spread beef and chile mixture over refried beans. Place tomatoes in a circle around outer edge of pizza. Place green onions in circle inside tomatoes. Place coarsely chopped green pepper in center. Sprinkle cheeses over pizza. Bake 20 minutes or until crust is golden brown on edges. Serve with sour cream and taco sauce or guacamole. Makes 4 to 6 servings.

## CORNMEAL CRUST

In a large bowl, mix together flour, cornmeal, baking powder and salt. Cut in shortening or margarine until mixture resembles fine crumbs. Stir in milk and mix until dough forms into a ball. Turn dough onto a well-floured board. Knead until smooth, 10 to 12 times.

Roll dough into 13-inch circle. Fold into quarters. Place dough on ungreased cookie sheet or pizza pan. Unfold. Pinch edge of circle to form a 1-inch rim. Set aside until ready to use.

(For a more traditional crust, substitute a basic pizza crust.)

---

An expert is someone who is called in at the last
minute to share the blame.

## COCA COLA BASTED HAM

1 (10-pound) precooked ham
    (not cured or canned)
6 cups Coca Cola
1 cup dark brown sugar
1 tablespoon dry mustard
2 tablespoons Dijon mustard
2 cups fine dry bread crumbs

Preheat oven to 325 degrees. Place ham fat side down in a shallow pan. Pour Coke into pan 1/2 inch deep. Bake 2 to 3 hours until ham can easily be pierced with a fork, basting with Coca Cola every 15 minutes. Center of ham will read 140 on a meat thermometer.

Remove ham from pan and cool. Cut away rind and fat with a sharp knife. Combine sugar, mustards and bread crumbs and enough Coke to form a thick paste. Add remaining Coke to bottom of pan. With oven at 375 degrees, bake 45 minutes longer, basting every 10 minutes, until sugar-mustard paste has melted into a dark glaze. Let stand at room temperature 30 minutes before slicing.

Serves 12 to 15.

## CHICKEN FRIED STEAK

1-1/2 pounds round steak, tenderized
Salt and pepper
2/3 cup flour
1 teaspoon paprika
1/2 teaspoon salt
1/4 teaspoon sage or poultry seasoning
2 eggs, beaten

Cut the steak into four portions and season with salt and pepper. Dust the steaks with about 2 tablespoons of the flour.

Combine remaining flour with paprika, salt and sage. Dip steaks in egg and then in seasoned flour. Repeat for a thicker crust.

Fry steaks in 1/4 inch oil in a skillet until browned on each side. Serve with cream gravy if desired.

## SAUSAGES OF SEVILLE

2 pounds link sausage
1 cup sherry or Montilla wine
1/4 cup brandy
2 tablespoons honey
1 orange, sliced

Place sausages in a large skillet with a cover. Pour over sherry, cover and simmer 10 minutes. Pour off liquid and fat. Saute sausages a few minutes, uncovered, to brown and add honey and orange slices. Stir all until glazed and hot.

Remove from heat and ladel over warm brandy. Flame at table and serve as buffet dish, with eggs, on toast or rice, or on top of waffles or hot cakes.

## KOFTA KEBABS
### (from the Gitanjali Indian Restaurant)

2 pounds of finely ground lamb
2 eggs
2 teaspoons of salt
2 teaspoons cumin powder
1/2 teaspoon ground black pepper
1 tablespoon of finely chopped fresh
    coriander leaves

Mix all above items together and leave in refrigerator overnight. Make patties or balls (size of your choice) and lay on baking sheet. Brush with mixture of melted butter and lemon juice just before baking in preheated oven at 400 degrees for 10 minutes.

## End of Summer Barbecue
## BEST EVER HAMBURGERS

2 pounds lean ground beef
1/4 cup oil
2 tablespoons Worcestershire sauce
2 tablespoons vinegar
2 envelopes Sloppy Joe mix
Toasted buns

Shape beef into patties and place in a shallow dish. Combine remaining ingredients, except the buns and pour over meat. Marinate at least 2 hours, turning patties occasionally. Place patties on the grill, turning only once, and serve on toasted buns.

Serves 6.

## BAKED HAM IN A BLANKET

1 (12 to 15-pound) ham
4 cups flour
1 cup brown sugar
2 tablespoons ground cloves
2 tablespoons cinnamon
2 tablespoons Dijon mustard
1 teaspoon pepper
Water or apple juice

Have your butcher cut off the small end of ham. (I save this for baked beans or split pea soup.) Trim off rind and excess fat. Place ham fat side up in an open roasting pan. Combine remaining ingredients, adding enough apple juice or water to make a stiff dough. Roll dough into a large sheet. Cover ham with dough. Place in a cold oven and bake at 300 degrees for 25 minutes per pound.

Serves 15.

This is great for any festive occasion.

# Poultry

## EASY STIR FRY
## CHICKEN AND VEGETABLES

1-1/2 pounds of chicken breasts, boned and skinned
1/2 teaspoon cornstarch
1 tablespoon safflower oil
Salt to taste
1/2 cup chicken bouillon
1/2 pound mushrooms, sliced
1/2 cup jicama, thinly sliced
1/2 pound fresh pea pods
1 bunch green onions, chopped
Pepper to taste
2 teaspoons soy sauce
1 packet sugar substitute
1 teaspoon sesame oil
1-1/2 teaspoons cornstarch dissolved in 1 tablespoon cold water

Cut chicken into squares. Toss in cornstarch. Heat wok or frying pan and add oil. Add chicken and salt to taste. Stir fry one minute. Add stock, mushrooms, jicama, pea pods and onions. Cover pan and cook 2 minutes. Add remaining ingredients and cook, stirring until thickened.

About 210 calories per serving. With a little melon for dessert, this is so easy and good for you.

Serves 4.

## HONEY CHICKEN WITH APPLES

2 fryers, cut into pieces
Salt, pepper and garlic powder to taste
6 tablespoons margarine, melted
8 apples, cored, peeled and quartered
1/2 cup honey
1/2 cup apple juice
2 tablespoons brown sugar
2 teaspoons grated lemon rind
2 teaspoons grated orange rind
1/2 cup orange marmalade
1/4 cup sherry

Sprinkle chicken pieces with salt, pepper and garlic powder. Melt the margarine. Place the peeled apples around edges of a 9″ x 13″ casserole. Place chicken in the center. Drizzle all with melted margarine. Roast in 325° oven for 45 minutes. Drain liquid.

Heat together the apple juice, honey, brown sugar, lemon and orange rind, and sherry. Baste chicken and apples with mixture. Bake 30 minutes longer, basting every 10 minutes until rich, golden brown. Brush orange marmalade over chicken and apples and bake 5 to 10 minutes to glaze.

Serve apples as an accompaniment to chicken. Extra apples can be glazed in separate pan, if desired, to serve with chicken or meat.

Serves 8.

# POLYNESIAN BAKED CHICKEN

2 fryers, cut into serving pieces
1 cup flour
1-1/2 teaspoons seasoned salt
1/4 pound butter
1 cup orange juice
2 tablespoons lemon juice
1/2 cup brown sugar
1 tablespoon cornstarch
1 tablespoon soy sauce
1 fresh pineapple, cubed
1 fresh papaya, cubed

Shake chicken parts in paper bag with flour and seasoned salt. Melt butter. Place chicken parts into a large baking pan and coat each piece with butter. Bake for 50 minutes at 350°, or until chicken is browned.

Meanwhile, combine juices, sugar, soy sauce and cornstarch in a sauce pan and bring to a boil, stirring constantly. Remove from heat when clear and thickened. Add fruit. Pour mixture over chicken, coating each piece, and bake 10 minutes longer. Serve garnished with chopped parsley or green pepper and toasted sesame seeds.

Serves 6.


# ITALIAN CHICKEN

4 boneless chicken breast halves, skinned
2 thin slices sandwich ham, cut in half
4 ounces mozzarella cheese, cut in 4 slices
4 (1-inch) fresh sage or dill sprigs
1/2 cup flour
1 egg, beaten
1-1/2 cups fresh bread crumbs
Oil for frying
Additional herbs if desired

Arrange each chicken piece between 2 pieces of waxed paper; pound with a mallet or rolling pin to flatten to about 1/4-inch thick.

Place a piece of ham on top of each chicken piece. Add a slice of cheese and a sprig of sage or dill to each chicken piece. Roll up each chicken piece halfway; fold in sides envelope-style and continue rolling. Secure with a wooden pick.

Roll each chicken piece in flour, then in beaten egg, then in bread crumbs.

Pour oil to 1-inch depth in a large skillet. Heat oil to 365° F. or until a 1-inch bread cube turns golden brown in 60 seconds. Fry chicken until light brown on all sides.

Serve with green beans and sliced tomatoes.

Serves 4.

# CHICKEN WITH ARTICHOKE HEARTS

1 fryer or chicken parts
Salt and pepper to taste
1/2 teaspoon paprika
5 tablespoons margarine or oil
1/4 pound mushrooms, sliced
1 can artichoke hearts, drained
2 tablespoons flour
2/3 cup chicken broth
3 tablespoons sherry
1/2 teaspoon dried rosemary
    or 1 tablespoon fresh rosemary

Sprinkle chicken pieces with salt, pepper and paprika. Brown in oil and remove to casserole. Saute mushrooms (you may need to add a little more oil). Arrange artichoke hearts amongst the chicken pieces. Sprinkle flour over the mushrooms; stir in the broth, sherry and rosemary.

Cook, stirring until thickened. Pour over chicken. Cover and bake for 30 minutes at 375°. Serve with rice, a green steamed vegetable and a fruit salad.

Serves 4.

# CHICKEN TAMALE BAKE
# FOR OSCAR NIGHT, 1986

1 tablespoon butter
2 whole chicken breasts, skinned, boned
    and cut into 1/2" cubes
1 onion, chopped
2 cloves garlic, crushed
1 teaspoon oregano
Salt to taste
1/2 teaspoon marjoram
1/8 teaspoon white pepper
3 tablespoons flour
1 cup milk
1 tomato, peeled and cut into 1/2" cubes

For tamale mixture, combine 3 cups milk, 2/3 cup yellow cornmeal and 1/2 teaspoon salt in a saucepan. Cook over medium heat, stirring constantly, until mixture comes to a boil and is thickened. Remove from heat and stir in 3 tablespoons butter and 1/4 cup grated Parmesan cheese.

Melt butter in a skillet. Add chicken, onion, garlic, oregano, salt, marjoram and pepper. Saute over high heat for 4 minutes. Stir in flour, then milk. Cook over medium heat until mixture comes to a boil and is thickened. Remove from heat and stir in tomato.

Cover the bottom of a buttered 2-quart shallow baking dish with half the tamale mixture. Top with the chicken mixture. Spoon remaining tamale batter over top in 3 diagonal strips. Bake at 350° for 20 minutes.

Serves 4 to 6.

## CHINESE NEW YEAR'S CHICKEN*

3 large chicken breasts, boned and skinned
1 egg white, lightly beaten
2 teaspoons cornstarch
Salt to taste
2 tablespoons bean sauce
1 tablespoon hoi-sin sauce
1 tablespoon chili paste (Szechwan paste)
2 tablespoons sugar
1 tablespoon red wine vinegar
5 cloves garlic, crushed
6 dried red peppers, cut in half and seeded
1 cup raw unsalted peanuts
2 cups peanut oil

Cut chicken into cubes. Combine with the egg white, cornstarch and salt to taste. Chill for 30 minutes.

Combine the bean sauce, hoi-sin, chili paste with garlic, sugar and wine vinegar. Set aside.

Heat 2 cups oil in wok and when it is almost boiling hot but not smoking, turn off heat and add the peanuts. They should turn a light brown. If not, you can turn on the heat briefly, watching carefully as they cook fast. Remove and reserve oil.

Heat 1 cup oil in wok (you can save the rest) and cook chicken 45 seconds but do not brown. Now pour off all but 2 tablespoons of oil from the wok. Add peppers, cook until dark — it takes 15 seconds — add sauce and the chicken, cook 1 minute more.

Serve sprinkled with peanuts — 6 servings.

This is great with rice and stir-fried vegetables.

*Year of the Tiger.


## CHICKEN IN BARBECUE SAUCE

2 egg yolks
1/4 cup honey
1/4 cup soy sauce
1/4 cup lemon juice
1/4 cup melted margarine
Salt to taste
1 tablespoon paprika
1/2 teaspoon pepper
10 pieces of frying chicken of your choice

Combine all ingredients except chicken. Dip chicken into sauce and place in a shallow baking dish. Bake uncovered at 400° for 30 minutes, basting once. Turn chicken over and pour remaining sauce over all and bake another 30 minutes, basting once more.

Serves 4.

## COQ AU VIN IN THE MICRO

1/4 pound bacon, diced
3/4 pound small white onion, peeled
1/2 pound mushrooms, thickly sliced
1 teaspoon thyme leaves
3/4 cup burgundy wine
1 (3-pound) chicken, cut in serving pieces
1 teaspoon salt
Sprinkling of pepper
1 tablespoon dried parsley flakes
1 bay leaf, crumbled
1/4 cup brandy (optional)
2 tablespoons flour
Water as needed

Cook the bacon in the microwave in a small open casserole until browned and crisp, about 4 minutes. Spoon out bacon and drain on paper towels.

Layer the onions in a 9" x 12" baking dish. Cut any large ones in half. Sprinkle mushroom slices over the onions, then the thyme. Pour in the wine. Place the chicken, skin side down, over mixture, with the fleshy part to the outside. Add the bacon, salt, pepper, parsley flakes and brandy.

Cover with waxed paper and cook on high for 15 minutes. Turn the chicken over, rotate the dish, cover with waxed paper and cook on high for another 10 minutes. Remove chicken to a serving dish.

Add enough water to the flour to make a medium paste. Work a little of the hot mixture into the flour/water, then stir it into the wine broth. Cook on high 2 minutes, giving a stir now and then. Pour sauce over chicken and let stand a few minutes before serving. Serves 4 to 6.

A classic French recipe that you can do anytime ... and it is *so good!* Bon Appetit!

## CHICKEN MARENGO

4 small, whole chicken breasts
Salt and pepper
1/4 cup oil or butter
2 onions, thinly sliced
1 garlic clove, crushed
2 large tomatoes, peeled and chopped
3/4 cup white wine
1 cup sliced, fresh mushroom caps

Wash chicken breasts and wipe dry. Sprinkle with salt and pepper. Saute in oil until golden brown on both sides. Remove to a platter. Saute onions and garlic until onions are tender. Add tomatoes and cook until mushy. Return chicken to skillet. Season with salt and pepper to taste. Pour in wine and cook, covered, for 30 minutes. Season with paprika and add mushrooms, and cook for 7 to 10 minutes.

Serves 4.

## CHICKEN DELLA ROBBIA

2 to 3 fryers, cut up
4 tablespoons butter
2 tablespoons salad oil
2 onions, sliced
1-1/4 cups water
1/2 teaspoon chicken bouillon
1/2 pound mushrooms, sliced
1 cup white raisins
2 teaspoons salt
1/4 cup lemon juice
1 clove garlic, minced
1/2 teaspoon ground cloves
1/2 teaspoon allspice
1/2 teaspoon ginger
1/4 cup brown sugar
1 cup walnut halves
1/2 cup water
1 tablespoon cornstarch
2 cups green seedless grapes
2 cups orange sections
12 cherries

In a large Dutch oven or fryer, saute chicken pieces in butter and oil until golden brown. Add onions and saute.

Combine 1-1/4 cups water with 1/2 teaspoon instant chicken bouillon. Add with mushrooms, raisins, salt, lemon juice, garlic, spices and brown sugar. Simmer, covered, turning 1 or 2 times, for 35 minutes or until tender. Add walnut halves. Push chicken to side of pan.

Blend cornstarch with 1/2 cup water and stir into pan liquid. Heat until smooth and thickened. Add grapes, oranges and cherries and heat through for 2 to 3 minutes. Serve at once on heated platter or in a chafing dish.

Serves 8 to 12.


## THAI CHICKEN

8 cloves garlic
2 tablespoons peppercorns, freshly ground
2 tablespoons coriander roots
6 pieces chicken
Oil for deep frying

Grind or pound the garlic, peppercorns and coriander roots to a paste.

Wash and thoroughly pat dry the chicken. Rub the paste all over the chicken and let stand to marinate for at least 30 minutes.

Heat oil in a wok to 375° F. and deep-fry the chicken until golden and tender. Drain the chicken on paper towels. Serve hot with rice and Sweet and Hot Chili Sauce.

Yield: 2 to 3 servings.

# COUNTRY CAPTAIN CHICKEN

President F. D. Roosevelt liked a chicken dish called "Country Captain" which was part of the fare served when he was in residence at Warm Springs, Georgia. Of East Indian origin, it is thought the dish found its way into this country along with spice shipments to Savannah.

1 (2-1/2 to 3-pound) fryer
1/4 cup flour
1 teaspoon salt
1/4 teaspoon pepper
1/3 cup butter
1 small onion, finely chopped
1/3 cup green pepper, thinly slivered
1 clove garlic, crushed
1-1/2 teaspoon curry powder
1/2 teaspoon thyme
1 teaspoon lemon rind, grated
1 (1-pound) can tomatoes
2 tablespoons currants
1/4 cup cashews
1/4 cup chutney

Cut chicken into serving pieces and coat in a mixture of flour, salt and pepper. Brown in butter in a large heavy skillet. Remove chicken from the skillet. To skillet add onion, green pepper, garlic, curry powder, thyme and lemon rind. Cook slowly for 25 minutes, or until chicken is tender. If mixture becomes dry, add small quantities of dry white wine. Add currants, heat and serve with cashew nuts and chutney.

Serves 4.

# LEMON CHICKEN

3 chicken fryers
1 cup oil
3/4 cup lemon juice
Salt to taste
2 teaspoons paprika
2 teaspoons onion powder
1 teaspoon garlic powder
2 teaspoons crushed sweet basil
2 teaspoons crushed thyme

Have the butcher split the chicken and remove wings, backbone and tail. Save for the stockpot. Place chickens in a shallow pan. Combine remaining ingredients in jar. Cover and shake well. Pour over chicken and cover tightly.

Marinate overnight in the refrigerator, turning occasionally. Let stand at room temperature for 1 hour. Cook chicken over hot coals for 15 to 20 minutes on each side, basting frequently with marinade.

Serves 6.

# APPLE CHICKEN

2 tablespoons butter
2 tablespoons oil
6 chicken breasts
1/4 cup cognac
2 onions, chopped
4 medium apples, peeled, cored and sliced
1 cup cider
1 cup sour cream
1 tablespoon flour
1/3 cup golden raisins
2 tablespoons chopped parsley
1 teaspoon tarragon
1 teaspoon salt
1/4 teaspoon pepper
1/2 teaspoon paprika

Heat oil in skillet; add chicken and brown. Remove chicken and place in a 9" x 12" baking dish.

Warm cognac, ignite and pour over chicken. Allow flame to burn out.

Saute the onion in the butter until tender. Add onions and apples to chicken in the baking dish. Combine remaining ingredients and pour over chicken. Bake uncovered at 350° for 1 hour.

Serves 4 to 6.

A fabulous make-ahead dish — wonderful served with brown rice, fruit salad and a yeast roll, with chocolate mousse for dessert.

# PAPER BAG BARBECUED CHICKEN

1/4 cup catsup
1/4 cup white vinegar
1/4 cup Worcestershire sauce
1/4 cup lemon juice
1 tablespoon chili powder
1 tablespoon Dijon mustard
Salt to taste
1 tablespoon paprika
1/3 cup water
Dash of pepper
1/4 cup butter, melted
2 chicken fryers, cut into pieces

Combine all ingredients, except chicken. Stir ingredients over low heat until butter is melted. Place chicken in a large brown paper bag. Pour sauce into bag, and roll top of bag down. Secure with paper clips.

Place bag in roaster, cover and bake at 500° for 15 minutes. Reduce heat to 350° and bake for 1 hour and 15 minutes more.

Serves 6.

# CHINESE BURRITOS FOR NEW YEAR'S EVE

8 (10-inch) flour tortillas
2 tablespoons sesame oil (or use regular oil)
3/4 pound boneless chicken breast
1/4 cup green onions, chopped
1/2 teaspoon ginger-root, minced
1 to 2 cloves garlic, minced
1 cup fresh bean sprouts
1/2 cup chicken broth
3 tablespoons soy sauce
1 tablespoon dry sherry
2 teaspoons sherry
2 teaspoons sugar
2 teaspoons cornstarch
1/2 cup Hoisin sauce

Preheat oven to 350°. Lay tortillas out flat on oven rack, two deep if necesary. Warm tortillas 5 minutes.

Heat oil in a wok or skillet. Cut chicken into narrow strips. Stir-fry for 3 minutes or until chicken is done. Stir in the next four ingredients.

In a small bowl combine the broth, soy sauce, sherry, sugar and cornstarch. Add to wok, stir until meat is coated and sauce is thickened.

Spread warmed tortillas with the Hoisin sauce. Spoon 1/4 cup chicken mixture in the center of each tortilla. Fold up bottom end and then each side and roll. Serve warm.

These will serve four as an entree but at parties I cut them into bite-sized pieces and use them for appetizers and I just can't make them quick enough. I usually make a big bunch, wrap them in waxed paper, and heat them for about 30 seconds in the microwave to serve.

# LESLIE FOSTER'S FANTASTIC CHICKEN BARBECUE MARINADE

1 cup white wine vinegar
1 cup olive oil
1/2 cup dry white wine
1 teaspoon salt
1 teaspoon oregano
1/2 teaspoon thyme
1/4 teaspoon Tabasco
1 tablespoon parsley or cilantro, chopped
Garlic to taste, minced
2 chickens, cut in half

Mix all marinade ingredients and marinate chicken halves at least 1 hour. Barbecue over medium heat cut side down to begin with, for at least 25 minutes, basting and turning often.

Serves 4.

# FRUITY ORANGE CHICKEN

3/4 cup flour
2 teaspoons salt
1/2 teaspoon pepper
1 teaspoon tarragon
8 half chicken breasts, boned
6 tablespoons butter
1 clove garlic, pressed
1 pound fresh mushrooms, sliced
3 cups chicken stock
1 chicken bouillon cube
2 tablespoons Curacao or Cointreau (or more)
2 (11-ounce) cans mandarin oranges
1/2 pound green seedless grapes or 1 (16-ounce) can

Mix flour, salt, pepper and tarragon. Dredge clean, wiped chicken breasts with the flour mixture, reserving leftover mixture. Let stand a short while.

Melt 4 tablespoons butter in skillet and add garlic. Brown the chicken just until golden brown; it does not have to be cooked. Place in baking dish. Add 2 tablespoons butter to skillet, brown the mushrooms and put them on the chicken.

If necessary, add more butter to skillet and make a roux with the remaining flour mix, about 1/4 cup. Add the stock slowly, then the bouillon cube and Curacao or Cointreau.

Pour sauce over the chicken. (May be frozen at this point). Cover tightly with foil and bake 1 hour at 325° 15 minutes longer if it has been frozen and thawed, or refrigerated.

Before serving, heat the oranges and grapes in their own juice and drain. Arrange chicken on platter and place fruit over it.

Serves 8.

# SAUTEED CHICKEN LIVERS

Crush 1 clove of garlic into a little chopped parsley and mix it with 3 finely chopped shallots. Set it aside.

Cut 6 fresh chicken livers into halves.

Place 3 tablespoons of butter into a frying pan and when it begins to sizzle add the chicken livers. Be careful, the hot butter may spatter. Turn the livers often and don't cook longer than 8 minutes.

Make 2 slices of toast to be ready when the livers are done. Place toast on a hot serving platter and arrange the sauteed livers over them. Sprinkle the prepared garlic/parsley and shallots over the top. Sprinkle with a pinch of salt and freshly ground pepper.

Put 1 tablespoon of butter into the frying pan in which the livers were sauteed and when it comes to a bubbling boil, pour it over the finished dish. Season to taste.

## SWEET AND SOUR CHICKEN

3 tablespoons oil
3 chicken breasts, boned, skinned,
    cut into 1/2-inch strips
1 (13 1/2-ounce) can pineapple chunks,
    syrup reserved
1 cup chicken broth
1/2 cup vinegar
2 tablespoons soy sauce
1/4 cup brown sugar
3 tablespoons cornstarch
1 large green pepper, cut into chunks
4 small tomatoes, cut in eighths

Heat oil in pan over high heat. Add chicken and cook until chicken turns white and is cooked through, stirring frequently. Add syrup, 1/2 cup broth, vinegar, soy sauce, and brown sugar. Continue heating until it boils. Combine cornstarch and remaining broth, add to sauce while stirring, and cook until thickened. Add pineapple, green pepper and tomatoes, and cook over low heat only until heated through.

Serve with rice or chow mein noodles.

Makes 4 to 6 servings.

## COMPANY CASSEROLE

8 ounces brown and serve sausage links
2 tablespoons flour
2 cups cooked, cubed chicken
4 large tomatoes, peeled and choped
1 cup strong chicken broth
1/2 cup sliced green onions
1/4 teaspoon savory
1/4 teaspoon thyme
1/4 teaspoon Tabasco sauce
1 pound fresh asparagus
1/2 cup slivered almonds

Cut sausages into quarters and fry in skillet until golden brown. Add flour and cook a few minutes more. Combine with chicken, tomatoes, broth, onions and seasonings in a buttered 2-quart baking dish.

Trim asparagus and drop into boiling salted water and boil until crisp-tender, from 3 to 10 minutes, depending on size. Drain and arrange in a row on top of casserole.

Sprinkle almonds in a row along center. Bake covered at 375° for 35 minutes, or until hot and bubbly.

Serves 4.

## PARMESAN SESAME CHICKEN

2 fryers, cut up
1 cup flour
2 eggs, lightly beaten
3 tablespoons milk
1-1/4 cups grated Parmesan cheese
2/3 cup sesame seeds
2 teaspoons salt
1/4 teaspoon pepper
2 teaspoons paprika
2/3 cup bread crumbs
2 tablespoons shortening (liquid)
2 tablespoons butter
1/4 cup melted butter

Remove skin from chicken (don't use chicken wing tips). Preheat oven to 400.° Use extra salt to salt chicken.

Mix flour, 2 teaspoons salt, pepper and paprika and coat the chicken. Combine eggs and milk; dip chicken in it. Combine Parmesan, seeds, bread crumbs and roll the chicken in mix. Melt 2 tablespoons butter and shortening in jelly roll pan 15 x 10 x 1 inches. Place chicken bone side down. Drizzle with 1/4 cup melted butter.

Bake 1 hour.

Cool and then chill.

## A Touch of Europe
## POULET SAUTE AU RIESLING

1 fryer (2-1/2 to 3 pounds)
1 tablespoon peanut oil
4 tablespoons butter
1/4 pound mushrooms, sliced
3 ripe tomatoes, peeled, seeded and chopped
1/2 bottle dry white wine
2 tablespoons brandy
2 tablespoons consomme
Salt
Cayenne pepper
3 tablespoons parsley, chopped
2 garlic cloves, chopped

Cut the chicken into serving pieces. Heat the oil and butter in a casserole. Brown the chicken until golden on all sides. Add the mushrooms and the tomatoes, reduce the heat slightly and cook for 5 minutes Add the wine, the brandy and the consomme. Season with salt and pepper and a little cayenne. Bring to a boil, cover the casserole, and simmer for 25 minutes. Transfer the chicken to a hot serving dish and keep warm. Skim the fat off the pan juices, add the parsley and the garlic. Bring it to a boil and cook over high heat until the sauce has reduced. Pour over chicken and serve very hot.

Serves 4.

## CHICKEN HAWAIIAN

6 chicken breasts, or 2 cut-up fryers
1/2 cup flour, seasoned with 1/2 teaspoon
    black pepper, 1 teaspoon paprika
    1 teaspoon curry powder
1 (1-pound, 4-ounce) can pineapple chunks
1/4 cup butter
2 cups green pepper strips
1 chicken bouillon cube
1 cup boiling water
2 teaspoons cornstarch
1 tablespoon soy sauce
2 tablespoons vinegar
1/3 cup sugar
1 jigger gin

Melt butter in large frying pan. Dust the chicken lightly with the seasoned flour and brown it in butter. Remove chicken, add more butter to pan if necessary. Drain syrup from pineapple and set aside (you should have about 1 cup). Cook pineapple chunks in butter for 3 minutes. Measure out 2/3 cup pineapple syrup and pour one-half of it over pineapple. Add green pepper strips, cover and simmer 10 minutes (some tastes like shredded onion also, use it optionally). Dissolve bouillon cubes in boiling water and stir into pineapple chunks. Mix cornstarch with remaining 1/3 cup pineapple syrup and stir in. Add soy sauce, vinegar and sugar. Cook, stirring constantly, until thick and clear. Add chicken and gin and remaining 1/2 cup pineapple syrup.

Serve over rice.

## HOLIDAY STUFFED CHICKEN

6 cups fresh bread cubes
6 tablespoons butter or margarine
1/2 cup sliced celery
1/4 cup sliced green onions
3/4 cup water or wine
1 cup fresh or frozen cranberries, halved
2 tablespoons chopped parsley
1 tablespoon grated orange peel
1/2 cup chopped walnuts
3 tablespoons sugar

Arrange the bread cubes on a cookie sheet and toast in a 350° oven for about 30 minutes. In a large saucepan, melt butter and cook the celery and onions until tender; add remaining ingredients and toss.

This will stuff a 5 to 7-pound fowl.

———————————————

Middle-age is when you can do just as much as ever but don't.

# CHICKEN WITH ALMONDS & GRAPES

6 chicken breasts
1/2 cup flour
3/4 teaspoon salt or 1 teaspoon seasoned salt
1/2 teaspoon pepper
1 teaspoon paprika
2 tablespoons butter
2 tablespoons oil
2 tablespoons finely chopped shallots or
      3 tablespoons chopped onion & 1 clove
      finely chopped garlic
1/2 cup sliced mushrooms (optional)
1/4 cup brandy
1/4 cup dry vermouth
1/2 cup chicken stock
1/2 cup seedless grapes (can use canned grapes)
1/2 cup almonds or cashews or walnuts

Mix together the flour, salt & pepper and paprika and lightly flour the chicken breasts. Combine oil and butter in a heavy saute pan and when bubbly and hot add the chicken pieces. Add the shallots (or onion & garlic) and the mushrooms. Turn chicken so it browns evenly on both sides. When nice and brown add the brandy. Allow to heat and flame it. When the flame dies down add the wine, stock and grapes. Cover and simmer 15 minutes. Add the nuts and serve immediately.

Serves 6.

This can be prepared ahead of time waiting for the nuts until the last minute, when you reheat.

# VONS CHICKEN BREASTS

4 chicken breasts, skinned, boned, and cut
      into bite-sized pieces
1 small onion
1 teaspoon ginger
1 tablespoon oil
1 tablespoon soy sauce
1 teaspoon Dijon mustard
Juice of 1 orange or lemon
1/2 cup jelly (plum, apricot, apple, etc.)
Cooked rice

Preheat oven to 475 degrees. Place chicken on the bottom of a baking pan. Combine remaining ingredients in a food processor and process until smooth. Pour mixture over chicken and marinate for 30 minutes at room temperature, turning pieces occasionally. Bake, uncovered, 10 to 12 minutes, or until a lovely golden brown. Serve over rice. This is a delightful dish that's easy and fast and it goes well with a green steamed vegetable.

Serves 4.

# CHICKEN TETRAZZINI

| | |
|---|---|
| 2 chickens | 2 cans chicken broth |
| 1/4 pound noodles | 1/2 pound mushrooms |
| 1 teaspoon salt | 2 tablespoons butter |
| 2 tablespoons butter | 1 tablespoon grated |
| 4 tablespoons grated |     Romano cheese |
|     Parmesan cheese | Salt and pepper |

Minced garlic

Simmer chicken in chicken broth until tender. Remove meat from bones. Cook noodles in unsalted gently boiling water about 10 minutes. Drain noodles and season with 1 teaspoon salt, butter, Parmesan cheese and 1 cup tetrazzini sauce.

Saute mushrooms in butter for 3 to 4 minutes, then season with salt, pepper and garlic to taste and cook gently several minutes.

Spread noodles in greased, shallow baking dish. Add mushrooms and chicken and pour remaining sauce over all. Sprinkle Parmesan cheese and Romano cheese over top and bake at 350° for 30 minutes.

Serves 6.


# TETRAZZINI SAUCE

1/4 cup butter
1/3 cup flour
2 cups cream or half-and-half
1 cup stock from chicken
1/2 cup sauterne or vermouth
Salt to taste

Melt butter in skillet in flour, then slowly add cream, stock, salt and wine. Cook gently, stirring often, about 5 minutes.


# CHICKEN DIABLO

Quarter 2 chickens, weighing about 2-1/2 pounds each. Rub them with lemon and brown in melted butter and oil. When the chicken is brown, add 2 tablespoons chopped onions, 1/2 teaspoon chopped garlic, 4 large mushrooms, sliced and 1/2 teaspoon thyme. Simmer until vegetables are soft and transparent. Sprinkle with 1-1/2 teaspoons paprika, add 1/4 cup sherry, cover and let steam for 25 minutes additionally until chicken is done and tender. Remove chicken pieces to a hot platter.

## Sauce:

Add 1 cup brown sauce to skillet with 1 teaspoon Worcestershire sauce, 1/2 teaspoon dry mustard, 1 teaspoon lemon juice and 2 tablespoons heavy cream. Let simmer slowly for 5 minutes. Serve over chicken pieces.

## CHICKEN OR TURKEY HASH

3 cups chicken or turkey,
   cut into pieces
2-1/2 cups rich poultry broth
1 cup rice
1 large onion, chopped
2 garlic cloves, minced

3 tablespoons oil or margarine
1 dried red pepper
Salt and pepper to taste
2 tablespoons sherry
Handful of chopped parsley
1 cup of beans or peas (optional)

1 small (3-ounce) jar pimientos

### Sauce:

1-1/2 tablespoons flour
1-1/2 tablespoons chicken fat or butter
1-1/2 cups chicken stock or 3/4 cup stock and
     3/4 cup milk if you like white gravy
Salt and pepper to taste

Cook rice, uncovered, in the chicken broth over low heat for 20 minutes or until broth is absorbed. Taste for seasoning.

In a flameproof casserole, saute onion and garlic in oil until clear. Add red pepper, salt and pepper to taste, sherry and parsley. Combine with chicken, stir and keep over low heat. Add peas or beans if you wish.

Make a roux of flour and chicken fat, then mix with broth (or half broth and half milk), then cook until thick, add to rice and chicken mixture. Lastly add small jar of pimientos for color. Taste and adjust seasoning. Serve hot.

This is a great way to use up leftover poultry and you can feed 6 in less than 30 minutes. My family loves this with coleslaw. Easy and good.

## KENTUCKY FRIED CHICKEN
### (Gloria Pitzer)

In a plastic bag:
3 cups self-rising flour
1 tablespoon paprika
2 envelopes Tomato Cup of Soup
2 packages Good Seasoning Italian Dressing Mix

Shake well.

Spray 2 pans with Pam.

Run chicken pieces under cold water and drain well.

Dredge chicken, one piece at a time, in flour mixture to coat.

Place chicken, skin side up, on prepared pans and drizzle with 2 tablespoons of cooking oil.

Bake uncovered one hour at 350 degrees until golden brown.

Yield approximately 32 pieces or 4 fryers (legs, thighs, breasts and wings).

# CREPES A LA MEXICANA

1/4 pound plus 2 tablespoons butter
2 cups fresh mushrooms, sliced
1 cup green onions, chopped with some green
1-1/2 pounds cooked chicken, chopped into bite-size pieces
1/4 cup dry white wine
1 cup evaporated milk
3/4 cup fresh milk
6 tablespoons flour
1-1/2 teaspoons salt
1/4 cup minced fresh parsley
1/2 cup toasted slivered almonds
1 (4-ounce) can green chilies, chopped
12 crepes or flour tortillas
1 cup Monterey Jack cheese, grated
12 avocado slices

Preheat oven to 350°. Melt butter and saute mushrooms and onions until soft. Add chicken and simmer gently for 10 minutes.

In a blender mix wine, condensed milk, fresh milk, flour and salt. Pour into saucepan and cook over medium heat, stirring constantly, until thickened. Combine with chicken mixture and add parsley, almonds and chilies.

Place 1 to 2 tablespoons of filling on each crepe or tortilla and roll. Arrange in buttered baking dish, rolled edge down. Top with cheese. Bake covered 15 minutes. Remove cover, add avocado and bake an additional 3 minutes.

Serves 6 to 8.

# CHICKEN WITH LEMON & HERBS

1 cup fresh mint, dill & parsley in about
    equal proportions or to taste
2 cloves garlic, minced
6 boned chicken breasts, skinned and halved
    (about 4 pounds)
Salt and freshly ground pepper to taste
2 lemons
2 tablespoons butter or margarine
6 pieces of foil 12-inches square

Preheat oven to 350°. Mix the herbs and the garlic together in a small bowl. Flatten the chicken breasts slightly with the palm of your hand. Arrange breast pieces on foil and season with salt and pepper. Sprinkle herb and garlic mixture over the chicken breasts. Slice the lemons thinly and place 2 or 3 slices on each breast. Now dot with butter and seal the packets. Place packets on a baking sheet. Place in the middle of the oven and bake for 30 minutes. Transfer to serving plates and let guests open packets at the table.

This is good hot or cold. A nice entree for a picnic or perhaps the Hollywood Bowl.

Serves 6.

# ENCHILADAS VERONIQUE

2 cups chopped onion
1/2 cup butter
1/2 cup flour
1 teaspoon salt
4 cups milk
1 (4-ounce) can chopped
    green chilies

2 cups cooked, diced chicken
2 (8-ounce) cans seedless grapes, drained,
    or 2 cups fresh seedless grapes
2 cups shredded Monterey Jack cheese
1/2 pound fresh mushrooms,
    sliced and sauteed
12 corn tortillas

1/2 cup toasted slivered almonds

Make white sauce: Saute onion in butter until onion is tender. Add flour, salt and milk to make a medium-thick sauce. Add the green chilies and set aside.

In a separate large bowl, toss together the chicken, grapes, cheese and mushrooms.

Warm the tortillas. Cold tortillas tend to crack when rolled, so flip each tortilla back and forth in a greased, hot skillet over low heat until they are warm and pliable.

Place a spoonful of chicken mixture across the center of each warm tortilla. Roll tortillas around the filling and place seam side down in two lightly-greased

Make white sauce: Saute onion in butter until onion is tender. Add flour, salt and milk to make a medium-thick sauce. Add the green chilies and set aside.

In a separate large bowl, toss together the chicken, grapes, cheese 7" x 11" baking dishes.

After all the tortillas are filled and rolled, pour sauce over enchiladas. Bake at 350° for 25-30 minutes, or until heated through. Sprinkle toasted almonds over top during last 5 minutes of baking. Makes 12 enchiladas.


# TARRAGON CHICKEN AND VEGETABLES

1 each carrot and onion, chopped
1 tablespoon butter
1 broiler-fryer, cut up (about 3 pounds) or
    chicken breasts, thighs and drumsticks
1/2 pound small whole mushrooms
3/4 cup dry white wine
1/2 cup chicken broth
1 teaspoon each salt and tarragon
3/4-pound small boiling onions, peeled and parboiled,
    or 1 (10-ounce) package frozen onions, thawed

Using a large Dutch oven or flameproof casserole, saute carrot and onion in butter until glazed; push to the sides of the pan. Add chicken pieces and brown on all sides.

Add mushrooms to pan and saute quickly in drippings. Add wine, broth, salt, tarragon and onions.

Bake in a 375° oven for 45 minutes or until chicken is just tender, basting once or twice with pan juices.

Makes 4 to 6 servings; about 250 to 300 calories per serving.

# LOW CALORIE TURKEY MEATBALLS

1 pound raw ground turkey
2 egg whites
6 tablespoons chopped water chestnuts
1 tablespoon soy sauce
1 tablespoon pale dry Sherry
2 cloves garlic, minced
3/4 teaspoon salt
2 slices freshly chopped ginger
2 teaspoons cornstarch
1/2 tablespoon whipped margarine
Special Sauce

For meatballs, mix together all ingredients except margarine. Shape into 1 1/2-inch balls for entree-size servings or 3/4-inch balls for appetizers.

Brown in margarine in a large frying pan, turning to brown on all sides. Transfer to a shallow baking dish. Pour Special Sauce over it and bake in a 350° oven for 10 minutes.

Makes 4 entree servings or 30 appetizer servings. Contains about 235 calories per entree serving and 30 calories per appetizer serving.

## Special Sauce:

Mix together 3 tablespoons unsweetened pineapple juice or apple juice, 1 tablespoon soy sauce, 1-1/2 tablespoons catsup, 2 teaspoons vinegar, 1 clove minced garlic, a few drops sesame oil, and 1 slice freshly chopped ginger.

## IMPROVISED GRAVY

When you don't have enough natural pan juices and drippings to make a gravy or you need gravy to create a tasty dish out of leftover meat, here is a basic recipe that will serve well. You can add compatible seasonings like fresh herbs or a little duxelles. Use beef bouillon for red meat and chicken for poultry.

2 tablespoons minced shallots, scallions or onion
3 tablespoons butter
3 tablespoons flour
1/4 cup red wine or dry vermouth (optional)
1-1/2 cups beef or chicken broth
Leftover drippings or additional tablespoon butter
Salt
Freshly ground pepper

Saute the minced shallots or onion in the butter until translucent. Stir in the flour and, cooking slowly, stir until it turns light brown. Remove the pan from the fire, add the wine if you are using it, and an equal amount of broth. Stir until smooth; return to the fire and slowly add the remaining broth, stirring constantly. Continue to cook, stirring often, for another 5 minutes. Stir in leftover drippings or butter, salt and pepper to taste.

# JACKIE'S CHICKEN AND DUMPLINGS

1 (3 to 5-pound) stewing hen
3 sprigs parsley
3 celery stalks with leaves
1 carrot, sliced
1 onion, sliced
2 teaspoons salt
1/2 teaspoon pepper

## Dumplings:

1 cup milk
1 egg, beaten
1-1/2 cups flour
2 heaping teaspoons baking powder
1 teaspoon salt
1 teaspoon sugar
3 tablespoons minced parsley

Place chicken in a Dutch oven, cover with water, add parsley, celery, carrot, onion, salt and pepper. Bring to a boil. Boil 5 more minutes; now simmer 2 hours or until tender. You may have to add more water. Remove chicken and vegetables from broth. Bone chicken and cut into serving pieces.

For dumplings mix milk and egg. Sift together flour, baking powder, salt and sugar. Combine milk and egg with the dry ingredients. Drop by tablespoon into the boiling broth. Cover pan tightly and cook for 15 minutes. NO PEEKIE. Add chicken and parsly before serving.

Old-fashioned goodness.

Serves 6 to 8.

# BASIC TURKEY GRAVY
### Makes 2 cups

1/4 cup turkey fat (from drippings)
4 tablespoons flour
2 cups turkey stock (from giblets)
   or broth

1/2 teaspoon salt
1/8 teaspoon pepper
1/4 teaspoon poultry seasoning
   (optional)

Heat fat in bottom of the turkey roasting pan, scraping loose any cooking crusts. Stir in flour to make a paste and cook a minute. Add stock and stir to deglaze pan and blend with flour mixture. Pour mixture into a sauce pan if desired. Cook until gravy thickens and boils lightly. Simmer a few minutes; keep warm until serving time.

Brown Gravy Variation — Add 1/4 teaspoon Kitchen Bouquet or Gravy Master for darker color. Stir in 1/4 cup tomato paste or currant jelly for richer flavor.

Cream Gravy — Prepare Basic Turkey Gravy using 1 cup turkey stock and 1 cup cream or half-and-half.

Thickening may be half flour and half cornstarch for glossy gravy.

# WOODY'S WORLD CLASS WHITE CHICKEN CHILI

For six hearty eaters or eight sort of regular eaters you will need:

6 chicken breasts
1 diced onion
12 corn tortillas
3/4 cup corn oil
3 Anaheim green chiles
    (or a 7-ounce can
    of diced green chiles)
1 (12-ounce) can of Mexicorn
    (drained)

1 (10-ounce) bottle of green
    taco sauce
3-1/2 cups of grated Monterey
    Jack cheese
1 (8-ounce) container of sour cream
1/2 cup grated Parmesan cheese
2 teaspoons salt
1 teaspoon of white pepper
1 can green ripe olives (pitted)

Now just follow these easy steps and you will make a dish that your family and friends will want you to do over and over again.

1.   Boil the chicken breasts in a couple quarts of water with a diced onion for about a half an hour or until done. Remove from the pot and let cool.

2.   Cut the tortillas in half and then place the two halves on top of each other. Cut about 1/4 inch off of each end and off the round part of the back of the stack. Throw these cuts away. Then cut the stack into 3/8-inch wide strips.

3.   Heat the oil in a small skillet and cook the tortilla strips 20-30 at a time until they are just starting to get crisp. It won't take but about 15-20 seconds for each batch. Remove the strips to a paper towel to drain.

4.   Roast and remove skin and seeds from three green chiles and chop sort of fine (abou 1/4-inch squares) or use one 7-ounce can of diced green chiles.

5.   Cut the pitted green ripe olives in half lengthwise

6.   In a large bowl put the olives, the green chiles, the drained corn, the salt and pepper, the bottle of green taco sauce, the sour cream and two cups of the grated Monterey Jack cheese.

7.   By now chicken should be cool enough so that you can remove the skin and bones and dice it. It should be cut into about 1/2-inch pieces.

8.   Add the chicken to a large bowl and mix up all of the ingredients.

9.   In the bottom of a shallow two-quart baking dish, spread out half of the tortilla chips. They will just about cover it if you spread them out good.

10.   Pour all of mixed ingredients from bowl into the shallow baking dish.

11.   Use 1-1/4 cups of remaining grated Monterey Jack cheese to cover mixture. Spread it out evenly over entire surface. You will still have 1/4 cup left.

12.   Now cover the cheese with the remaining tortilla chips. Spread them out evenly over the whole area.

13.   Next sprinkle the remaining 1/4 cup of grated Monterey Jack cheese over the tortilla chips. This is partly for looks and partly to hold the chips together.

14.   Then sprinkle the remaining 1/4 cup of grateed Parmesan cheese over the top of the whole area of the baking dish.

15.   Put it in a 325-degree oven for about 30 minutes or until the top is a sort of golden color and the sides are bubbling a bit. Or you can keep it in the icebox overnight and cook it tomororow. ENJOY!

# Seafood

## Down Home Good
## CRAB TOSTADAS

1 avocado, peeled and sliced
2 tablespoons lime juice
1/4 teaspoon garlic salt
1 large head iceberg lettuce
1 (1-pound, 4-ounce) can refried beans
Corn tortillas, fried crisp
1 cup mild cheddar cheese, shredded
1 pound crabmeat
2 medium tomatoes, sliced
1/2 cup pitted ripe olives
Taco sauce

Mash avocado in blender and blend in lime juice and garlic salt. Line 4 plates with the outer leaves of the lettuce, then shred the inside head and mound on plates. Heat the beans until they start to bubble. Arrange a tortilla on top of the greens on each plate and spoon over each the hot beans. Sprinkle with the cheese and cover with a layer of crabmeat (save some for the garnish). Spoon on avocado mixture, garnish with a few crab pieces. Surround with sliced tomatoes and ripe olives.

Serves 4.

## SALMON STUFFED EGGPLANT

2 good sized eggplants
Oil
2 medium onions, chopped
1/2 cup cooked brown rice
1-1/2 teaspoons paprika
1 cup canned tomatoes
1/2 teaspoon oregano
Tabasco sauce
1 (7-ounce) can salmon,
    bones and skin removed
1/2 cup Parmesan cheese
1/4 cup margarine, melted

Cut eggplants into two lengthwise pieces. Score, sprinkle with salt, place cut-side down on a towel for 30 minutes. Preheat oven to 350°. Wipe eggplant dry and place pieces on a cookie sheet cut-side down. Bake about 10 minutes and cool.

In a large skillet, heat some oil and stir in onions. When limp, stir in rice, paprika, tomatoes, oregano and Tabasco to taste. Cook to a thick pulp, stirring now and then.

Scoop out pulp from eggplant, reserving shells. Place pulp in fry pan with tomato mixture and add salmon and Parmesan cheese. Place mixture into eggplant skins and drizzle with the melted margarine. Garnish with a little paprika. Bake about 20 minutes or until thoroughly heated through.

Serves 4.

## FISH AND CHIPS

1 pound fresh or frozen fish filets
1 pound baking potatoes, peeled (3 medium)
Fat for frying
1/4 cup all-purpose flour
1/2 teaspoon salt
2 tablespoons water
1 tablespoon cooking oil
1 egg yolk
1 stiffly beaten egg white
1/4 cup all-purpose flour
Salt
Malt vinegar

Thaw frozen fish; cut into serving-size pieces. Pat dry with paper toweling.

Cut potatoes in uniform strips slightly larger than French fries. Fry a few at a time in deep hot fat (375°) until golden, 5 to 6 minutes. Remove; drain and keep warm.

In a bowl stir together 1/4 cup flour and salt. Make a well in center of dry ingredients. Add water, oil and egg yolk; beat smooth. Fold in egg white.

Dip fish in 1/4 cup flour and then in batter. Fry fish in deep hot fat (375°) until golden brown, 1-1/2 to 2 minutes on each side. To serve, season fish and chips with salt and drizzle with malt vinegar.

## STIR-FRIED SHRIMP AND ASPARAGUS

1 pound asparagus, stem ends trimmed
2 slices fresh ginger, minced
2 teaspoons cornstarch
2 tablespoons water
2 tablespoons sherry
1 tablespoon soy sauce
3 tablespoons peanut oil
1 pound uncooked shrimp, peeled and deveined
1 clove garlic, minced
3 scallions, cut into 1-inch lengths

Slice asparagus diagonally 1/4-inch thick. Add minced ginger to shrimp and toss. Blend together cornstarch, water, sherry and soy sauce and add to skillet. To heated oil in large skillet or wok, add asparagus, shrimp and garlic. Stir-fry 2 minutes. Add scallions and fry 1 minute longer. Cook, pour in cornstarch mixture, stirring until sauce boils and thickens. Turn onto serving dish and serve over rice.

Note: Snow peas, string beans, zucchini or broccoli may be substituted for asparagus.

Serves 4.

# FILLETS IN CREAM

1 teaspoon lemon juice
1 scallion or shallot, diced
1/3 cup dry white wine
5 to 6 fish fillets
1/4 pound mushrooms, sliced
1 clove garlic, minced
1/4 teaspoon dry tarragon
1 tablespoon parsley, chopped
6 tablespoons butter
3 tablespoons flour
1/2 cup milk
1/2 cup cream
Salt and pepper to taste
1/3 cup grated Swiss cheese

Butter a shallow baking dish, add the lemon juice, shallot or scallion, and wine. Lay in the fillets and cover with foil or a lid.

Steam bake in a 350° oven 12 minutes. Remove fillets and keep warm. Strain the poaching liquid and save it.

Saute the mushrooms, garlic, tarragon and parsley in the butter for 3 minutes over medium heat. Stir in the flour and cook 1 minute. Remove pan from heat and stir in the milk, cream, and 1/2 cup of the fish broth. Return to heat and cook until the sauce begins to thicken, stirring constantly, and adding more fish stock if needed. Season to taste.

Stir in Swiss cheese and let it melt. Pour sauce over the fillets and brown under the broiler.

Serves 4.

This recipe is good with any fish fillet, fresh or salt water.

# SALMON AND MUSHROOM BAKE
## (On the BBQ)

2 pounds salmon steaks or fillets
1 teaspoon salt
Pepper to taste
1/4 cup butter, melted
1/4 cup mushrooms, sliced
2 tablespoons lemon juice
2 tablespoons onion, grated

Combine all seasoning ingredients. Place pieces of salmon in separate packages made of double sheets of heavy-duty aluminum foil and, just before sealing, spoon sauce onto each fish. Place on preheated grill. Cook at MEDIUM 35 minutes, or until fish flakes easily with fork.

Serves 6.

## SCALLOP-STUFFED SHRIMP

1 dozen raw jumbo shrimp
6 ounces scallops, minced
1/4 cup fresh bread crumbs
1/4 cup grated Parmesan cheese
Paprika for garnish
1 clove garlic
3 tablespoons melted butter
1/4 cup dry white wine or dry sherry (optional)

Preheat oven to 350.°

Shell the shrimp, leaving the tails intact. Devein and butterfly them. Stuff each with 1/2 teaspoon of chopped scallops; arrange them in a buttered baking dish.

Combine the bread crumbs and cheese, sprinkle over the scallop stuffing. Top each with a light dash of paprika.

Put the garlic clove through a press, add to the melted butter, and drizzle over the shrimp. Bake for 15 minutes. Baste with white wine or dry sherry.

Serves 2 as an entree or 4 as an appetizer.

## GRAND CENTRAL OYSTER PAN ROAST

The Oyster Bar of New York's Grand Central Station has been a landmark for travelers since it opened with this dish in 1912. Oyster Pan Roast (a stew, despite its name) is still served there today, made according to this original recipe.

16 freshly opened oysters, liquor reserved
1/2 cup reserved oyster liquor
1/4 cup clam juice
4 tablespoons butter
2 dashes celery salt
2 teaspoons Worcestershire sauce
1 cup milk
1 cup heavy cream
Paprika

Put the oysters, oyster liquor, clam juice, 2 tablespoons of the butter, celery salt and Worcestershire sauce in the top of a double boiler and set pot over boiling water. The bottom of the pan should not touch the water.

Whisk or stir briskly for about 1 minute until the oysters plump up and their edges begin to curl. Add the milk and cream and continue stirring briskly until liquid approaches the boil. Do not let it boil.

Remove from heat immediately, ladle into pre-heated bowls, and top each serving with a remaining tablespoon of butter, dusted with paprika. Serve immediately with oyster crackers.

Serves 2.

# WONDERFUL SEAFOOD CASSEROLE

1/4 cup margarine
3/4 cup rice
1/3 cup golden raisins
2 cups chicken stock
1 teaspoon salt
1/4 teaspoon pepper
4 tablespoons margarine
1 cup mushrooms, sliced
1-1/4 teaspoons curry powder
1/2 teaspoon ginger
1 pound mixed cooked seafood of your choice
1/4 cup sherry
4 tablespoons margarine
1/4 cup flour
1/8 teaspoon white pepper
1/4 teaspoon dry mustard
2 cups half-and-half
1 cup grated Swiss cheese

Heat oven to 400.° Butter a casserole dish. Heat 1/4 cup margarine in a large saucepan. Cook rice until golden, then add raisins and chicken stock. Bring to a boil; simmer, covered, for 20 minutes or until liquid is absorbed. Season with salt and pepper and toss lightly with a fork. Spread rice on the bottom of the casserole.

Melt 4 tablespoons margarine and saute mushrooms, curry and ginger; cook gently for 3 minutes. Remove from heat and add seafood and sherry. Spoon over rice.

Melt 4 tablespoons margarine; add flour, pepper, mustard and let bubble. Remove from heat and add half-and-half. Return to low heat and stir until thick and smooth. Pour over seafood. Sprinkle with cheese, and bake for 25 minutes.

Serves 4 to 6.


# SCALLOPS IN BAKED CREAM

1 cup cracker crumbs
1-1/2 teaspoons salt
1/4 teaspoon pepper
1/2 teaspoon basil
1/2 teaspoon oregano
1 tablespoon finely chopped parsley
2 pounds scallops
1 cup heavy cream

Preheat oven to 375.° Butter 11" x 7" baking pan.

On piece of waxed paper, combine crumbs, salt, pepper, basil, oregano and parsley. Use to coat scallops. Arrange in pan. Pour cream over scallops. Bake in preheated oven for 25 minutes, or until bubbling and lightly browned.

Serves 4.

# SPANISH FISH FILLETS

1/4 cup whole blanched almonds
1 tablespoon chopped onion
1 minced garlic clove
2 tablespoons oil
2 tablespoons fresh bread crumbs
1 cup tomatoes, chopped (fresh or canned)
2 teaspoons lemon juice
Salt
1/3 cup water or white wine
1/2 pound fish fillets

Preheat oven to 400.° Grind almonds in blender.

Combine onion, garlic and oil in saucepan. Cook gently until onion turns limp. Stir in almonds, bread crumbs, tomatoes and 1 teaspoon lemon juice. Add about 1/4 teaspoon salt. Simmer about 25 minutes, stirring often.

Meanwhile, combine water and remaining lemon juice in a shallow casserole. Sprinkle fish fillets with salt and roll. Place fish rolls, seam side down, in casserole. Cover and bake 25 minutes.

Remove fish and stir about 1/4 cup fish broth into the tomato mixture. Then spoon sauce over fish and sprinkle with chopped parsley. Serves 2.

Start your dinner with avocado halves filled with Russian dressing. Then Spanish fish fillets, buttered rice, sauteed zucchini strips. Finish with lemon ice cream and cookies. A special dinner for that special person.

# BAYOU BAKED BASS SUPERB

2-1/2 to 3 pounds bass or other fish
2 cans crab, drained
1/2 cup bread crumbs
1/3 cup mayonnaise
2 tablespoons lemon juice
1/4 cup capers, drained
1 tablespoon Worcestershire sauce
1 teaspoon dry mustard
1/2 teaspoon salt
1/4 cup butter, melted
2 tablespoons lemon juice

Make a large cavity in the fish. Combine the next 9 ingredients for stuffing; stuff fish.

Make a sauce with remaining ingredients. Baste fish. Place fish in baking pan and bake at 350° for 20 minutes. Baste fish and bake 20 minutes more or until done.

Baste fish again and garnish with parsley. This is lovely served with a Hollandaise sauce.

Serves 4 to 6.

A real salute to the Bayou cuisine...

# BAKED TROUT WITH MUSHROOMS

4 trout, cleaned with heads and tails left on
Salt and freshly ground pepper
Flour
1/2 cup butter
2 tablespoons olive oil
1 pound fresh mushrooms, thinly sliced
1 teapoon lemon juice
3/4 cup thinly sliced green onions (with 2-3 inches green part)
1/4 cup fresh bread crumbs

Season trout lightly with salt and pepper. Roll in flour and brush off excess. In a heavy 10 to 12-inch skillet, melt 2 tablespoons butter with the olive oil over high heat. When foam subsides, add the trout and cook for 4 to 5 minutes on each side, or until golden brown. Carefully transfer trout to a plate or platter.

In a stainless steel or enameled skillet, melt about 4 tablespoons butter over moderate heat. Add mushrooms, sprinkle with lemon juice and cook 3 minutes until slightly soft, stirring constantly with a wooden spoon. Remove mushrooms to a buttered 9 x 13-inch oven-proof baking dish.

Melt 1 tablespoon butter in skillet and add green onions. Cook one minute. Remove to a bowl. Lightly brown bread crumbs in remaining butter.

Place trout on mushrooms, then top with green onions and bread crumbs. Bake at 425° for about 10 minutes or until trout is white and flakes.

Makes 4 servings.


# SZECHUAN SHRIMP

2 tablespoons peanut oil
1 pound extra-large raw shrimp, shelled and deveined
1/4 cup minced green onion
2 tablespoons minced fresh ginger
3 cloves garlic, finely minced
2 tablespoons dry sherry
2 tablespoons soy sauce
2 teaspoons sugar
1/2 teaspoon salt
2 to 3 tablespoons catsup
2 tablespoons chili sauce
1 teaspoon red pepper flakes

Heat oil in a wok or large, heavy skillet. Add shrimp, green onion, ginger and garlic. Stir-fry until shrimp are pink. Add sherry, soy sauce, sugar and salt. Stir well and blend in catsup, chili sauce and red pepper flakes. Serve with piping hot rice.

Makes 6 to 8 servings.

# CHINESE NEW YEAR'S SHRIMP

2 pounds large shrimp, shelled, deveined and butterflied
1/4 cup hoisin sauce
1/4 cup dry sherry
2 tablespoons rice wine vinegar
2 tablespoons soy sauce
1 clove garlic, minced
2 cups flour
1/2 cup ground macadamia nuts
2 teaspoons baking soda
1 teaspoon salt
1-1/4 cups coconut milk
1 egg, beaten
2 cups grated coconut
Vegetable oil

Combine shrimp, hoisin sauce, sherry, vinegar, soy sauce and garlic in a large bowl and marinate 2 hours or longer.

Combine nuts, flour, baking soda and salt in a medium bowl. Beat coconut milk with egg and combine with the flour mixture, stirring with a whisk. Batter should be thick enough to coat shrimp. Cover batter and let stand 2 hours.

Drain shrimp and pat dry with paper towels. Dip shrimp in batter (should coat thickly), shake off excess batter, then roll in coconut. Place on waxed paper-lined cookie sheet and chill.

Pour 2 inches of oil into a skillet or wok. Bring oil to 375°. Fry shrimp, three at a time, until golden and crisp. Drain on paper towels. Serve hot with Plum Dipping Sauce. Also terrific with curried bananas and crumbled bacon. With a little steamed rice, it's a nice way to start Chinese New Year.

Serves 6.


# TURBOT EN YOGURT

1 pound turbot or sole fillets
Salt and pepper to taste
1/2 cup low-fat yogurt
2 tablespoons dry white wine
1 egg yolk
1 green onion, chopped
1/8 teaspoon garlic salt
3 tablespoons minced parsley

Lay fish fillets in a lightly greased baking dish and sprinkle with salt and pepper.

Stir together the yogurt, wine, egg yolk, onion, garlic salt and parsley and spread over the fish, covering completely.

Bake in a 375° oven for 20 minutes, or until fish flakes with a fork.

Serves 4 at 150 calories per serving.

## SCALLOPED OYSTERS

2-1/2 cups coarse cracker crumbs
1 teaspoon salt
Pepper to taste
Butter
1 pint oysters, drained
1 cup celery, chopped
1/2 teaspoon Worcestershire sauce
1/2 cup heavy cream
Chopped parsley

Combine cracker crumbs, salt and pepper and 1/3 cup melted butter. Toss until crumbs are coated with butter. Spread 1/2 of the crumb mixture in a casserole. Cover with oysters.

Saute celery in small amount of butter until tender. Sprinkle celery over oysters. Cover with remaining crumb mixture.

Combine Worcestershire sauce and cream; pour over top. Bake at 350° for 20 minutes or until lightly browned. Sprinkle with parsley.

Serves 6.

## MAGIC CAJUN SAUCE WITH CRAWFISH OR SHRIMP

2 teaspoons salt
2 teaspoons cayenne
1 teaspoon white pepper
1 teaspoon black pepper
1 teaspoon dried basil
1/2 teaspoon dried thyme
Mix seasonings together and set aside.

1/4 cup onions, chopped
1/4 cup celery, chopped
1/4 cup bell pepper, chopped
Combine chopped vegetables and set aside.

7 tablespoons oil
3/4 cup flour
3 cups seafood stock
1/2 pound sweet butter
2 pounds crawfish or shrimp
1 cup green onions, finely chopped

Heat oil over high heat and mix in flour; cook until brown, about 3 to 5 minutes. Stir in the vegetables and 1 tablespoon of the seasoning mix and cook for 5 minutes over medium heat.

Bring stock to a boil and pour into roux and vegetable mixture. Stir until smooth; simmer 3 minutes.

In a frying pan, melt one stick butter and add crawfish or shrimp. Cook 1 minute, stirring the whole time. Add remaining butter to stock mixture and remaining seasoning and crawfish or shrimp mixture and simmer 4 minutes. Serve over rice. Serves 6.

# BUTTERFLIED COCONUT SHRIMP

1 pound large shrimp
Vegetable oil
1/4 cup flour
1/2 teaspoon salt
1/2 teaspoon dry mustard
1 egg
2 tablespoons cream of coconut* or 2 tablespoons light cream
3/4 cup flaked coconut or shredded fresh coconut
1/3 cup packaged bread crumbs
Chinese Mustard Sauce, (see below)

Shell and devein shrimp, leaving tails on. Slit shrimp with sharp large knife along curved side, cutting almost through. Place on paper toweling.

Pour oil into medium-sized saucepan to a depth of 2 inches. Heat to 350° on deep-fat frying thermometer.

While oil is heating, combine flour, salt and dry mustard in one small bowl; beat egg and cream of coconut in second small bowl. In third bowl combine coconut and bread crumbs.

Dip shrimp in flour mixture, then in egg-cream mixture, then in coconut-crumb mixture, coating well. Refrigerate until ready to cook. When oil is hot, fry shrimp a few at a time, turning once, for 2 minutes or until golden. Remove with a slotted spoon and drain on paper toweling. Keep warm in oven. Serve with Chinese Mustard Sauce and bottled Duck Sauce, if you wish.

*Available in some markets, most liquor stores stock 15-1/2 ounce can. Tastes good with light cream, as substitute.

## Chinese Mustard Sauce:

Mix 1/3 cup dry mustard with 1 tablespoon honey, 2 teaspoons vinegar and 1/4 cup cold water until well-blended. Keep refrigerated. Makes about 1/3 cup.

## EASY BAKED WHITE FISH

1 pound white fish fillets
Salt, pepper & fresh garlic to taste
1/2 cup parsley, finely chopped
3 green onions, chopped
1/2 teaspoon basil
1 teaspoon grated lemon peel
2 teaspoons oil
1 dozen cherry tomatoes, cut in half

Arrange the white fish in a lightly greased baking dish, and season with salt, pepper and garlic. Mix together the remaining ingredients, except the tomatoes and sprinkle over the top of the fish. Arrange the tomatoes cut side down, over the top of the fillets. Bake uncovered in a preheated 375-degree oven for 20 minutes.

Approximately 135 calories per serving. Easy and so good.

To microwave, cover with plastic wrap and cook on high power 8 to 10 minutes. Serves 4.

# SALMON SOUFFLE ROULADE
## Cake:

1/4 cup butter
1/4 cup flour
1/8 teaspoon salt
1-1/4 cups milk
4 egg yolks, lightly beaten
3 egg whites, room temperature
1 tablespoon grated Parmesan cheese

Preheat oven to 400.° Grease and line with foil a 15-1/2" x 10-1/2" x 1" pan, letting foil extend over the edge.

Melt butter over low heat and blend in flour and salt. Cook for 1 minute, stirring constantly. Gradually pour in milk. Cook over medium heat until mixture comes to a full boil, stirring constantly. Remove from heat, stir 2 tablespoons of the mixture into the egg yolks, and then gradually add yolks to mixture. Cool slightly.

In a large bowl, beat egg whites until soft peaks form. Add half the egg whites to the mixture and fold in gently. Add remaining whites and fold in. Pour into prepared pan and bake 15 to 20 minutes or until puffy and golden. Remove from oven and invert onto a clean towel that has been sprinked with the Parmesan cheese. Carefully peel off foil. Roll up cake in towel and place on rack to cool.

## Filling:

1 (15-ounce) can red salmon, drained
1 tablespoon lemon juice
1 tablespoon mayonnaise
1 (3-ounce) package cream cheese, softened
2 tablespoons dill weed

Combine all the ingredients. Unroll cooled cake and spread with filling ingredients to within 1/4 inch of the edges. Reroll. Wrap and chill for 2 to 4 hours.

To serve: cut into 1/2-inch slices and serve on melba or pumpernickel toast. Garnish with sour cream and dill.

Yield: 28 slices at about 80 calories per slice.


## POACHED SALMON IN THE DISHWASHER

Take one salmon and open the belly, season to taste with a little salt, pepper, melted butter, dry white wine and a few sprigs of fresh dill. Brush the outside of the fish with butter and season to taste.
Now, wrap salmon airtight in a double thickness of foil, envelope style. Place salmon packet in the top rack of the dishwasher and push the button for the full cycle. It works beautifully every time.

You can make individual vegetable packets as well and place them in the top rack with the salmon, so the whole dinner is cooked in the top of the dishwasher.

This is so easy and really a topic of conversation for your dinner party.

## SHRIMP ON THE SKEWER "MEXICANA"
### (As Prepared by Chef Raimund Hofmeister
### at the 1985 Food and Cooking Expo)

24 large red Spanish shrimp
2 medium-sized red onions, cut into 24 (3/4" squares)
2 large green peppers, cut into 24 (3/4" squares)
1/4 cup ginger in syrup, cut in julienne strips
1/2 cup fresh pineapple, cut in julienne strips
1/2 cup fresh tomato, cut in julienne strips
1/2 cup onions, cut in julienne strips
1/4 cup dry fume blanc
3 teaspoons butter
1/2 teaspoon chopped dill
1/2 teaspoon chopped parsley
1/2 cup tequila
Dash of tabasco, salt and pepper

### Marinade:

| | |
|---|---|
| 2 cups olive oil | 3 bay leaves |
| 1/2 teaspoon fresh rosemary | 1/4 teaspoon garlic |
| 1/4 teaspoon marjoram | Juice of 1 lemon |
| 1/4 teaspoon thyme | 1 tablespoon Worcestershire sauce |

Peel, devein and clean shrimp thoroughly. Alternate shrimp, onion and green pepper until there are 4 shrimp each on 6 skewers. Now mix olive oil, rosemary, bay leaves, marjoram, thyme, and a touch of fresh chopped garlic with lemon and Worcestershire. Marinate each skewer overnight.

The following day (when ready to serve), heat up a large skillet to fit the 6 skewers. Add 2 tablespoons butter and saute on both sides to a light brown color, but not quite cooked. Remove from skillet and put between 2 plates to keep warm. Now add the onions into the skillet and saute for 3 minutes on low heat. Deglaze with fume blanc; add salt, pepper, lemon juice, Worcestershire and dash of tabasco, and cook another 2 minutes. Add ginger, pineapple and tomatoes; heat up and flambe with tequila. Finally, mix in parsley, dill and 1 large tablespoon of butter. Serve on bed of rice and top with ginger, pineapple, onions and tomato.

## SHRIMP CURRY

| | |
|---|---|
| 1/3 cup butter | 3 cups cooked shrimp |
| 3 tablespoons butter | 1 tablespoon chopped candied ginger |
| 1 to 2 tablespoons curry powder | 1 tablespoon lemon juice |
| 1 teaspoon salt | 1 tablespoon sherry |
| 1/4 teaspoon paprika | 1 teaspoon onion juice |
| Dash of nutmeg | Dash of Worcestershire sauce |
| 2 cups light cream | |

Melt the butter, then blend in the flour, curry powder, salt, paprika and nutmeg. Stir in cream and cook until thick and bubbly. Add remaining ingredients, stirring continually from time you added the cream. When heated through, serve.

# GRILLED ANGLER WITH GARLIC BEURRE ROUGE*

1/2 cup fruity olive oil (light)
5 tablespoons lemon juice
4 cloves fresh garlic, peeled and slivered
1 bunch fresh cilantro, chopped to make 1/2 cup,
    reserving some whole leaves for garnish
Salt and freshly ground pepper to taste
6 (six-ounce) Angler fillets, about 3/4-inch thick
    (or any firm-fleshed fish)
1/4 pound sweet butter
1/4 cup chopped sweet red onion
2 small hot green chiles, finely minced
1 tablespoon finely minced fresh garlic
1 pound ripe tomatoes, peeled and chopped
Lemon wedges

Mix together olive oil, 4 tablespoons lemon juice, slivered garlic, 1/4 cup chopped cilantro and salt and pepper to taste. Add fish fillets and marinate for 1 hour or as long as overnight.

Meanwhile, prepare Garlic Beurre Rouge. In a frying pan over medium heat, melt 2 tablespoons butter. Saute onion, chiles and minced garlic until soft. Add tomatoes and the remaining 1 tablespoon lemon juice. Cook, stirring, for 10 minutes. Remove from heat and add salt and pepper to taste. Stir in remaining 1/4 cup chopped cilantro. Slowly stir in remaining butter until melted.

Barbecue fish over low glowing coals, about 7 minutes or until done to your liking, turning fish once. Remove to warm serving platter. Top with Garlic Beurre Rouge Sauce. Garnish with lemon wedges and reserved cilantro leaves.

Makes 6 servings.

*Finalist, 1984 Gilroy Garlic Festival Recipe Contest.


# RED ROOSTER TAVERN'S FILLET OF SOLE

4 fillets of sole (flounder)
Cracker crumbs
Salt and pepper to taste
4 bananas
Unsweetened grapefruit juice
Melted butter
Curry powder

Roll fillets and place them in a buttered casserole dish. Top with cracker crumbs. Salt and pepper to taste.

Place bananas around the sides of the dish. Pour a little grapefruit juice over the fish and fruit. Drizzle melted butter over all. (Butter prevents the bananas from over-browning.) Top with a sprinkle of curry.

Bake in a hot oven (400°) until fish flakes apart easily with a fork and bananas are puffed.

Makes 4 servings.

# SHRIMP AND CRAB SUPREME

1 onion, sliced
1 tablespoon dill seed
2 bay leaves
6 peppercorns
2 cans beer
2 pounds raw shrimp in shells
3 packages frozen chopped spinach
3 tablespoons grated onion
2 tablespopons lemon juice
Salt, pepper and cayenne to taste

12 ounces frozen crabmeat, thawed
8 tablespoons butter
1/4 cup flour
2 cups half and half
1 teaspoon garlic juice
2 teaspoons Worcestershire sauce
1/4 teaspoon hot sauce
1/4 teaspoon paprika
8 tablespoons sherry
Grated Parmesan cheese

Preheat oven to 325? Combine onion, dill seed, bay leaves, peppercorns and beer in a deep pot and bring to a boil. Add shrimp and boil 5 minutes. Drain, let cool, and shell. Set aside.

Cook spinach, drain and mash as dry as possible. Season with grated onion, lemon juice, salt, pepper and cayenne. Make a cream sauce of butter, flour and cream. Add garlic juice, Worcestershire, hot sauce, paprika and sherry.

In a shallow casserole, alternately layer the shrimp, crabmeat, spinach and cream sauce. Generously sprinkle grated Parmesan cheese over top and heat for about 30 minutes.

Serves 6.

## Low Calorie Fish Entree
## SPICEY WHITE FISH

1 pound white fish fillets
1/4 teaspoon oregano
1/4 teaspoon cumin
1/8 teaspoon dried red pepper flakes
1 to 2 cloves garlic, crushed
3 green onions, chopped
1/2 bell pepper, chopped
2 tomatoes, peeled and chopped
2 tablespoons parsley, chopped
2 tablespoons cilantro, chopped
1 teaspoon fresh ginger root, chopped
1 avocado, sliced
1 lemon, sliced

Place fish fillets in a lightly greased baking dish. Combine remaining ingredients except avocado and lemon and sprinkle over the fish fillets. Bake in a preheated 375-degree oven for 20 minutes, uncovered.

Garnish with avocado and lemon slices.

Serves 4. Approximately 180 calories per serving.

To microwave, cover dish with plastic wrap and cook on high power about 8 to 10 minutes.

# FISH IN PEAR SAUCE ON THE LIGHT SIDE

4 firm Bartlett pears
4 tablespoons margarine
1/2 teaspoon salt
1/2 teaspoon dry mustard
1/4 teaspoon dried basil, crumbled
2 tablespoons fresh dill weed, chopped
1/8 teaspoon seasoned pepper
1 chicken bouillon cube, crumbled
1 cup onion, thinly sliced
1 cup carrots, julienne cut
4 (1-inch) fish steaks, about 2 pounds
    (sea bass or any firm fish may be used)
2 small tomatoes, peeled and sliced
1 lemon, thinly sliced

Halve, core and quarter the pears. Melt 2 tablespoons of the margarine and mix with salt, mustard, basil, dill weed and pepper. Pour over pears and reserve. Melt remaining margarine in a skillet and add bouillon, onion and carrot and mix thoroughly. Cook slowly, covered, for 5 to 10 minutes. Add fish steaks, pears with butter mixture, tomato and lemon slices. Cover and cook for 10 minutes.

Serves 4.

Love this with brown rice and pine nuts and watercress.

## Fun with Mushrooms
# TUNA AND MUSHROOM PIE

4 cups fresh mushrooms, sliced
1/2 cup onion, chopped
2/3 cup celery, sliced
2 tablespoons lemon juice
1/3 cup margarine
1/3 cup flour
3-1/2 cups milk
2 (7-ounce) cans tuna
1 tablespoon Worcestershire sauce
1 package pie crust mix

Melt margarine and saute mushrooms, onion, celery and lemon juice 5 minutes. Blend in flour and gradually stir in milk, cooking until thickened. Add tuna and Worcestershire sauce. Turn into a buttered 2-quart casserole and top with prepared pie crust. Bake at 425 degrees for 30 minutes, or until crust is browned.

Great lenten dish that serves 6 to 8.

# Breads

# CARRINGTON'S CORNBREAD

1/2 pound butter
1 cup sugar
4 eggs
1 (4-ounce) can green chilies, chopped
1 (16-ounce) can cream-styled corn
1/2 cup Jack cheese, grated
1/2 cup sharp cheddar cheese, grated
1 cup flour, sifted
4 teaspoons baking powder
1/4 teaspoon salt
Pinch of dry red pepper flakes
1 cup yellow cornmeal
Butter and honey

Cream butter. Add sugar and eggs one at a time . Mix well. Stir in peppers, corn and cheeses and mix well. Sift together flour, baking powder and salt. Mix with pepper flakes and cornmeal. Add to butter mixture. Pour into a greased 8" x 12" baking dish.

Preheat oven to 350°. Place bread in oven, then reduce heat to 300° and bake for 1 hour. Serve with butter and honey and fried chicken.


# CHEESE ONION BREAD

1 package dry yeast
1/4 cup warm water
2 tablespoons dry minced onion
3 tablespoons water
2 cups milk, scalded
2 tablespoons margarine
2 tablespoons sugar
2 teaspoons salt
6 cups flour
1/2 teaspoon celery salt
1/4 teaspoon ground sage
1 cup grated sharp cheese

Dissolve yeast in warm water.

Soften minced onion in the 3 tablespoons water and set aside.

Scald milk, add margarine, sugar and salt. Cool to lukewarm, then add yeast.

Mix celery salt, sage and grated cheese with 2 cups of the flour. Add onion, milk and yeast mixture and beat until smooth. Add enough of the remaining flour to make a medium stiff dough.

Knead until smooth, about 10 minutes. Cover and let rise in a warm place until double in bulk. Punch down; let rest about 15 minutes before shaping into 2 loaves. Place loaves in 2 greased 7-1/2 x 3-1/2-inch pans and let rise for 1 hour, or until double in bulk.

Bake at 350° for about 1 hour.

# FABULOUS RYE BREAD

4 packages yeast
1/8 teaspoon ginger
2 cups warm water
1 cup dark molasses
4 teaspoons salt
4 tablespoons caraway seed

4 cups rye flour
1/2 cup cocoa
4 tablespoons oil
2-/1/2 cups white flour
2-1/2 cups whole wheat flour
Cornmeal to dust pans

Mix together the yeast and the 1 cup warm water and the ginger.

In a separate bowl, mix 2 cups warm water, dark molasses, salt and the caraway seed. Add rye flour, cocoa, oil, white flour and the yeast mixture. Beat until smooth. Spread whole wheat flour onto a board. Place sticky batter on flour and knead together about 10 minutes. Place in an oiled bowl, turning to grease all sides. Cover with a cloth and let rise in a warm place about 2 hours or until doubled in bulk. Punch down and let rest 10 minutes.

Divide and shape into loaves. Place in 9 x 5 x 3-inch pans which have been dusted with cornmeal. Bake at 375° in a preheated oven for 45 minutes, or until a tap on the top of the bread produces a hollow sound.

Makes 2 loaves.

This bread is simply wonderful just buttered and then spread with cream cheese. A whole meal with your favorite soup.

# FAVORITE BRAN MUFFINS

1 cup boiling water
1-1/2 teaspoons baking soda
1/2 cup shortening
1 cup brown sugar
2 eggs
2 cups buttermilk
1/2 teaspoon salt
1-1/2 cups flour
1 cup 40% Bran Flakes
2 cups All Bran
1 cup nuts, chopped
1 cup dates, chopped

Add soda to boiling water and let cool. Cream shortening and sugar. Add eggs, milk, salt and flour. Stir in water and soda. Cream for 1 minute. Stir in bran flakes, bran, nuts and dates. Grease small pyrex bowls. Bake at 375° for about 35 minutes. Makes 18 large muffins.

This would be a dynamite way to start your morning with a steaming hot cup of coffee and a nice piece of melon.

## BUTTERMILK RAISIN BREAD

1-1/2 cups buttermilk
1 package dry yeast
1/4 cup sugar
2 eggs
1/2 cup butter, melted
5 to 5-1/2 cups unbleached white flour
1-1/2 teaspoons salt
1/2 teaspoon baking soda
1 cup seedless raisins

Heat buttermilk to warm, add yeast and sugar, stir until yeast is dissolved.

Slightly beat eggs and add cooled butter. Stir into yeast mixture.

Sift dry ingredients together; add by thirds to yeast-egg mixture, beating well after each addition.

Turn out on well-floured board and knead until dough is smooth and elastic. Knead in raisins at the last. Place dough in oiled bowl, brush with melted butter; cover and let raise in a warm place until double in bulk (about 1 hour).

Punch down dough and turn out on floured board. Divide dough in half and let rest 15 minutes. Shape into loaves and place in greased bread pans. Cover and let rise until double (1 hour).

Bake at 400° for 30 to 35 minutes. Makes 2 loaves.


## DATE NUT BREAD

1 cup boiling water
1 cup dates, chopped
1 teaspoon baking soda
4 tablespoons shortening
3/4 cup brown sugar
1 egg
1-1/2 cups sifted flour
1/2 cup salt
1 cup chopped walnuts

In a mixing bowl, pour water over dates. Stir in baking soda and let stand 5 minutes. Cream together shortening and sugar, then egg, beating well. Stir in flour, salt and nuts. Stir in dates. Line a 10-inch loaf pan with waxed paper and pour in batter. Bake in a preheated 300-degree oven, 45 to 60 minutes, or until firm.

---

It's better to slip with the foot than with the tongue.

## CALIFORNIA APRICOT LOAF

1/2 cup (1 stick) butter
1/2 cup sugar
3 eggs
1/2 cup fresh orange juice concentrate
Grated rind of 1 fresh orange
1 cup chopped dried apricots
2-2/3 cups crushed graham crackers
1/2 teaspoon baking powder
1/2 teaspoon baking soda
1/2 teaspoon salt
1 cup chopped walnuts

Melt butter in a large saucepan. Stir in sugar. Add eggs one at a time, and stir until mixture is smooth. Stir in remaining ingredients in the order listed. Mix thoroughly. Turn into a greased loaf pan (8-1/2" x 4-1/2"). Bake in a moderate oven (300°) for 55 minutes or until toothpick inserted in center comes out clean. Allow to cool in pan for 5 minutes. Then turn out on rack to cool thoroughly before slicing.

Makes 1 loaf.

### Apricot Crunch:

Toss 1-1/2 cups plump-cooked apricots coarsely cut, with 2 tablespoons fresh orange juice; turn into shallow baking dish. Thoroughly mix 1 cup rolled uncooked oats, 3/4 cup brown sugar and 6 tablespoons melted butter. Sprinkle over fruit. Bake in 400° oven 15 minutes or until topping is Brown. Cool slightly. Makes 6 servings. Serve warm. Pass heavy cream or top with ice cream.

## EASY MONKEY BREAD

3 medium cans buttermilk biscuits
1/2 cup sugar
1/2 teaspoon cinnamon
1 stick margarine
3/4 cup sugar
3/4 teaspoon cinnamon

Cut biscuits into quarters and roll into the 1/2 cup sugar and 1/2 teaspoon cinnamon. Pile into a greased and floured bundt pan. Melt margarine and add remaining sugar and cinnamon. Pour over biscuits. Bake at 350° for 30 to 35 minutes.

---

He who blows his stack adds to the world pollution.

---

Man is never too old to yearn.

# JACKIE'S FABULOUS GARLIC LOAF

1 (1-pound) loaf sweet French bread
1/2 cup butter
6 cloves fresh garlic, crushed
2 tablespoons sesame seeds
1-1/2 cups sour cream
2 cups cubed Monterey Jack cheese
1/4 cup grated Parmesan cheese
2 tablespoons dried parsley flakes
2 teaspoons lemon pepper seasoning
1 (14-ounce) can artichoke hearts, drained
1 cup shredded cheddar cheese
1 (6-ounce) can pitted ripe olives
Tomato slices and parsley sprigs for garnish

Cut French bread in halves lengthwise. Place halves on aluminum foil covered baking sheet. Tear out soft inner portion of bread in large chunks, leaving crusts intact. Melt butter in a large skillet and stir in garlic and sesame seeds. Add bread chunks and fry until bread is golden and butter is absorbed. Remove from heat.

Combine sour cream, Jack cheese, Parmesan cheese, parsley flakes and lemon pepper seasoning. Stir in drained artichoke hearts and toasted bread mixture. Mix well. Spoon into bread crust shells and sprinkle with cheddar cheese.

Bake at 350 degrees for 30 minutes. Meanwhile drain olives. Remove bread from oven and arrange olives around edges of bread and tomato slices and parsley sprigs down center.

Makes 8 servings of cheesey, garlic goodness.


## A Salute to Octoberfest
## RAISIN BEER BREAD

2 cups beer
1 (15-ounce) package raisins
5 cups sifted flour
1-1/4 cups sugar
1 tablespoon baking soda
1/2 teaspoon salt
1-1/2 teaspoon nutmeg
3 eggs, well beaten
2-1/2 cups American cheese, grated
2 cups walnuts, chopped

Heat beer to boiling and pour over raisins. Let stand until cool and raisins plumped. Mix flour with sugar, soda, salt and nutmeg. Stir in beer and raisins, eggs, grated cheese and walnuts. Mix well. Spoon batter into 2 greased 9 x 5-inch loaf pans. Bake at 350 degrees for 45 minutes or until toothpick inserted in center comes out clean. Serve warm or cold with butter, cheddar or cream cheese.

# FLOWERPOT BREAD

1 large potato, peeled and diced
1 teaspoon salt
1 cup water
1/2 cup butter
1/2 cup sugar
1/2 cup powdered skim milk
3 eggs, beaten
2 packages yeast
1/4 cup warm water
1 teaspoon sugar
5 cups flour, more or less
   (or 1/2 cup soy flour and
    1/2 cup wheat germ may
    be substituted for part of flour)

Put potato into water with salt and boil until tender. Remove from heat, add butter and sugar to water, and mash all together. Blend in the powdered milk and beaten eggs.

Dissolve yeast in warm water with sugar, and add to mixture. Slowly add flour until a soft dough is achieved.

Knead until dough is smooth and elastic, then put into a well-buttered bowl, turn once, cover with a damp cloth, and allow to rise until doubled in bulk. Punch down, knead again, and store covered in the refrigerator until needed. It will last for up to 10 days.

Before using, allow dough to rise at room temperature for about two hours. Using flowerpots that are either new or thoroughly washed in an automatic dishwasher, butter pots, line with wax paper, butter the paper and fill about two-thirds full with dough. Allow dough to rise.

Preheat oven to 400° and bake at this temperature for 10 minutes, lower heat to 325° and continue baking until done, about 1/2 hour to 3/4 hour.

This healthful bread makes a delightful conversation piece and an unusual house gift — pot and all.

# MASHED POTATO DINNER ROLLS

1/2 cup shortening
1 cup hot mashed potatoes
1 teaspoon salt
2/3 cup sugar

2 cups lukewarm milk
1 package dry yeast
2 eggs
6 cups flour (or thereabouts)

Mix shortening, potatoes, salt and sugar. Dissolve yeast in milk. Add to potatoes. Beat eggs in a large bowl. Pour in potato mixture and stir well with a spoon. Add enough flour to make a soft dough. Rub surface with a little oil. Cover with dish towel and leave in a warm place until doubled in bulk. Use hands to form rolls about the size of a large egg. Place in large greased muffin tins. Let rise again and bake in a 450-degree oven for 10 minutes.

Makes 5 dozen great rolls for a Holiday Fare.

# HOUSKA BREAD
## (Czechoslovakian Holiday Bread)

1 package active dry yeast
1/4 cup warm milk (about 110°)
1/3 cup milk, scalded then cooled to lukewarm
1/4 cup butter, melted
2 eggs
1/3 cup sugar
1/2 teaspoon salt
1 teaspoon grated lemon peel
1/4 teaspoon nutmeg
1/2 teaspoon cinnamon
3 cups regular all-purpose unsifted flour
2/3 cup white raisins
1/2 cup blanched almonds
1 egg white, beaten with 1 tablespoon water
1 teaspoon sesame seeds

In a large bowl of an electric mixer, blend yeast and water and let stand 5 minutes. Add milk, butter, eggs, sugar, salt, lemon peel, nutmeg, cinnamon and half the flour. Blend on low speed until well mixed. Then beat for 2 minutes at medium speed.

With a spoon add remaining flour, raisins and almonds to form a stiff dough. Turn dough onto a floured board and knead until dough is smooth and slightly tacky, about 5 minutes. Place in a greased bowl, cover with a clean cloth, and let the dough rise in a warm place until almost doubled, about 1-1/4 hours.

Punch down the dough and divide into 4 equal portions. Roll each to form a rope about 21 inches long. Place ropes side by side diagonally across a greased baking sheet. Pinch tops together at one end and braid loosely as follows: Pick up one rope on right, bring it over the next one, under the third, and over the fourth.

Repeat, always starting with the rope on the right until the braid is complete. Tuck ends under lightly and let rise until almost doubled, about 1 hour. Brush loaf with egg white mixture, sprinkle with seeds.

Bake in a preheated 350° oven until golden brown, 20 to 30 minutes, or until done. Serve warm or reheated.

# MEXICAN CORNBREAD

1 cup corn meal
1 cup milk
1/2 teaspoon salt
1 cup cream style corn
1/2 teaspoon soda, added to milk
2 eggs
1/2 cup oil
3 jalapeno peppers, minced
1 cup cheddar cheese, grated

Mix all ingredients and bake in a large skillet at 350 degrees for about 40 minutes.

Serves 6.

## HOLIDAY CRANBERRY BREAD

2 cups all-purpose flour
1 cup sugar
1-1/2 teaspoons baking powder
1/2 teaspoon baking soda
1 teaspoon salt
Juice and grated rind from 1 orange
2 tablespoons shortening
Boiling water
1 egg, well beaten
1 cup chopped nuts
1 cup halved raw cranberries

Sift dry ingredients together.

In a separate bowl, combine juice, rind, shortening and enough boiling water to yield a total of 3/4 cup. Cool; add beaten egg.

Blend liquid into dry ingredients, stirring only until the flour mixture is dampened. Blend in nuts and cranberries.

Pour into greased loaf pan. Push batter into corners, leaving the center slightly indented. Bake in a preheated 350° oven 60 to 70 minutes.

Makes 1 loaf.

## RHUBARB STICKY MUFFINS

1 cup finely chopped rhubarb
1/4 cup butter
1/2 cup firmly packed brown sugar
1/3 cup butter
1/3 cup sugar
1 egg
1-1/2 cups flour
2 teaspoons baking powder
1/2 teaspoon salt
1/2 teaspoon nutmeg
1/2 cup milk

Combine rhubarb, 1/4 cup butter and brown sugar in a small bowl and mix with a fork until blended. Put in the bottom of 12 large greased muffin cups.

Beat 1/3 cup butter, sugar and egg until fluffy. Sift flour, baking powder, salt and nutmeg. Add to butter-sugar mixture alternately with milk. Stir just to blend. Spoon on top of rhubarb. Bake in a 350° oven for 20-25 minutes. Invert pan on rack and let stand for a few minutes. Remove pan. Serve warm.

Makes 12 large muffins.

-------------------

Experience is what you get while looking for something else.

# GRISWOLD'S BRAN MUFFINS
## Muffin Spread

1/4 cup butter or margarine
6 tablespoons brown sugar
6 tablespoons granulated sugar
2 tablespoons honey
1 tablespoon water

Cream butter, gradually beat in sugars, add honey and water and beat until fluffy. Set aside.

## Muffin Batter

1/2 cup whole wheat flour
3/4 cup cake flour
6 tablespoons sugar
1/2 teaspoon salt
1/2 teaspoon cinnamon
1/2 teaspoon baking soda
1/2 cup raisins
2 eggs
1/4 cup honey
1/4 cup oil
1/4 cup drained crushed pineapple
3 cups whole bran cereal
1-1/2 cups buttermilk

Combine dry ingredients, add eggs, honey, oil and buttermilk. Mix well. Fold in pineapple and bran cereal. Place 2 teaspoons of muffin spread in each muffin tin and then fill two-thirds full with batter. Bake at 400° for 18 to 20 minutes. Remove from oven and invert immediately on cooling rack.

Yield: 18 muffins.

# APPLESAUCE NUT BREAD

1 cup sugar
1 cup applesauce
1/4 cup oil
3 egg whites
3 tablespoons skim milk
2 cups flour
1 teaspoon soda
1 teaspoon baking powder
1/2 teaspoon salt
1/2 teaspoon cinnamon
1/4 teaspoon nutmeg
1/2 cup nuts, chopped

Preheat oven to 350 degrees. Combine all ingredients until well blended. Fold in nuts. Spread batter into an oiled and floured 9 x 5 x 3-inch loaf pan. Bake 45 minutes or until toothpick comes out clean.

# CRANBERRY NUT BREAD

2 cups sifted flour
1 cup sugar
1-1/2 teaspoons baking powder
1/2 teaspoon baking soda
1 egg, well beaten
1 cup cranberries, coarsely chopped
1 teaspoon salt
1/4 cup shortening
3/4 cup orange juice
1 tablespoon grated orange rind
1/2 cup chopped nuts

Sift together flour, sugar, baking powder, soda and salt. Cut in shortening until mixture resembles coarse corn meal. Combine orange juice and grated rind with well-beaten egg. Pour all at once into dry ingredients, mixing just enough to dampen.

Carefully fold in chopped nuts and cranberries. Spoon into greased loaf pan (9 x 5 x 3). Spread corners and sides slightly higher than the center.

Bake in a preheated oven at 350 degrees about one hour. Remove from pan and cool. Store overnight for easy slicing.

# LEMON GRANOLA BREAD

Granola Streusel Topping
1 cup sugar
3/4 cup all-purpose flour
3/4 cup whole wheat flour
1 tablespoon baking powder
1/2 teaspoon salt

1/2 cup butter, melted
2 eggs, slightly beaten
1/2 cup water
Grated peel and juice of 1 lemon
     (3 tablespoons juice)
1 cup granola

Prepare Granola Streusel Topping, set aside. In large bowl, combine sugar, flours, baking powder and salt. Combine butter, eggs, water, lemon peel and juice; add to dry ingredients, stirring just until all flour is moistened. Stir in granola. Pour into well-greased 9 x 5 x 3-inch loaf pan. Sprinkle with Streusel. Bake at 350° for 45 minutes or until toothpick inserted in center comes out clean. Cool 10 minutes; remove from pan. Cool on wire rack.

## Granola Streusel Topping:

1 tablespoon flour
1 tablespoon sugar
1-1/2 teaspoons butter or margarine

Grated peel of 1/2 fresh lemon
2 tablespoons granola

In small bowl, with fork blend together flour, sugar and butter. Stir in lemon peel and granola.

# ORANGE CARROT LOAF

1-1/4 cups whole wheat flour
1 teaspoon ground cinnamon
1/2 teaspoon baking powder
1/2 teaspoon baking soda
1/4 teaspoon salt
2 eggs, slightly beaten

Grated peel and juice of 1 orange
  (1/3 cup juice)
1/3 cup honey
1/4 cup salad oil
1 cup shredded carrots
1/2 cup chopped walnuts
1/2 cup raisins

In large bowl, combine flour, cinnamon, baking powder, baking soda and salt. Combine eggs, orange peel, juice, honey and oil; add to dry ingredients, stirring just until all of flour is moistened. Stir in carrots, walnuts and raisins. Pour into well-greased 9 x 5 x 3-inch loaf pan.

Bake at 350° for 1 hour or until toothpick inserted in center comes out clean. Cool 10 minutes; remove from pan. Cool on wire rack.

## Salute to Johnny Appleseed
# CRUNCHY APPLE TOP MUFFINS

2 cups flour
3 teaspoons baking powder
1/2 teaspoon salt
1/2 teaspoon cinnamon
1/2 teaspoon nutmeg

1/2 cup sugar
1 egg
4 tablespoons shortening
1 cup milk
1 cup finely chopped apple

## Topping:

1/2 cup finely chopped apple
1/2 teaspoon cinnamon
1/4 cup sugar

Sift together the dry ingredients. Add shortening, egg and milk. Mix until well blended and fold in 1 cup chopped apples. Put in well greased muffin tins. Sprinkle over the 1/2 cup chopped apples, then shake over a mixture of the cinnamon and sugar. Bake at 400 degrees 20 to 25 minutes.

Makes 12 to 16.

# SUPPER MUFFINS

1/2 cup sour cream
1/2 cup cheddar cheese, grated
1/4 cup onion, chopped
1 tablespoon butter or margarine
1 (14-ounce) package corn muffin mix

Mix sour cream and cheese in a small bowl, set aside. Saute onion in the butter over low heat until limp. Prepare corn muffin mix according to package instructions, stir in onion. Spoon batter into greased muffin tins, filling 2/3rds full. Top each with 1-1/2 teaspoons of the reserved cheese mixture. Bake as directed on package until tops are bubbly and edges golden, 15 to 20 minutes.

Makes 1 dozen.

# CRANBERRY MUFFINS

1 cup coarsely chopped cranberries
2 tablespoons sugar
2 cups flour
1/2 cup sugar
3 teaspoons baking powder
1/4 teaspoon salt
1 cup milk
1 teaspoon vanilla
1/4 cup butter, melted
2 eggs

Add 2 tablespoons sugar to cranberries; set aside. Mix flour, remaining sugar, baking powder and salt in a large bowl. Set aside.

Beat together eggs, milk, vanilla and butter. Make a well in the center of the flour. Pour in liquid all at once, stirring quickly with a fork just until mixed. Do not beat; batter will be lumpy. Fold in cranberries. Fill greased 2-1/2-inch muffin tins two-thirds full and bake in 400° oven 25 to 30 minutes.

Makes 12 muffins.

# IRISH BRAN BREAD

12 ounces bran
4 ounces flour
3/4 teaspoons baking soda
1/2 teaspoon cream of tartar
1/2 teaspoon salt
1 teaspoon powdered sugar
1 ounce margarine
11 ounces buttermilk

Sift together dry ingredients; stir in bran and mix well. Cut in margarine. Make a well in the center and pour in buttermilk. Mix well. Place dough in a greased 9-inch round springform pan. Smooth top with a knife dipped in milk and make a cross on top with the knife. Bake at 425° for 15 minutes, then lower temperature to 325° and bake for 1 hour.

## Natural and Good
## OATMEAL MUFFINS

1 cup whole wheat pastry flour
1/4 cup brown sugar
1/4 cup raw wheat germ
1/4 cup instant milk powder
1/2 teaspoon salt
1 tablespoon baking powder

3 tablespoons margarine
1 cup rolled oats
1 egg, beaten
1 cup milk
1/2 cup raisins

Preheat oven to 425 degrees. Mix together the first 6 ingredients. Cut in margarine. Add oatmeal and blend. Add eggs and milk stirring lightly. Fold in raisins. Pour into lightly greased muffin tins and bake 15 minutes, or until done.

Makes 12-16 muffins. Super with homemade jam.

## GRANDMA'S EASY NO KNEAD PEASANT BREAD

2 cups lukewarm water
1 package dry yeast
1 tablespoon sugar
2 teaspoons salt
4 cups bread flour (if you like, use all-purpose flour)
1 tablespoon cornmeal
Melted butter

In a large bowl, combine the water, yeast, sugar and salt. Stir until dissolved. Stir in bread flour. Turn the dough out onto a floured plate. Clean the bowl and grease with butter. Return the dough to bowl and cover with a damp towel. Let rise in a warm place for 45 minutes or until double in bulk.

Grease a baking sheet and spinkle it with cornmeal. Flour your hands and divide the dough into 2 parts, shaping each into an oblong loaf, but do not knead. Let the loaves rise another 45 minutes until almost doubled.

Preheat oven to 425°. Brush the tops of the loaves with melted butter and bake 10 minutes. Reduce temperature to 375° and bake 20 minutes more. While the loaves are still hot, brush with more butter and serve with your favorite jelly. Yum!

You will love the feeling of doing this bread and everyone will want your recipe.

Yield: 2 loaves.

## SWEET POTATO BREAD

2 eggs
2/3 cup shortening
2-2/3 cups sugar
1 (16-ounce) can sweet potatoes, mashed
2/3 cup water
3-1/3 cups flour
2 teaspoons soda
1-1/2 teaspoons salt
1/2 teaspoon baking powder
1 teaspoon cinnamon
1 teaspoon cloves
2/3 cup nuts, chopped
2/3 cup raisins

Preheat oven to 350 degrees. Grease 2 (9 x 5 x 3-inch) loaf pans. In a large bowl, cream sugar and shortening. Stir in eggs, sweet potato and water. Blend in flour, soda, salt, baking powder, cinnamon and cloves. Stir in nuts and raisins. Pour into pans. Bake about 70 minutes or until wooden pick inserted in center comes out clean.

Yields 2 loaves.

## QUICK CINNAMON ROLLS

1/2 cup hot milk
3 tablespoons shortening
3 tablespoons granulated sugar
1-1/2 teaspoons salt
1 envelope active dry yeast
1/2 cup warm water
1 egg, lightly beaten
3-1/4 cups presifted flour
Softened butter, brown sugar and cinnamon

In a mixing bowl combine milk, shortening, sugar and salt.

Soften yeast in water. Add to milk mixture. Add egg. Stir in flour to make a soft dough.

Turn onto lightly floured board. Knead lightly until smooth.

Grease 13" x 9" x 2" baking pan. Roll out dough into a rectangle. Spread with butter; sprinkle with brown sugar and cinnamon. Roll up lengthwise like a jelly roll. Cut into 1-inch thick slices. Arrange in pan. Let rise for about 1 hour.

Preheat oven to 350°. Bake in prehated oven for about 30 minutes.

Makes 24 rolls.

## BANANA NUT BREAD

3 medium bananas
Lemon juice
1/2 cup butter or margarine
1 cup sugar
2 eggs, beaten
1/2 teaspoon salt
2 cups flour
1 teaspoon soda
2 teaspoons vanilla
1 cup pecans, chopped

Preheat oven to 350 degrees. Mash bananas and sprinkle with lemon juice. In a separate bowl, cream butter and sugar. Add eggs and salt, beat well. Add flour and soda. Beat well; add vanilla, pecans and mashed bananas. Grease and flour a loaf pan (9" x 5" x 3"). Pour batter into pan and bake for 45 minutes or until toothpick comes out clean. Do not overbake. To successfully slice nut bread, cool several hours or overnight or if you can't wait, partly freeze. Now you can slice without crumbling.

An optimist is someone who tells you to cheer up when things are going his way.

# ZUCCHINI FRUIT LOAF

3 eggs, well beaten
1 cup oil
2 cups sugar
2 teaspoons vanilla
2 cups grated zucchini
1 cup canned fruit (peaches, pears,
     apricot, pineapple or fruit
     cocktail) drained thoroughly
3 cups flour
2 teaspoons baking soda
1/2 teaspoon baking powder
1 teaspoon salt
1-1/2 teaspoons cinnamon
1 teaspoon nutmeg
1 cup raisins
1 cup nuts

Beat eggs, oil, sugar and vanilla together. Add zucchini and fruit. Combine the dry ingredients and add to egg mixture. Fold in raisins and nuts. Bake in 2 greased 5"x9" loaf pans. Bake at 350° for 1 hour. Cool in pans 10 minutes before turning out onto cooling racks.


# LITTLE RUSS RAISIN BRAN MUFFINS

1 (15-ounce) box raisin bran cereal
3 cups sugar
2 cups white flour
3 cups whole wheat flour
5 teaspoons baking soda
2 teaspoons salt
4 teaspoons cinnamon
4 eggs, beaten
1 quart buttermilk
1 cup corn oil

Mix dry ingredients. Add liquids and combine. Refrigerate covered. When ready to bake, fill muffin cups half full. Bake at 400° for 15 minutes (or microwave on high for 2 minutes, 10 seconds). This will keep in the refrigerator for 6 weeks.

# SWEETS
## and
# TREATS

*Candy*
*Pies*
*Cakes*
*Cookies*
*Desserts*

# HOLIDAY ALMOND TOFFEE

1 cup butter
1 cup sugar
2 tablespoons water
1 tablespoon white corn syrup

1/4 teaspoon salt
1 cup sliced blanched almonds
1/2 teaspoon vanilla
1 (8-ounce) milk chocolate bar

In heavy skillet, melt butter. Remove from heat; add sugar and stir until sugar is dissolved. Add water, corn syrup and salt. Cook to 293°.

Line cookie sheets with aluminum foil. Spread with 3/4 of the nuts or enough to thinly cover cookie sheet. Pour candy over nuts. Spread with chocolate which has been cut into small pieces. Sprinkle with remaining nuts and cool.

When candy is cold, break into pieces and pack between layers of waxed paper in an airtight container. Cover and keep in a cool place for two to three weeks.

## Back to School Favorites
## CARAMEL APPLES

1 (14-ounce) can sweetened condensed milk
1 cup sugar
1/2 cup light corn syrup
1/8 teaspoon salt
1 teaspoon vanilla
6 medium apples
6 wooden skewers

Mix the first 4 ingredients together in a heavy 2-quart saucepan. Cook over low heat, stirring constantly until mixture comes to a rolling boil and the sugar is dissolved. Continue cooking over low heat stirring constantly for about 30 minutes or until temperature reaches 230 degrees on a candy thermometer. Remove from heat and stir in vanilla. Cool for 5 minutes. Insert wooden skewers in apples, dip in caramel until well coated, tilting pan as needed. Cool on lightly greased baking sheet.

Yields 6.

My children always knew when mom was getting serious about the fall holidays when the first caramel apples were made. I love cooking for my family so much that I couldn't wait to begin.

# GLAZED ORANGE SLICES

2 large navel oranges
2 tablespoons butter or margarine
1/3 cup light brown sugar, firmly packed
1/4 teaspoon ground allspice
1 tablespoon light corn syrup

Cut ends off oranges and cut crosswise into 1/2-inch slices. In large skillet, heat butter, brown sugar, allspice and corn syrup, stirring constantly until mixture is smooth. Add orange slices. Cook 10 minutes on each side or until oranges are shiny and glazed.

# OLD FASHIONED PEANUT BRITTLE

2 cups granulated sugar
1 cup light corn syrup
1/2 cup water

1 cup butter
2 cups raw Spanish peanuts
1 teaspoon soda

Combine sugar, corn syrup and water in a 3-quart saucepan. Cook and stir until sugar dissolves. When syrup boils, blend in butter. Stir frequently after mixture reaches 230°.

Add nuts when temperature reaches 280° and stir constantly until temperature reaches 305°. Quickly stir in soda, mixing thoroughly.

Pour into two cookie sheets. As candy cools, stretch it out thin by lifting and pulling from edges using two forks. Loosen from pan as soon as possible. Break into pieces. Store in airtight container.

Makes 2-1/2 pounds.

# TERRIFIC TAFFY

3 tablespoons butter
1/3 cup vinegar
1 cup cold water

3 cups sugar
1 teaspoon vanilla
Red food coloring

Melt the butter in a 4-quart saucepan. Add the vinegar, water and sugar. Stir until it dissolves.

Wash down the sides of the pan by putting the lid on the pan and boiling for 3 minutes. Continue to cook, without stirring, to soft crack stage (about 270°).

Pour into a buttered baking pan that has straight sides. Turn in the edges as it cools. Add vanilla and a drop or two of red food coloring to make a delicate shade of pink.

Begin stretching as soon as you can handle the candy. (It will still be very hot.) Stretch with the finger tips until it cools and is hard to pull.

Stretch into ropes approximately 1/2 to 3/4-inch thick. Cut or break into pieces. Wrap in waxed paper.

# CHOCOLATE CREAMS

1 (8 squares) package Baker's semi-sweet chocolate
1 cup confectioner's sugar, sifted
1 egg, well beaten
1 tablespoon milk

Melt chocolate in saucepan over low heat, stirring constantly. Remove from heat. Add sugar, egg and milk. Beat until smooth. Chill until firm enough to handle (about 30 minutes).

Shape into 1/2" balls, ovals or logs. Roll in decorations*. Pecan halves may be pressed into confection tops instead of rolling confections in chopped almonds.

Makes 5 dozen.

*Use coconut, colored candy crystals, jimmies, etc.

## ENGLISH TOFFEE

1-3/4 cups sugar
1/8 teaspoon cream of tartar
1 cup cream
1/2 cup butter
1 teaspoon vanilla (or 1 tablespoon rum)
1/4 pound melted semi-sweet chocolate
1/4 cup finely chopped nuts

Combine sugar, cream of tartar and cream in a large heavy saucepan and stir over quick heat until sugar is dissolved. Stir and boil ingredients for about 3 minutes. Add the butter and continue cooking the syrup until light colored and stick to the soft-crack stage 285-290 degrees. Remove from heat and add vanilla. Pour candy into a buttered pan and cool. Then spread the melted chocolate over candy. Sprinkle with chopped nuts while chocolate is still warm. Cool completely and cut into squares.

Makes about 1-1/2 pounds.

## CANDIED POPCORN

6 cups popped corn
2/3 cup sugar
1/2 cup water
2-1/2 tablespoons white corn syrup
1/8 teaspoon salt
1/3 teaspoon vinegar

Combine last five ingredients and stir until the sugar is dissolved. Bring to a boil and cover. Cook covered for about 3 minutes (the steam from the cooking will wash down the sides of the pan). Remove cover and without stirring bring to the hard crack stage (290°). Be sure the fire is not too hot.

Add coloring (if more than one color is desired, divide the sugar syrup and color as desired). Use plenty of coloring dye. Pour the syrup over the popped corn, stir with a wooden spoon until well coated. When it is cool enough to handle and still somewhat sticky, mold with the hands which have been lightly buttered.

This can be forced into molds. Be sure you ram the corn tightly into the nooks and crannies of the mold.

## Natural and Good
## HONEY-NUT BALLS

1/2 cup sesame or non-hydrogenated
   peanut butter
1/4 cup honey
1/2 cup milk or soy powder

1 tablespoon sunflower seeds
1 tablespoon walnuts, chopped
1 tablespoon raisins
3 tablespoons sesame seeds

Mix peanut butter and honey until well blended. Gradually add powdered milk until mixture resembles bread dough. Stir in remaining ingredients except sesame seeds. Roll mixture into small balls and roll into sesame seeds. Refrigerate until needed. Makes about 18 balls.

Great snack for the kiddies after school.

# ORANGE CANDIED NUTS

2 cups sugar
1/2 cup orange juice
1 tablespoon white vinegar
1/4 cup grated orange peel (from about 3 large oranges)
1/2 pound pecan halves
1/4 pound whole blanched almonds

Butter a 15-1/2 x 10-1/2 x 1-inch jelly roll pan and set aside.

Place the sugar and orange juice in a 3- to 4-quart saucepan. Bring the mixture to a boil over moderately high heat. Insert a candy thermometer, add the vinegar, and boil the syrup until it reaches 300° on a candy thermometer, or until the syrup reaches the hard crack stage.

Remove from heat and add the orange peel and nuts to the syrup. Stir to coat nuts evenly. Press mixture into prepared pan, flattening with a spatula into a single layer. Cool to room temperature. Separate the nuts by breaking into pieces.

May be stored in airtight containers for several months. Makes 4 cups nuts.

# "STINGY'S P-NUT BUTTER BALLS"

(A lady caller said her good friend in Arizona refused to share a recipe for p-nut butter balls. Three listeners called in after the show and gave us three versions, all below.)

## Basic Recipe:

1 pound margarine
2 pounds creamy p-nut butter
3 pounds powdered sugar
12 ounces semi-sweet chocolate chips

Mix first three ingredients (by hand) and roll into small walnut-sized balls. Chill 3 hours or overnight.

Melt the chocolate and using a toothpick, dip 1/2 or 2/3 of each ball into the chocolate and place on a waxed sheet chocolate side down, let cool or chill. Makes 200.

## Version #2:

You can add 1 pound of graham cracker crumbs to the p-nut mixture, and 1/2 bar of parafin wax to the chocolate. Some dip the balls partially in the melted chocolate, some totally.

## Version #3:

You can add 1-1/2 cups of Rice Crispies to the p-nut butter mix.

1 or 2 teaspoons of vanilla in each recipe couldn't hurt!

## PEACH UPSIDE DOWN PIE

1 (12-inch) square aluminum foil
2 tablespoons softened butter
2/3 cup toasted almonds or pecan halves
9 tablespoons brown sugar
Pastry for double crust 9-inch pie, unbaked
5 cups fresh peaches (about 8 medium-sized),
    peeled and sliced
3/4 cup granulated sugar
2 tablespoons quick-cooking tapioca
1/2 teaspoon nutmeg
1/4 teaspoon cinnamon
1 egg white, slightly beaten

Line a 9-inch pan with foil. Let excess foil overhang edge. Spread butter on bottom of foil; press nuts and 5 tablespoons brown sugar into butter. Fit a layer of pastry over nuts and brown sugar in pie pan.

Mix peaches with granulated sugar, 4 tablespoons brown sugar, tapioca and spices; pour into pastry shell. Cover with another layer of pastry, pricked to allow steam to escape; seal and flute edges. Brush with egg white.

Bake in a 450°oven for 10 minutes, then lower heat to 375° and bake 35 to 40 minutes longer or until done. Turn out upside down.

## BUTTERMILK PECAN PIE

1/2 cup butter
2 cups sugar
2 teaspoons vanilla
3 eggs (medium)
3 tablespoons flour
1/4 teaspoon salt
1 cup buttermilk
3/4 to 1 cup chopped pecans
1 (9-inch) unbaked pie shell
Sweetened whipped cream

Cream butter and sugar, adding 1/2 cup sugar at a time. Blend in vanilla. Stir in eggs, one at a time. Combine flour and salt; add to creamed mixture a little at a time. Stir in buttermilk. Sprinkle pecans in bottom of pie crust; pour custard mixture over pecans.

Bake at 300 degrees for 1 hour and 30 minutes. Best served at room temperature with sweetened whipped cream.

---

The 30-day diet has become very popular — that's the one people decide they'll start on in 30 days.

## BALI HAI BANANA CREAM PIE

3/4 cup sugar
3 tablespoons cornstarch
1/4 teaspoon salt
2 cups milk
3 egg yolks, slightly beaten
2 tablespoons butter

1 teaspoon vanilla
1 (9-inch) baked pastry shell
3 large bananas
3 egg whites
1/2 teaspoon vanilla
1/4 teaspoon cream of tartar
6 tablespoons sugar

In saucepan, combine sugar, cornstarch and salt; gradually stir in milk. Cook and stir over medium heat until bubbly. Cook and stir 2 minutes. Remove from heat.

Stir in small amount of hot mixture into egg yolks; immediately return to hot mixture; cook 2 minutes, stirring constantly. Remove from heat. Add butter and vanilla.

Slice 3 bananas into bottom of pastry shell. Pour cream mixture over bananas.

Beat egg whites with vanilla and cream of tartar until soft peaks form. Gradually add sugar, beating until stiff and glossy peaks form and all sugar is dissolved.

Spread meringue over hot filling, sealing to edge of pastry. Bake at 350° for 12 to 15 minutes, or until meringue is golden. Cool.

## SOUR CREAM RAISIN PIE

Pastry for a 1-crust pie
2 eggs
3/4 cup sugar
1/4 teaspoon salt
1 teaspoon cinnamon

1/2 teaspoon nutmeg
1/4 teaspoon cloves
1 cup commercial sour cream
1 cup seedless raisins

Prepare pastry and line an 8-inch pie pan. Refrigerate it while you make the filling.

Beat the eggs lightly, then stir in sugar, salt, cinnamon, nutmeg, and cloves. Stir in sour cream and raisins and pour into chilled pastry shell. Bake in a preheated 450 degree oven for 10 minutes, then reduce heat to 350 degrees, and bake 30 minutes longer or until a knife inserted in center comes out dry.

Serve warm.

## EASY NO BAKE LEMON PIE

1 prepared 9-inch pie shell
1 (14-ounce) can sweetened condensed milk
3 egg yolks
1/2 cup lemon juice
1 teaspoon grated lemon juice

Mix together the sweetened condensed milk, egg yolks, lemon juice and grated rind. Pour into prepared pie shell and chill. Will take 3 hours to set.

## CHOCOLATE MINT PIE

2 squares unsweetened chocolate
1/2 cup butter
1 cup powdered sugar
2 eggs
1/4 teaspoon essence of peppermint
Chocolate Cookie Pie Shell
Sweetened whipped cream
Grated chocolate

Melt chocolate in top of double boiler over hot water; set aside to cool.

Cream butter and powdered sugar until light and fluffy. Add unbeaten eggs, one at a time, beating until smooth. Add melted chocolate and mint flavoring. Spread in Chocolate Cookie Pie Shell. Chill for several hours or overnight.

Just before serving, top with sweetened whipped cream and garnish with grated chocolate.

## CHOCOLATE COOKIE CRUMB CRUST

1 cup finely crushed chocolate cookie crumbs
3 tablespoons sugar
1/4 cup butter, melted

Combine cookie crumbs and sugar. Add butter and blend until all crumbs are evenly moist. Pat over bottom and side of 9-inch pan. Bake at 350° for 6 minutes. Cool.

## RACE DAY PIE

1/2 cup sweet butter
2 extra large eggs, lightly beaten
Pinch of salt
1 cup sugar
1/2 cup flour
1 cup chocolate bits
1 cup pecans or walnuts, chopped
2 tablespoons 100-proof bourbon or 2 teaspoons vanilla
1 cup heavy cream, whipped

Preheat oven to 350°. Melt butter and set aside to cool. When butter is at room temperature, stir in beaten eggs. Stir in salt and sugar. Sift in flour and mix well. Fold in chocolate bits and nuts. Stir in bourbon or vanilla. Pour into 9″ pie shell and bake 30 to 35 minutes.

The pie will have a glistening crust and a tester inserted in the middle will come out clean but glossy. Set aside for 2 to 5 hours. Before serving, reheat pie for 10 minutes in 300° oven. Cover with whipped cream and serve.

Serves 8 to 10.

# EILEEN'S PUMPKIN PIE
## Crust:

1 (9-inch) Pillsbury "All-Ready" Pie Crust
1 egg yolk, slightly beaten

Ease crust into a 9" glass pie plate. Flute edges and generously prick bottom and sides with a fork. Microwave on an inverted pie plate for 5 minutes on High. Remove pie from oven and brush prick holes with egg yolk. Prepare filling.

## Filling:

3 cups of canned pumpkin
1 cup evaporated milk
2 eggs, slightly beaten
3/4 cup sugar
1/4 teaspoon salt
1 teaspoon cinnamon
1/2 teaspoon ginger
1/4 teaspoon cloves

Combine pumpkin and evaporated milk in a 2-quart casserole. Microwave on High for 5 minutes. Stir well.

In a 2-quart bowl, combine eggs, sugar, spices and hot pumpkin mixture. Stir. Pour into baked shell. Place pie on inverted plate and microwave for 15 minutes at 50% (Medium) power and 6 minutes at 100% (High) power. Rotate 2 to 3 times during microwaving.

Let cool completely.

# LEMONADE PIE AND STRAWBERRIES

1 can sweetened condensed milk
1 (6-ounce) can frozen concentrated lemonade (thawed)
Grated rind of 1 lemon
4 teaspoons lemon juice
1 (9-ounce) carton Cool Whip
Pastry shell
Sweetened fresh strawberries

Blend milk, lemonade, rind and lemon juice. Fold in Cool Whip. Pour into pastry shell, chill. Serve in wedges; top with strawberries.

# GIRDLE-BUSTER PIE

3 cups Rice Krispies
1/2 cup white Karo syrup
1/2 cup peanut butter

Mix together and spread in a pie pan; freeze.

Add softened vanilla ice cream; refreeze.

Top with fudge sauce.

# JACKIE'S LEMON MERINGUE PIE
## Crust:

1-1/2 cups flour
1 teaspoon salt
1-1/2 teaspoons sugar
1/2 cup vegetable oil
2 tablespoons milk

Put sifter in a 9" pie pan. Into sifter, place the flour, salt and sugar. Make a well in the center of dry ingredients and pour in the oil and milk. Stir all together with a fork. Push evenly in the pan, covering the bottom and sides. Flute the edge and prick bottom with a fork. Bake at 450° for 12 minutes, or until lightly browned. Cool.

## Filling:

| | |
|---|---|
| 1/4 cup flour | 3 egg yolks |
| 1/4 cup corn starch | 1/3 cup lemon juice |
| 1-1/2 cups sugar | 1 tablespoon butter |
| 1-1/2 cups hot water | 1 teaspoon grated lemon rind |

In a double boiler, cook the first 4 ingredients, stirring with a wire whisk about 20 minutes. Add remaining ingredients and cook until thick, about 10 minutes. Cool. Pour into prepared pie shell. Top with Klein's Magic Meringue (see recipe below).

# KLEIN'S MAGIC MERINGUE

This meringue will *not* bead or create a wateriness between the meringue and the custard. In addition, the meringue will stand up for the second day, if the instructions are followed carefully.

## Ingredients:

| | |
|---|---|
| 3 egg whites | 1 teaspoon baking powder |
| 3 tablespoons ice water, or shaved ice | 6 tablespoons granulated sugar |

## Procedure:

Place the first three above ingredients in a medium bowl, and beat vigorously with wire beater or electric mixer until egg whites are very stiff (test with a fork; if the fork will stand up vertically in the whites, the mixture has been beaten sufficiently.)

Now, fold in each tablespoon of sugar gradually, and when completed, whip the mixture again until stiff.

When covering the pie, make sure that the crust is covered, and bake in a preheated oven, at 425 degrees for at least 5 minutes, and not over 7 minutes. Be careful to watch the baking time for the degree of browness desired.

Cool on wire rack and refrigerate as usual.

## BANANA-APPLE PIE

1 cup brown sugar (packed)
2 tablespoons flour
2 eggs, well beaten
1 tablespoon lemon juice
3 cups grated apples
2 cups banana slices
1/2 teaspoon cinnamon
1/4 cup orange juice
1 tablespoon orange rind, grated
1 tablespopon lemon rind, grated

Combine apples and bananas. Mix sugar, flour and cinnamon. Stir in eggs, fruit juices and rinds. Add this liquid mixture to fruits and mix lightly. Turn into pie pan and cover with top crust. Bake at 425° for 45 to 50 minutes.

## MUD PIE

1 small box (8-1/2 ounces) chocolate wafers
4 tablespoons melted butter
1-1/2 quarts coffee ice cream, softened
1-1/2 cups chocolate fudge sauce
1 cup heavy cream
Toasted slivered almonds

Coarsely crush chocolate wafers and mix with butter. Press into a 9-inch pie pan. Place pan in freezer for 10 minutes.

Spread softened ice cream into pie shell and freeze until firm.

Remove from freezer and spread chocolate sauce over all. Store overnight or at least 10 hours in freezer.

Before serving, place whipped cream mound over top of pie and sprinkle with toasted almonds.

## KENTUCKY BOURBON CAKE

5 eggs, separated
6 tablespoons bourbon
1 box powdered sugar
2 sticks butter
16 chopped pecans
2-3 dozen lady fingers
1 pint heavy cream

Beat egg yolks. Add bourbon. Beat in sugar and cold, cut-up butter another bowl, beat egg whites and add nuts. Fold egg white mixture yolk mix.

Line a springform pan with waxed, buttered paper. Open lady finger out. Line sides and bottom of pan. Fold in mixture and refrigerate Remove from pan, the waxed paper. Fill with whipped cream.

# PUMPKIN CAKE ROLL

3 eggs
1 cup granulated sugar
2/3 cup pumpkin
1 teaspoon lemon juice
3/4 cup flour
1 teaspoon baking powder
2 teaspoons cinnamon
1 teaspoon ginger
1/2 teaspoon nutmeg
1/2 teaspoon salt
1 cup chopped pecans
Powdered sugar

## Filling:

1 cup powdered sugar
2 (3-ounce) packages cream cheese
4 tablespoons margarine
1/2 teaspoon vanilla

Beat eggs on high speed of mixer for 5 minutes. Gradually beat in granulated sugar. Stir in pumpkin and lemon juice. Stir together flour, baking powder, cinnamon, ginger, nutmeg and salt. Fold into pumpkin. Spread in greased and floured 15 x 10 x 1-inch pan. Top with chopped pecans. Bake at 375° for 15 minutes. Turn out on towel sprinkled with powdered sugar. Starting at narrow end, roll towel and cake together; cool. Unroll. Combine ingredients for filling and spread over cake; roll. Chill. Slice into 8 servings.

# PINK LEMONADE CHEESECAKE

1 package white cake mix
1 cup sour cream
1 (6-ounce) can pink lemonade frozen
    concentrate, thawed
1 (3-ounce) package softened cream cheese
3 eggs
1/4 cup sugar
 ½p sour cream

 rease and flour a 12-cup fluted tube pan (bundt pan). In
 top five ingredients, blending until moistened, then
 r 4 minutes. Pour batter into bundt pan and bake
 ck to check for doneness. Cool upright in pan.

 ogether to make the topping. Remove the cake
 pping. Refrigerate until served.

In
into
s inside
vernight.

# DARK FRUITCAKE

1 cup light molasses
1/2 cup water
2 pounds seedless raisins
2 pounds mixed candied fruit, chopped
1 cup butter
1-1/4 cups sugar
6 eggs
1 tablespoon grated orange rind

2-1/2 cups sifted flour
1/4 teaspoon baking soda
1 teaspoon salt
1-1/2 teaspoons cinnamon
1-1/4 teaspoons nutmeg
3/4 teaspoon allspice
1/2 teaspoon cloves
1/2 cup orange juice
3 cups coarsely chopped nuts

Blend molasses and water together in a large saucepan. Bring to a boil at medium heat, stirring constantly. Add raisins and bring to a boil again while stirring. Reduce heat to low and simmer for 5 minutes. Remove from heat, mix in candied fruit and set aside to cool.

Cream butter and add sugar. Gradually beat in eggs, one at a time, and add orange rind. Add sifted dry ingredients alternately with orange juice to creamed mixture. Stir in fruit mixture and nuts.

Pour into 2 greased 9" x 5" x 3" pans lined with waxed paper. Grease paper. Bake in 275° oven for about 3 hours.

Makes two 3-1/2 pound fruitcakes.

# ORANGE CHRISTMAS CAKE

1-1/2 cups buttermilk
1 cup butter
4 cups flour
1 pound dates, chopped
1 pound candied orange slices, chopped
1 teaspoon salt
1/2 cup grated orange peel
4 eggs, beaten,
2 cups pecans, chopped
2 cups sugar
1 teaspoon baking soda
1 cup white raisins

Cream eggs, butter and sugar. Mix in flour, soda and buttermilk. Add fruits, nuts and orange slice pieces and mix well. *Bake in greased, waxed paper-lined pans two-thirds full. Leave in pans and mix 1 cup orange juice and 1-1/2 cups sugar. Pour over cakes and let stand at least 20 minutes.

*If you use the small loaf pans, bake at 250° for 1-3/4 to 2 hours. For larger sized pans, bake at 250° for 2-1/2 to 3 hours. Do not overbake. Test with a toothpick.

## JACKIE'S CHOCOLATE MOCHA ICE CREAM CAKE

24 Oreo or Hydrox chocolate cream
   sandwich cookies, crushed
1/3 cup melted butter
1/2 gallon coffee ice cream
3 ounces unsweetened chocolate
2 tablespoons butter or margarine
1 cup of sugar
Dash of salt
2 (5-1/2 to 6-ounce) cans evaporated milk
1/2 teaspoon vanilla
1-1/2 cups heavy cream, whipped
1-1/2 ounces Kahlua liqueur
Powdered sugar to taste
3/4 cup nuts, chopped

Combine cookie crumbs and 1/3 cup butter and press into the bottom of a buttered 9" x 13" baking pan. Refrigerate. When chilled, spoon on softened ice cream and freeze.

Melt chocolate and 2 tablespoons butter. Add sugar, salt and milk. Bring to a boil, stirring constantly. Boil, stirring, until thickened.

Remove from heat and add vanilla. Chill, then spread on top of ice cream. Freeze. Whip cream and add Kahlua and powdered sugar to taste. Spread over chocolate layer and sprinkle top with chopped nuts. Freeze.

What can I say, dear, after I say I'm sorry . . . . Simply fabulous!

## PEACH UPSIDE-DOWN CAKE

1/3 cup shortening
2/3 cup sugar
2/3 cup milk
1 teaspoon vanilla
2 eggs
2 teaspoons baking powder
1-2/3 cups flour
1/8 teaspoon salt
1/4 teaspoon almond flavoring

Cream shortening and sugar. Add remaining ingredients and beat well. Pour over peach mixture.

### Peach Mixture:

1/3 cup butter
1 cup light brown sugar
1-1/2 cups sliced peaches

Place butter and sugar in a sheet cake pan and heat slowly, constantly until well browned. Add peaches. Cover with cake batter and bake 45 minutes at 350°. Turn out of pan, peach side up. Serve hot or cold with whipped cream. Other fruits may be substituted for the peaches.

Serves 6.

# MEL'S BAILEY'S CHEESECAKE
## Graham Cracker Crust:

1-1/2 cups graham cracker crumbs
6 tablespoons butter, melted
1/4 cup granulated sugar

Combine all the ingredients in a mixing bowl. Blend well. Press the crumb mixture onto the bottom and partly up the sides of a greased 9″ springform pan. Chill 10 minutes.

## Cheesecake Filling:

1 (5-ounce) bar milk chocolate (be choosy)
1-1/2 pounds cream cheese
2/3 cup powdered sugar
4 large eggs
1/3 cup Bailey's Irish Cream
4 tablespoons butter, melted
1 cup sour cream

Preheat your oven to 350°. Melt the chocolate in the top of a double boiler. Meanwhile, beat together the cream cheese and sugar in a large mixing bowl. Beat in the eggs, one at a time, mixing thoroughly after each egg.

Stir in the melted chocolate, then add the Bailey's, butter and sour cream. Blend well. Pour the mixture in the graham cracker crust and bake for 45 minutes. Now prop open the oven door and let the cake cool to room temperature.

# OREGON RAISIN RUM POUND CAKE

2 cups flour
1-1/4 cups sugar
1-1/2 teaspoons baking powder
1 teaspoon salt
1/2 teaspoon cream of tartar
Juice and rind of 1 small orange,
    plus water to make 1/2 cup
1/2 cup shortening
2 eggs
3/4 cup raisins

## Sauce:

1/4 cup sugar
1/4 cup orange juice
2 teaspoons rum extract

Sift together the dry ingredients. Add orange rind, juice and shortening. Add eggs and beat 2 minutes. Fold in raisins.

Pour into a greased foil-lined loaf pan. Bake at 350° for 1 hour or until done. Remove cake from pan. Top with sauce ingredients which have been mixed together. Yield: 1 loaf.

## OLD FASHIONED OATMEAL COOKIES

2 cups old fashioned oatmeal
1 cup shortening, melted
2 eggs
1 cup sugar
1/4 cup milk
2 cups all purpose flour
1 teaspoon soda
1 teaspoon baking powder
1 teaspoon cinnamon
1 teaspoon cloves
1 teaspoon vanilla
1/2 cup walnuts
1 cup raisins (optional)

Melt shortening and pour over oatmeal. Add sugar, eggs, milk and vanilla. Stir well and add sifted dry ingredients. Add nuts and raisins and drop by spoonfuls on oiled cookie sheet.

Bake 15 minutes at 350 degrees.

## MARSHMALLOW BROWNIES FOR THE HOLIDAYS

1 cup butter
2 cups sugar
1/3 cup cocoa
4 eggs
1-1/2 cups flour
2 teaspoons vanilla
1 (16-ounce) package miniature marshmallows
1/4 cup butter, softened
3 cups powdered sugar
1/3 cup cocoa
1/3 cup whipping cream
1 teaspoon vanilla

Cream the 1 cup butter, 2 cups sugar and 1/3 cup cocoa. Beat in eggs one at a time. Stir in flour. Add vanilla and mix well.

Pour into a greased 9″ x 13″ baking pan. Bake at 350° for 25 minutes. Remove from the oven and top with the marshmallows. Return to the oven for 5 minutes, or just long enough to melt and brown the marshmallows. Cool.

Blend together the 1/4 cup butter, powdered sugar, 1/3 cup cocoa, the cream and vanilla. Spread over cooled brownies. Let stand for 12 hours before serving.

Yield: 2 dozen.

A treat your family will never forget. The secret is to let them stand for 12 hours before cutting. Happy Holidays!

# PUMPKIN SQUARES

1 cup soft butter or margarine
1 teaspoon vanilla
2 cups brown sugar
1/2 cup pure maple syrup
2 eggs, beaten
1 cup canned pumpkin
2 cups flour
1 teaspoon baking powder
1/4 teaspoon baking soda
1 teaspoon cinnamon
1/2 teaspoon ginger
1/4 teaspoon allspice
1 cup flaked coconut
1 cup chopped walnuts

In a large bowl, cream together butter and vanilla. Add sugar and beat until fluffy. Add syrup, eggs and pumpkin. Beat well. Sift together flour, baking powder, baking soda and spices. Stir gradually into pumpkin mixture. Blend in coconut and nuts.

Spread batter in a greased 10" x 15" baking pan (jelly roll pan) and bake for 35 minutes at 350°. Cool in the pan. Cut into 32 bars or squares.

# CHRUSCIK
## (Polish Bow Cookies)

9 egg yolks
3 tablespoons sour cream
1 tablespoon rum
1 tablespoon vanilla
Powdered sugar
3 cups flour, sifted
1/2 teaspoon baking powder
1/2 teaspoon salt
3 tablespoons sugar
Oil for deep frying

Beat egg yolks with sugar until well blended. Add sour cream, rum and vanilla, and mix until smooth. Sift flour, baking powder and salt, and add to egg yolk mixture a little at a time.

On a heavily floured surface, knead dough vigorously, punching, squeezing as much flour into it as it will take until dough is no longer sticky (could take 1/2 hour). Separate dough into several portions and roll very thin. Turn dough and loosen often while cutting (dough should look like parchment paper). Cut dough into strips approximately 4" x 1-1/2" long. Make slit close to one end and bring longer end into slit; pull to form bow.

Heat oil to 375° and fry quickly, only a few seconds, until golden (not brown). Turn only once. Drain on paper towels and dust with confectioners sugar.

Makes 8 dozen.

# GIANT CHOCOLATE CHIP COOKIES

1-1/2 cups sifted flour
1/2 teaspoon salt
1 teaspoon baking soda
1/2 teaspoon cinnamon
1-1/2 sticks unsalted butter
1-1/2 teaspoons vanilla
1 teaspoon lemon juice
2/3 cup light brown sugar, firmly packed
1/2 cup granulated sugar
2 large eggs (may use extra large)
1/4 cup quick cooking oats (not instant)
1-1/2 cups walnuts, chopped
1 cup chocolate chips

Adjust two racks to divide oven into thirds and preheat oven to 350°. Cut aluminum foil to fit cookie sheets.

Sift together the flour, salt, baking soda and cinnamon. Set aside.

In a large bowl of electric mixer, cream butter. Add vanilla, lemon juice and both sugars. Beat in eggs one at a time. On low speed of mixer, add sifted dry ingredients, rolled oats, scraping bowl as necessary with rubber spatula. Beat only until mixed. Remove from mixer and fold in nuts and chocolate chips.

Now work next to the sink so you can wet your hands while shaping cookies. Spread out piece of waxed paper or foil. Use 1/4 cup of dough for each cookie. Form 12 to 15 mounds of the dough. Wet hands with cold water, shake water off but not dry, pick up mound of dough, roll into a ball, flatten to 1/2-inch thickness and place on the prepared foil. Do not place more than 4 cookies on a cookie sheet. These spread to gigantic proportions.

Slide a cookie sheet under the foil. Bake two sheets at a time for 16 to 18 minutes, reversing the sheets top to bottom to ensure even baking. If you bake one cookie sheet at a time, bake on the higher rack. Watch as they brown easily.

When you remove cookies from the oven, let them stand for at least a minute until they are firm enough to be moved. With a wide metal spatula, transfer to racks to cool. If racks are not 1/2 inch from surface, place on cake pan to allow more air to circulate.

When cool, you may wrap them, bottoms together, two to a package in plastic wrap and freeze.

Makes 12 to 15 large cookies.

---

If you think you have troubles just watch a dachsund trying to walk through deep snow.

## SUGAR DROP COOKIES WITH OIL

2-1/2 cups all-purpose flour
1-1/2 teaspoons double-acting baking powder
3/4 teaspoon salt
1 teaspoon cinnamon or 1/4 teaspoon freshly grated nutmeg
1 cup sugar
3/4 cup cooking oil
2 eggs
1 teaspoon vanilla
Granulated sugar

Sift together first 4 ingredients. In a separate bowl, combine the sugar and cooking oil. Add the eggs and vanilla and beat well. Add the flour mixture all at once and beat well.

Shape the dough into 1/2" balls. Dip the balls in the granulated sugar or flatten the balls as thin as you can between very lightly floured hands. (To give a corrugated effect, score them in parallel lines with a fork dipped in flour and sprinkle with granulated sugar.)

Bake in preheated 375° oven for 10 to 12 minutes on a lightly greased baking sheet.

Makes 5 dozen cookies.

## MOM'S DIETETIC COOKIES

1 stick corn oil margarine
1 cup Twin brown sugar
2 eggs
1 teaspoon vanilla
1 teaspoon baking soda

Cream all ingredients add:
1 cup flour
2 cups quick oats
1 cup chopped nuts

Drop on ungreased cookie sheet by teaspoonfuls. Bake 15 minutes at 350°.

## CRANBERRY CRUNCH SQUARES

1 cup quick cooking oats
3/4 cup brown sugar
1/2 cup sifted flour
1/2 cup moist angel flake coconut
1/3 cup butter or margarine
1 (1-pound) can cranberry sauce
1 tablespoon fresh lemon juice

Mix together oats, brown sugar, flour and coconut. Cut in butter until crumbly. Place half in a 8" x 8" x 2" greased baking dish. Combine cranberry and lemon juice, and place on top of mixture in baking dish. Top with remaining crumbs.

Bake for 40 minutes at 350°. Cut in squares; serve hot with vanilla ice cream.

Serves 6 to 8.

# TOFFEE DROPS

2-1/4 cups flour
1 teaspoon baking soda
1 teaspoon salt
1-1/4 cups butter
3/4 cups granulated sugar
1 cup brown sugar, packed
1 teaspoon almond extract
2 eggs
1 (12-ounce) package mini semi-sweet morsels
1 (6-ounce) package Heath Bits O' Brickle chips

Sift flour, baking soda and salt together and set aside. Beat batter, sugars and extract in a large bowl with an electric mixer until creamy. Beat in eggs one at a time. Stir in flour mixture with wooden spoon. Stir in chocolate and brickle pieces.

Drop dough by rounded teaspoons 2 inches apart onto an ungreased cookie sheet. Bake at 375° for 8 to 10 minutes. Cool on wire racks.

Makes 8 dozen.

# BUTTER COOKIES

1 cup butter
3/4 cup sugar
1 egg
2-1/4 cups sifted flour
1/2 teaspoon baking powder
Dash of salt
1-1/2 teaspoons almond extract

Cream sugar and butter until fluffy. Mix in egg, baking powder, salt, almond extract and flour. Bake at 375° for 8 to 10 minutes. Use a cookie press. If decorating with candies, place on cookie sheets before baking.

Yields 5 dozen.

# SNICKERDOODLES

1 cup shortening (part butter)
1-1/2 cups sugar
2 eggs
2-3/4 cups flour
2 teaspoons cream of tartar
1 teaspoon baking soda
1/4 teaspoon salt

Combine the first 3 ingredients and beat until light and fluffy. Sift together the remaining ingredients and combine with the sugar mixture. Roll into balls and roll each ball in a mixture of 2 tablespoons sugar and 2 teaspoons cinnamon. Place each ball 2 inches apart on an ungreased cookie sheet. Bake at 400 degrees for 8 to 10 minutes.

Makes 5 dozen cookies.

# INDEX

## APPETIZERS AND BEVERAGES

Beef Cubes Oriental .......................... 12
Cheese Fondue ............................... 11
Aphra de Jacques*
   (Fried Jack Hors d'Oeuvres) ................ 16
Fried Jack Cheese ........................... 13
Appetizer Cheesecake ........................ 11
Buffalo Chicken Wings
   With Bleu Cheese Sauce ................... 15
Honey Baked Chicken Wings ................. 10
Corned Beef Canapes ........................ 13
Guacamole Stuffed Celery .................... 8
New Years Eve Crab Mold ................... 14
Adobe Hacienda Dip .......................... 6
Hot Broccoli Dip ............................. 16
Pot Luck Dip ................................. 5
Spicy Tuna Dip .............................. 7
Hungarian Surprises ......................... 8
Little Mushroom Turnovers ................... 4
Meatballs a La Cafe .......................... 9
Mexican Cheese Fondue ...................... 7
Mushroom Filling ............................ 4
Marinated Mushrooms ........................ 4
Onion Bites (Appetizer) ...................... 9
Resolution Meatballs ......................... 6
Low Calorie Pate ............................ 10
Best Ever Chicken Liver Pate ................ 12
Mock Liver Pate ............................. 8
Spinach and Cheese Appetizers ............... 9
Swiss 'n Rye Boat for Super Bowl Sunday ...... 14
California Sushi Roll ......................... 5
Chutney Tuna Pupus ........................ 7
Acapulco Shrimp ............................ 13
Mike Roy's Champagne ...................... 19
Bride's Champagne Punch ................... 19
Wedding Champagne Punch .................. 18
Brandy Egg Nog Deluxe ..................... 20
Old Fashioned Egg Nog ...................... 20
How to Make Bailey's Irish Cream ............ 17
Gin Sparklers for the Fourth ................. 19
Liqueurs .................................... 18
Frozen Berry Liqueurs ....................... 18
Banana Liqueur .............................. 18
Orange Michael (Julius' poor relation)
   (Mike Roy's Special) ...................... 17
Holiday Punch ............................... 20
Sangria ..................................... 17
Simple Syrup ................................ 17
Easy Whisky Sours for Party Time ........... 17

## SOUPS AND SANDWICHES

Cream of Asparagus Soup .................... 26
Avocado Bisque .............................. 24
Easy Old-Fashioned Bean Soup ............... 36
Harvest Bean Soup .......................... 22
Borscht ..................................... 32
Bouillabaisse ................................ 29
Summertime Beet and Zucchini Soup ......... 22
New York Cream of Cabbage Soup ........... 33
Quick Chicken Broth ........................ 24
Chicken and Coconut Milk Soup
   (Gaeng Dom Yam Gai) .................... 33
Chicken and Egg Noodle Soup ............... 26
C.V. Wood's World-Championship Chili ....... 28
Woody's Everyday Chili ..................... 25

Chili for Hot Dogs .......................... 23
Easy Cheese Chowder ....................... 34
Jackie's Cioppino ............................ 27
Jellied Consomme Madrilene .................. 30
Consomme Madrilene ........................ 29
Creamed Corn Soup ......................... 24
She Crab Soup .............................. 30
Substitute for Cream Soups ................... 25
Cold Cucumber Soup ........................ 25
Cucumber Soup a La Scandia ................ 31
Creole Gumbo ............................... 27
Hearty Lentil Soup .......................... 32
Summer Lime Soup .......................... 31
Sopa De Lima ............................... 36
Main Dish Minestrone Soup .................. 23
Hot and Sour Shrimp Soup (Thai) ............ 34
Kansas City Steak Soup
   (From the Mulebach Hotel) ............... 35
Easy Italian Vegetable Soup .................. 35
Creme Vichyssoise ........................... 30
Sausage Filled Baguettes ..................... 40
Back to School Favorites
   Ham Biscuits ............................. 42
   Barbequed Brisket ........................ 38
   Avocado Burgers ......................... 41
   Burrito Dog .............................. 39
   Cheese-stuffed Rolls ...................... 37
   Chicken Salad Sandwiches ................ 37
   Gyro Sandwich ........................... 39
   Barbequed Hamburgers for a Large Party .... 38
   Devilled Steak in Pita Rolls ............... 40
   Summer Pita Pocket Sandwiches ........... 42
   Shrimp Sandwiches ....................... 37
   Homemade Sloppy Joes ................... 41

## SALADS AND DRESSINGS

Apple Cider Salad Mold ...................... 62
A Salute to Octoberfest
   Octoberfest Applesauce Salad .............. 49
Apple Walnut Salad .......................... 61
Apricot-Marshmallow Delight ................. 53
Artichoke Grapefruit Salad .................... 59
Fresh Green Bean Salad ..................... 49
Sour Cream Bean Salad ..................... 49
Griswolds Bean Sprout Salad ................. 50
Beet Jello Salad ............................. 59
Sour Cream Horseradish Sauce ............... 59
Ceviche Sacramento ......................... 58
Bing Cherry Salad Mold ..................... 63
Heavenly Cheese Salad Mold ................. 56
Freezer Coleslaw ............................ 63
Low Calorie Shredded Chicken Salad ......... 54
Fresh Cranberry Salad ....................... 54
Molded Chicken Cranberry Salad ............. 48
Holiday Cranberry Salad ..................... 61
Fresh Fruit Salad ........................... 53
Holiday Green Salad ......................... 60
Hot Weather Guacamole Salad ................ 56
Jicama Salad ................................ 57
Mandarin Salad ............................. 62
Mushroom, Cheese and
   Watercress Salad ......................... 60
Nectarine Chicken Salad ..................... 58
Kathy Gallagher's
   Seafood/Pasta Salad ...................... 51

# INDEX (Continued)

Different Potato Salad .......................... 50
Holiday Potato Salad ........................... 55
Seven-Layer Salad ............................. 52
Papaya and Shrimp Salad ...................... 51
Curried Buffet Slaw ............................ 57
Molded Spinach Salad ......................... 50
Party Spinach Salad for Graduation ............ 55
Summer Steak Salad ........................... 52
Taboluh Salad ................................. 63
Salad of Arugula and Cherry Tomatoes ......... 64
Watergate Salad ............................... 56
Marie Callendar's Hot Bacon Dressing ......... 48
Cream Dressing in the Food Processor ......... 47
Hawaiian French Dressing ...................... 46
Tomato French Dressing ....................... 46
Creamy Mustard Vinaigrette ................... 64
Honey Mustard Dressing ....................... 44
Grandma's Boiled Mustard Dressing ........... 44
Magic Pan Oil and Vinegar Salad Dressing ..... 45
Poppy Seed Dressing .......................... 64
Steak Salad Dressing .......................... 52
Sweet and Sour Dressing ...................... 47
Basil Wine Vinegar ............................ 45
Dill Wine Vinegar ............................. 46
Red Raspberry Vinegar ........................ 44
Sesame Oil Dressing ........................... 54
Tarragon Wine Vinegar ........................ 45

## SAUCES AND MARINADES

Rick Royce's Original BBQ Sauce .............. 71
Low Sodium BBQ Sauce ....................... 75
Blender Bearnaise Sauce ....................... 74
Low Calorie Bearnaise Sauce .................. 69
Bleu Cheese Sauce ............................ 74
Brandy Sauce ................................. 69
Cumberland Sauce ............................ 67
Curry Sauce ................................... 74
Grand Marnier Sauce .......................... 75
Western Herb Sauce ........................... 73
Blender Hollandaise Sauce ..................... 74
Honey Basted Ham ............................ 71
Elsie's Cranberry Sauce ........................ 70
Creamed Horseradish Sauce ................... 73
Sour Cream Horseradish Sauce ................ 66
Jezebel Sauce ................................. 72
Lemon Mustard Sauce ......................... 75
Orange Honey Sauce and Glaze ............... 72
Szechuan Peppercorn Sauce ................... 68
Plum Sauce ................................... 76
Sauce Provencale (Microwave) ................. 76
Sweet and Sour Basting Sauce ................. 73
Sauce Tartare ................................. 67
Teriyaki Sauce ................................ 67
Jackie's White Sauce .......................... 69
The Sorcery of Saucery
    Bechamel Sauce ........................... 78
    For a Cheese Sauce ........................ 78
    For a Mornay Sauce ........................ 78
    For a Cream Sauce ......................... 78
Orange Butter ................................ 76
Fresh Peach or Plum Chutney ................. 77
Honey Basted Ham ............................ 66
Improvised Gravy .............................. 78
Beef Palace Meat Marinade .................... 73
Mr. Muller's Marinade for a Crusty Roast ....... 68
Holiday Lamb Rub ............................ 72

Gloria Pitzer's Merry Cool Whip ............... 70
Salsa Fria ..................................... 68
Green-Chili Salsa .............................. 70
Hot Fudge Topping for Sundae Bar ............ 77
Chocolate Syrup for Sundaes .................. 77

## EGGS, CHEESE, PASTA, PIZZA, ETC.

Beer Batter for Vegetables ..................... 81
Canneloni .................................... 95
Chili-Ghetti ................................... 81
Apple Harvest Dressing ....................... 81
Chestnut & Sausage Dressing ................. 84
Oyster Dressing ............................... 85
Tex-Mex Stuffing .............................. 92
Wild Rice Dressing ............................ 83
Potato Dumplings ............................. 98
Bacon and Eggs Supreme ..................... 86
Eggs Florentine with Cheese Souffle Sauce ..... 84
Ragout of Eggs and Mushrooms ............... 90
Seafood Fettucini with
    Garlic and Mushrooms ..................... 91
Baked Hungarian Noodles ..................... 82
Kroppe Kaker ................................. 83
Anne Bancroft's Lasagna ...................... 89
Elegant Lasagna for a Special Occasion ........ 96
California Mexican Lasagna .................... 97
Speedy Spinach Lasagne ...................... 82
Santa Barbara Linguine ....................... 90
Linguine with Zucchini and Tomatoes .......... 89
Back to School Macaroni Casserole ............ 80
Apple Pancakes ............................... 87
Cheese Pancakes ............................. 88
Fresh Strawberry Puff Pancake ............... 88
Impossible Pie ................................ 92
Mushroom Pie Madeira ....................... 85
Super Bowl Onion Pie ........................ 80
Easy Party Pizza .............................. 95
French Bread Pizza ........................... 86
Eggplant Celery Pizza ........................ 94
Deep Dish Zucchini Pizza ..................... 98
Welsh Rarebit (Microwave) .................... 93
Tangy Rice Casserole ......................... 87
Spaghetti Mizithra (Greek-Style)
    From the Spaghetti Factory ................. 87
Jackie's Favorite Buffet Souffle ............... 94
Tempura (Batter-Fried Food) .................. 93
Fitzie's Famous French Toast ................. 91

## VEGETABLES

Stuffed Artichokes ........................... 101
Bourbon Baked Beans ........................ 104
Down Home Baked Beans ..................... 109
Wonderful Baked Beans ...................... 115
Beans for the Labor Day Picnic .............. 116
Marinated Green Beans ....................... 102
Green Beans Vinaigrette ...................... 100
Broccoli Casserole ........................... 113
Lemon Basil Carrots .......................... 100
Nebraska Carrots ............................ 112
Carrots and Parsnips ......................... 108
Baked Corn for the Holidays .................. 103
Barbecued Corn .............................. 104
Summer Vegetables Magic
    Heavenly Corn ............................ 113
Frozen Cucumbers ........................... 113
Rabbi Yale Butlers Vegetable Kugel
    for Passover .............................. 106

# INDEX (Continued)

Jackie's Meatless Meal for Lent ............... 105
Onion Casserole ............................. 114
Charcoaled Onions ......................... 111
French Fried Onion Rings .................... 107
Pickled Maui Onions ........................ 112
Holiday Peas .............................. 110
Barbequed Potatoes ........................ 102
Best Buffet Potatoes ....................... 107
Mashed Potatoes with Crater Gravy........... 116
Easter Orange Mashed Potatoes .............. 111
Creamy Party Potatoes ...................... 109
Picnic Potatoes ............................ 115
Czech Potato Pudding ....................... 107
Mom's Super Potato Casserole............... 114
Baked Sweet Potatoes and Pippins ........... 100
Sweet Potato Surprise ...................... 114
Spinach Souffle ............................ 108
Mardi Gras Spinach Strudel.................. 110
Cheese Crunch Spuds ....................... 105
Summer Vegetable Magic
    Pesto Stuffed Tomatoes.................. 106
Sun Dried Tomatoes......................... 111
Tomato Rings with Spinach ................. 101
Fresh Vegetable Casserole .................. 108
Stuffed Vegetables (Microwave) ............. 103
Yam and Apple Casserole .................... 112

## MEATS

Beef Bourguignonne
    in the Crock Cooker ..................... 137
Delmonicos Beef Rolls ...................... 125
One Dish Beef and Zucchini.................. 135
Easy Beef Brisket with Mustard Ring .......... 118
Mustard Ring .............................. 118
Father's Day Brisket with Barbecue Sauce
    Barbecue Sauce ......................... 141
Stuffed Cabbage Leaves .................... 127
Carne Asada ............................... 123
Cheeseburger Pie........................... 118
Chili-Ghetti ............................... 137
Chili Mex Casserole for Cinco de Mayo ....... 134
Common Sense Cooking .................... 124
Chorizo ................................... 126
Curing Corned Beef ........................ 138
Dried Fruit Curry .......................... 140
Enchiladas Cinco de Mayo .................. 139
    Sauce, Filling
Fajitas .................................... 125
Filo Wrapped Filet Mignons
    With Madeira Sauce ..................... 132
Madeira Sauce............................. 132
Baked Ham in a Blanket .................... 144
Coca Cola Basted Ham ..................... 143
Crock Pot Ham for Rice .................... 139
Baked Ham with Raisin Sauce............... 121
End of Summer Barbecue
    Best Ever Hamburgers................... 144
Hawaiian Potpourri ........................ 141
Kofta Kebabs
    (from the Gitanjale Indian Restaurant) ....... 144
Leg of Lamb in a Brown Paper Bag ............ 120
Stuffed Leg of Lamb for Easter .............. 128
Elegant Rack of Lamb....................... 132
Dinner Meat Loaf .......................... 124
Super Bowl Mexican Pie .................... 134
Curried Pork Chops and Apricots ............. 123
Porkraut Rollups........................... 119

"James Beard's Pork
    with Sauerkraut Noodles" .................. 136
Pineapple Pork Chop Pilau .................... 136
Leg of Pork with Red Cabbage ................ 131
Pumpkin and Pork Chop Casserole ............ 126
Stuffed Pork Tenderloin ...................... 131
Bolichi (Microwave)
    (Stuffed Round Steak) ................... 128
Sausage Stuffed Apples ..................... 122
Campfire Sausage and Beans ................. 130
Savory Super Bowl Sausages................. 129
Sausages of Seville......................... 143
Barbecued Country Style Spareribs ........... 121
Spareribs, Kraut and Dumplings............... 129
Tulsa Ribs ................................ 120
Barbecue Sauce ........................... 120
Dumplings................................. 129
Chicken Fried Steak ........................ 143
Flank Steak ............................... 130
Mother's Day Steaks........................ 133
Party Steaks .............................. 122
Easy Baked Stew .......................... 126
Everybody Loves this Beef Stew.............. 119
Scrumptuous Stroganoff .................... 127
Taco Pizza Pie
    Cornmeal Crust ........................ 142
Tortilla Flats .............................. 133
Jackie's Tortilla Casserole ................... 138
A Touch of France Mushrooms with Veal ....... 135

## POULTRY

Apple Chicken.............................. 153
Chicken with Artichoke Hearts............... 148
Chicken with Almonds and Grapes............ 159
Leslie Fosters Fantastic Chicken
    Barbecue Marinade..................... 154
Chicken in Barbecue Sauce ................. 149
Paper Bag Barbecued Chicken ............... 153
Vons Chicken Breasts ...................... 159
Chinese Burritos for New Years Eve........... 154
Woody's World Class White Chicken Chili...... 166
Chinese New Years Chicken ................. 149
Company Casserole ........................ 156
Country Captain Chicken.................... 152
Coq Au Vin in the Micro .................... 150
Crepes a la Mexicana ...................... 162
Chicken Della Robbia ...................... 151
Chicken Diablo Sauce ...................... 160
Jackie's Chicken and Dumplings
    Dumplings ............................ 165
Enchiladas Veronique ...................... 163
Chicken or Turkey Hash .................... 161
Chicken Hawaiian ......................... 158
Honey Chicken with Apples ................. 146
Italian Chicken............................. 147
Kentucky Fried Chicken
    (Gloria Pitzer) ......................... 161
Lemon Chicken ........................... 152
Chicken with Lemon and Herbs.............. 162
Sauteed Chicken Livers .................... 155
Low Calorie Turkey Meatballs
    Special Sauce ......................... 164
Improvised Gravy.......................... 164
Chicken Marengo.......................... 150
Fruity Orange Chicken ..................... 155
Parmesan Sesame Chicken.................. 157
Polynesian Baked Chicken .................. 147

# INDEX (Continued)

Poulet Saute Au Riesling ........................ 157
Easy Stir Fry Chicken and Vegetables .......... 146
Holiday Stuffed Chicken ....................... 158
Sweet and Sour Chicken........................ 156
Chicken Tamale Bake for
   Oscar Night 1986 .......................... 148
Tarragon Chicken and Vegetables .............. 163
Chicken Tetrazzini ............................. 160
Tetrazzini Sauce .............................. 160
Thai Chicken .................................. 151
Basic Turkey Gravy ............................ 165

## SEAFOOD

Grilled Angler with Garlic Beurre Rouge ........ 180
Bayou Baked Bass Superb ..................... 173
Fish and Chips ............................... 169
Down Home Good Crab Tostadas ............. 168
Fillets in Cream ............................... 170
Low Calorie Fish Entrees ...................... 181
Grand Central Oyster Pan Roast .............. 171
Scalloped Oysters ............................ 176
Fish in Pear Sauce on the Light Side............ 182
Salmon Stuffed Eggplant ..................... 168
Salmon and Mushroom Bake On The BBQ ..... 170
Poached Salmon in the Dishwasher ........... 178
Salmon Souffle Roulade ...................... 178
Scallops in Baked Cream ..................... 172
Wonderful Seafood Casserole ................. 172
Butterflied Coconut Shrimp .................... 177
Stir Fried Shrimp and Asparagus .............. 169
Magic Cajun Sauce with Crawfish or Shrimp.... 176
Shrimp and Crab Supreme .................... 181
Shrimp Curry ................................. 179
Shrimp on the Skewer "Mexicana"
   (As Prepared by Chef Raimund Hofmeister
   at the 1985 Food and Cooking Expo)........ 179
Chinese New Year's Shrimp.................... 175
Scallop Stuffed Shrimp ........................ 171
Szechuan Shrimp ............................. 174
Red Rooster Taverns Fillet of Sole ............. 180
Spanish Fish Fillets ........................... 173
Baked Trout with Mushrooms ................. 174
Turbot en Yogurt ............................. 175
Fun with Mushrooms
   Tuna and Mushroom Pie .................... 182
Easy Baked White Fish ....................... 177

## BREADS

Applesauce Nut Bread ........................ 192
California Apricot Loaf ......................... 187
Banana Nut Bread ............................ 197
Irish Bran Bread .............................. 195
Cheese Onion Bread.......................... 184
Quick Cinnamon Rolls ........................ 197
Carringtons Cornbread ....................... 184
Mexican Cornbread .......................... 190
Cranberry Nut Bread ......................... 193
Holiday Cranberry Bread ..................... 191
Date Nut Bread............................... 186
Lemon Granola Bread
   Granola Streusel Topping ................... 193
Jackie's Fabulous Garlic Loaf ................. 188
Flowerpot Bread .............................. 189
Houska Bread
   (Czechoslovakian Holiday Bread) ............ 190
Easy Monkey Bread .......................... 187
Crunchy Apple Top Muffins ....,............. 194

Favorite Bran Muffins .......................... 185
Griswolds Bran Muffins ........................ 192
Cranberry Muffins ............................ 195
Little Russ' Raisin Bran Muffins................ 198
Natural and Good Oatmeat Muffins ........... 195
Rhubarb Sticky Muffins ....................... 191
Super Muffins ................................ 194
Orange Carrot Loaf........................... 194
Grandma's Easy No-Knead Peasant Bread...... 196
Mashed Potato Dinner Rolls................... 189
Sweet Potato Bread........................... 196
A Salute to Octoberfest Raisin Beer Bread...... 188
Buttermilk Raisin Bread ....................... 186
Fabulous Rye Bread .......................... 185
Zucchini Fruit Loaf ........................... 198

## SWEETS AND TREATS:
### Candy, Pies, Cakes, Cookies, Desserts

Back to School Favorites Carmel Apples ....... 200
Chocolate Creams............................. 201
Natural and Good Honey Nutballs ............. 202
Orange Candied Nuts.......................... 203
Old Fashioned Peanut Brittle................... 201
Candied Popcorn ............................. 202
Terrific Taffy ................................. 201
Holiday Almond Toffee........................ 200
English Toffee................................. 202
Toffee Drops ................................. 218
Klein's Magic Meringue ....................... 208
Banana Apple Pie ............................ 209
Bali Hai Banana Cream Pie .................... 205
Chocolate Mint Pie ........................... 206
Race Day Pie ................................ **206**
Easy No-Bake Lemon Pie ..................... 205
Girdle Buster Pie ............................. 207
Lemonade Pie and Strawberries ................ 207
Jackie's Lemon Meringue Pie .................. 208
Eileen's Pumpkin Pie .......................... 207
Mud Pie ..................................... 209
Peach Upside Down Pie ....................... 204
Buttermilk Pecan Pie.......................... 204
Sour Cream Raisin Pie ........................ 205
Glazed Orange Slices ......................... 200
Kentucky Bourbon Cake....................... 209
Mel's Baileys Cheesecake ..................... 213
Pink Lemonade Cheesecake ................... 210
Jackie's Chocolate Mocha
   Ice Cream Cake........................... 212
Dark Fruitcake ............................... 211
Orange Christmas Cake ....................... 211
Peach Upside Down Cake
   Peach Mixture............................. 212
Oregon Raisin Rum Pound Cake ............... 213
Pumpkin Cake Roll ........................... 210
Marshmallow Brownies for the Holidays ........ 214
Butter Cookies ............................... 218
Giant Chocolate Chip Cookies ................. 216
Chocolate Cookie Crumb Crust ............... 206
Chruscik
   (Polish Bow Cookies) ...................... 215
Cranberry Crunch Squares .................... 217
Mom's Dietetic Cookies....................... 217
Old Fashioned Oatmeal Cookies ............... 214
"Stingys P Nut Butter Balls"................... 203
Pumpkin Squares ............................. 215
Snickerdoodles ............................... 218
Sugar Drop Cookies With Oil ................. 217